DEDICATION

This book is dedicated to the 58,320 brave souls, including eight women, whose names are inscribed on the U.S. Vietnam Memorial Wall as of May 2018. The original 57,939 names listed in 1982 have been updated. Both counts vary from the official tally of U.S. Vietnam war deaths, 58,220 as of May 2018. But regardless of the count, every participant deserves honor.

CONTENTS

AUTHOR'S NOTE

"When somebody else's opinion of me matters more than my opinion of myself, then I'm held hostage by them. When my opinion of myself matters more to me than what others think, then I'm free."

CHAPTER 1: ON THE HOMESTEAD

"I woke up early in the mornin'
Lookin' for the sun to come through
Golden flowers with ripe young faces
Heaven filled with mornin', mornin' dew..."

—John R. Black, *"Wake Up Sunshine"*

The military and its culture of duty were part of my life from the very beginning. I was born the day after Christmas, 1940, in Spokane, WA. My father, who was then a private first class in the Army's Fourth Infantry band, wasn't there at St. Luke's Hospital for my arrival that afternoon. Instead, John Wesley Black had that very day boarded a steamer to Alaska, where he'd soon be performing with the Fourth Infantry band. But I was named after him and his own father, John Horace Black. My middle name, Ronald, was borrowed from Ronald Colman, a 1930s movie actor that Mom and Dad loved.

My mother and her family more than made up for Dad's early absence. Juliana Agatha (Tomsha) Black, known to friends and family as June, welcomed me into a large and loving family centered around the family homestead near Jump Off Joe Lake, in the Colville Valley about 30 miles from Spokane. She was the eighth child to have been born to my grandfather, Jacob Tomsha, and grandmother, Manca (Marijana or Mary) Torker Tomsha.

These grandparents lived on the homestead originally chartered by my great-grandfather, Blasius "Blaze" Tomse, and his wife Marie A. Novak Tomse. (The original Slovene spellings of names, from great-grandpa Jakob Tomse's to my mother's middle name, Agata, gradually gave way to more Americanized spellings, although both are common in family records.) A

1

number of other family members lived on the same land or nearby, notably my uncle Louis, my mom's younger brother and my favorite uncle.

My parents married in Coeur D'Alene, Idaho, on January 11, 1939, but by the time I arrived, Dad had been deployed. Mom had me baptized in Spokane on Feb 2, 1941, with my uncle Louis and his wife Mary (May) Tomsha becoming my godparents.

The family homestead

I wouldn't meet Dad, who my mother called Jack, until later that spring. He came home on leave in April, and he and my mother took me to meet his parents near Gifford, Idaho, about 125 miles southeast of Spokane where they also were homesteaders. My grandfather Black was born in Missouri, and my grandmother Black in Illinois, but they'd both moved west before meeting.

Mom and Dad at American Lake

The Black family has been traced to County Tyrone in Northern Ireland, and they were probably there from around the 1600s. Research by family members and DNA testing undertaken by my sister Julie have traced our journey in the United States back to William Black, who was born in Pennsylvania in 1805. William's father was a descendent of Blacks in Country Tyrone, Northern Ireland, but as yet, we have not been able to identify his father, exactly when the branch came to the United States, or other specifics.

Grandpa John H. Black and Grandma Mary H. (Williams) Black in 1890

That said, DNA tracing through the male line places my Black ancestors as far back as 400 C.E. and the Inishowen region of northwestern Ireland, in County Donegal, as part of Clan Ui Neill (O'Neil). YDNA results show that my father was a descendant of Niall Noigiallach, also known as Niall of the Nine Hostages, who ruled as high king of Ireland from 377 to 404 C.E. His descendants created one of the foremost political dynasties in Ireland between the seventh and tenth centuries. Family ancestors had lengthy sojourns in the Dumfries/Galloway region of Scotland, too. Members of the Black family eventually also emigrated to Canada, New Zealand, Australia, and England, as well as helped to establish Fargo, North Dakota.

Me and Dad

After Dad returned to Alaska, my mother took an Alaska Steamship Company steamer, the S.S. Columbia, sailing on May 17, 1941, to Seward. It arrived on May 23, and we rode a train to meet him in Anchorage, near Fort Richardson where he was then stationed. While in Alaska we lived in a cabin and celebrated Christmas there. Mom later told me that we were all awakened one night with the cabin shaking back and forth.

"We thought it was an earthquake!" she said. "But it was a bear rubbing his back on the side of the cabin." Mom recalled that a number of times Dad was confronted by a bear as he walked to work.

Our Alaska cabin, where we celebrated my first Christmas

Because of the Pearl Harbor bombing earlier that month, all military dependents were evacuated out on December 30 and Mom and I had to take a troop train to the port and board the S.S. Columbia again. Then we were anchored at sea because of the fear of enemy submarines. The seas were so rough both Mom and I were seasick and vomiting, and she later said that it was a very frightening time for her. Eventually we got safely home to Washington.

Inside our Alaska cabin

Other than those months in Alaska, most of my preschool years were spent on the homestead. In many ways, the homestead was the heart of our family and had been for half a century. According to family lore, research by my sister Julie, and a book written by my uncle Louis called *For Whom the Bell Has Tolled*, the homestead was established by Great-Grandpa Blasius, who was born in 1842 and had immigrated from Slovenia (formerly Yugoslavia) at 41 years old in 1883. A tailor, he brought his wife and the four kids in their family by then. Those children included my eight-year-old grandfather, Jacob

Tomse. They made a brief stop in Pennsylvania and then moved to Minnesota, where they bought 40 acres, cutting wood and hauling it to St. Cloud for a living. Eventually they heard of the free homestead land in the Washington Territory. Great-Grandpa Blaze came west in the spring of 1886, leaving his wife and now six kids behind.

Mom with me at the homestead

Spokane, then known as Spokane Falls, was as far as the railroad went. Great-Grandpa Blasius followed the military road northwest from Spokane to Fort Colville to the land he would settle, past Loon Lake into the Grouse Creek area near Jump Off Joe Lake. He first staked a claim and built a cabin on Section 20 at TS 31 R 41 EWM, and his family came west to join him. This cabin is still standing. But within a year or two he found a better spot with lots of freshwater springs about two miles south, in the southeast quarter of Section 30 at TS 31 R 41 EWM.

After clearing the better land and building on it, he was eventually able to get his homestead patented on May 5, 1904. He would ultimately own 360 acres, which would pass to my grandfather Jacob. Chewelah, about 10 miles away, was the nearest village, though initially it wasn't much more than a stage and freight stopover. Still, it had a store and a small mission church. The family attended every Sunday, usually walking to get there, and often brought home what they needed from the store.

The rest of the time, they worked hard. To clear the land in the early years, they felled trees of up to six feet on the stump, burning them to get rid of them—there wasn't a market for the wood at that time. On no more than three acres, the family raised potatoes, cabbage, carrots, and other garden vegetables. My grandfather recalled that the first year, the spuds grew to the size of walnuts. Great-grandpa Blaze and homesteaders who'd come out with him all had experience farming, but they didn't know the land and soil conditions. There was much better land available but they couldn't see the rocks for the trees. Once cleared, it was full of stumps and boulders and wasn't easy to water.

Fortunately, after more cultivation, the gardens grew better, though hunting also helped keep the family fed. My grandfather Jacob, the family's second-oldest child, said he got a lot of pheasants and grouse. He recalled that many times, they had no money for bird shot for their muzzle loaders. Instead, they would sift out gravel about the size they needed and it worked fine. The family men also made money, about 50 cents a day between them, cutting wood for the railroad's steam engines and hauling it to the rails. Grandpa Jacob said, "We didn't get hipshot carrying that money around, but it bought us our beans and sowbelly."

Blasius Tomsha and his family

My great-grandmother, Marie, was apparently quite a busy-body. But this trait made her good at arranging marriages for her sons and daughters, including two more born in Washington. In 1907, Jacob married Mary Torker in the hamlet of Jump Off, which existed by then and featured not only a school but St. Joseph Church, built in 1905. (In fact, my great-uncle Matt Tomsha and his wife Frances Trampush were the first couple to be married there, and Grandpa Jacob was not far behind.)

Children quickly followed, though Jacob and Mary suffered the early loss of their first baby, Frank. By the time my mother was born in 1918, the family was large and money was tight, although a lush family garden helped sustain them. Christmas was celebrated with some candy and an orange, which my mother called "wonderful." The kids might also exchange wooden gifts they'd whittled for each other.

Life was tough for a lot of the family. During the years of World War II, my grandmother Mary Tomsha received letters from Cousin Vincent and Cecilia Lukezic, who were in Ljubljana, Slovania. After Grandma Mary passed away, my mother received the letters. Parts of one in particular, dated March 25, 1947, speak to how terrible and desperate the situation was for our family in Slovania and all of Europe.

> Dear Cousin June,
>
> Our life is very hard, from year to year it gets worse. This socialism is not very good. Thank you very much where you obtained for me $5.00 to buy vitamins. With your help from the Red Cross I received powdered milk and eggs. Because of you I also received help from the Yugoslav Agency in New York. My mother was deeply surprised when she learned that you are willing to buy her a pair of shoes. Could you also include in the package some razor blades and soap? We can't even buy blades here. We would also be appreciative to receive some food. How is your son Johnny and your small Juliana, is she still jumping around you so merrily? If you come to visit us you will see how hard we are living.

In one letter she acknowledged the passing of Grandma Tomsha and what a good woman she was. Other letters again pleaded for help: "You Americans, you can be satisfied, because your land was intact before the war.... Our factories have been destroyed... our civilians, mothers, and children were shot by the Germans or sent to concentration camps, you Americans, not so. We need your help, you can believe us."

Reading all the letters from during and after the war that are now in our family archives is sobering and depressing.

Mom, standing second from left, with her champion team

One Christmas during my mother's childhood, the original farmhouse burned to the ground. They rebuilt, with no family record of where or how they survived the winter in the meantime. During high school, Mom played forward on the Valley High School basketball team with her cousins Agnes and Margaret Tomsha, and they were the 1935 Stevens County champions. After graduating in 1936, she worked for a short time as a maid for a town doctor in Spokane, Washington, until he began chasing her around his bedroom. Within a few years, however, she'd met my father, who was nearly fifteen years her senior.

Mom (again standing second from left) with family and friends

My father also had grown up on a homestead, with two brothers and three sisters. Dad was born July 26, 1903, and attended Columbia College in Milton, Oregon. There, starting from when he was a freshman, he won contests as a proficient violinist, pianist, trombone player, and vocalist, as well as taking first place in an oratory contest against nearby Whitman College. He was asked to join a mixed quartet to tour Oregon, Montana, and Idaho to help advertise Columbia's music program.

After leaving school, he joined the U.S. Marine Corps on February 17, 1926. He served in what's now known as Beijing, China, as a member of the American Legion Guard Band. In a 1926 letter home, he wrote, "By the way I was picked to play piano for the Marine Orchestra. That means quite a bit as we get $12.00 a night for playing, each man, so I can save more money. I've got to have at least $300.00 when I get out."

Dad (standing) as a college performer

He often played at formal events for the American Legion—the era's version of the embassy. The band's audiences included Gian Galeazzo Ciano, an Italian diplomat and Mussolini's son-in-law who would become Minister of Foreign Affairs.

Another of his letters, this one dated April 21, 1927, was about the war taking place. "The trouble here is quieting down since the Russian Reds were run out of the Legation by International Soldiers. The Russians have caused all the trouble here so far. The other night we had a little trouble from Chinese students who tried to get into the Legation, but nothing since then, and I hope the trouble is over, but please don't worry as there isn't much danger."

Dad left the Marines in 1930 and on July 24, 1931, he enlisted in the U.S. Regular Army for the Fourth Infantry Division Band at Fort George Wright, initially for a three-year stint. He married my mother on January 11, 1939. His mother wrote her a letter that began, "Dear June: Gess [sic] I might as well get used to it if you are going to be my daughter and you are getting my very best son." Unfortunately (or perhaps not, with that beginning), she was too frail to travel to the wedding, but she did wish the new couple "all the joy this life can give and an abundant entrance into the next beautiful world."

My father as a U.S. Marine

My parents had a honeymoon at American Lake near Fort Lewis, Washington, that May. I was born as my parents' first child when Mom was 22. We initially lived on a rural mail route in Spokane where rent was about $50 a month and Mom could buy a loaf of bread for five cents. While most of her uncles, aunts, and siblings had gone off to lives that included careers in the Navy and the Air Force, her parents still lived on the homestead. My family would spend many of my childhood years living there, too, mostly in a house across the meadow from the original cabin, where first a ranch house and then eventually only a bunkhouse stood.

That land and my grandfather were important parts of my early life. He'd spent some years as a blacksmith before getting married and coming back to the homestead, and he was very handy with all types of tools. When he needed something special, he would make it, from drill bits to wagon wheels, wooden barrels, and even moonshine stills.

My grandmother Tomsha unfortunately died of cancer in 1945 when I wasn't yet five, so I don't remember much about her, though I have one vivid memory of waking from a nap and going out onto the side porch and outside. Wearing my long underwear, I looked down at Grandma, who was sitting there on a blanket under the cherry tree, eating cherries. She said, "Come and sit by me, Johnny, and have some cherries." I sat down beside her; it was very peaceful. Later I went with my mother to see Grandma at Sacred Heart Hospital in Spokane, where she was being treated for cancer. As we went into her hospital room, she was climbing back into bed. My next memory of her was when she was placed in bed at home for her wake. Her loss bewildered me and left me sad and lonely.

Grandma and Grandpa Tomsha, my first best friends

Fortunately, Grandpa Jacob was kind and gentle. He was my best friend growing up. He'd been crippled while helping another farmer load lime at our lime kiln near the homestead. Grandpa was standing at the back of the truck, and without looking, the farmer backed up and accidentally crushed Grandpa's back. After that, he had to get around on crutches. He would sit out on the lawn, chewing Peerless Chewing Tobacco. It came in a pouch, and

Grandpa would take a big wad and put in under his bottom lip. He loved it. Indoors, he spit into a can beside her chair; in the yard that wasn't an issue. He also liked to peel an orange or a lemon and put the whole thing into his mouth at once to eat it. I thought it was rather amazing he could do that, but I never tried it myself.

Outside with him, I flew paper airplanes, played with my dog, and just had fun. I'd have to remember to watch for my pet deer, who would run up behind me and jump on my back with his front hoofs. He was playing, but it hurt! And sometimes he'd knock the wind out of me.

Grandpa taught me something about responsibility and helping others, because his injury had made him incontinent. It was a close-knit community and everybody took care of everybody else. That went double at home. He would be sitting on his rocking chair and couldn't make it to the bathroom so he would pee his pants, terribly. When he was in his chair and that happened, I could pull off his socks and long underwear and put dry ones on him. He never complained.

One of my first real experiences of terror was being alone with him when a terrible thunderstorm descended on the ranch house, which had no window shades. I thought the world was coming to an end. I jumped up into my grandpa's lap, and he continued to read from his Slovenian Bible with me for a couple of hours, until the storm passed.

At times, he could've used some protection from me. There was no fence to keep the cattle from coming near the house, though they knew better than to actually come onto the lawn, and one day when grandpa was sitting in a chair on the lawn, the cattle were nearby. I don't know what got into me, but I stampeded them across the lawn toward him. They almost ran over my grandpa. My mother saw it, and it was the first time I ever got licked with a belt. A second time came after I was throwing rocks one day and hit him there, on the lawn, in the back of the head. Then I finally learned not to do that kind of stuff.

Mostly, though, we just spent good times together. My dad was kind and gentle, and he never laid a hand on me. All my grandparents also set wonderful examples of simplicity and spirituality that I fondly recall to this day.

Though my father had grown up in the Assembly of God tradition, my mother's family was Catholic. Grandpa Jacob read his Bible in Slovenian every day, and he and my grandmother taught me how to pray. I learned to say bedtime prayers starting when I was about five years old. "Now I lay me down to sleep…." During Lent, we prayed the rosary every night, lighting a candle and kneeling on the living room's wood floor. I really liked it. I knew that Grandma Mary Black read and prayed the Bible every day, too. My earliest memory of church was attending Mass at our Jump Off Joe mission church. We usually walked as a family through the meadow past the Peternell cabin—a short cut to church.

I began to learn much more about church when I started serving Mass as an altar boy and especially when I was confirmed at St. Mary of the Rosary church in Chewelah. Bishop White came from Spokane to preside over our confirmation ceremony. He asked if any of us being confirmed had any questions. I got right up and asked a question about the sacrament of extreme unction. The people in church laughed, I guess simply because I got right up and asked while no one else being confirmed had any questions.

We had a hardworking farm family who did everything, and relatively little had changed between the original homestead and my earliest years. We didn't have electricity until I was about nine, and my grandparents would never own a car. Grandpa told me that when they'd had business to do before I was born, they walked to Chewelah, ten miles away, or Colville, about 30 miles. The first car for anybody in the family was when Uncle Jake and Uncle Louis and Aunt May all came home after World War II, a few years after my birth. Uncle Jake bought a new Model T Ford, but later he and Uncle Louis were drinking and drove the car into the creek.

Even later, it was not easy to get home in the winter because you had to make it up steep Bulldog Grade. Many times I would be let out at the edge of the road at the beginning of the grade while car after car took a run at the hill. Cars would start sliding backwards and the adults would be cussing a blue streak as they slipped and fell and the car sometimes slid off the road. I picked up a lot of swear words from these incidents, and they unfortunately became part of my vocabulary. Every time I went to confession I had to tell the priest what I'd said recently. Usually my penance would be to say a rosary, not just of a couple of "Our Fathers."

We never really had much money, either, but everyone was happy. Mom made do with what we had. She loved her parents and was really a farm girl at heart. She raised a large garden and chickens, canned food, made sausage, and kept a very neat house. She also picked huckleberries with other family members in the Mt. Chewelah Peak area in the summer. For some reason, though, Mom would never let me go on those outings.

I loved country life.

I loved living in the country, which made it easy to have pets. I had about three dogs, including one named Sabi. My dog slept on my bed. Sometimes one of my dogs would disappear, having been eaten by wolves. I also had a stuffed dog, a little brown terrier, that I received on my third or fourth birthday. It was one of my favorite toys, and I still have it today.

We had three sheep dogs that would herd the cattle on the homestead and help me bring them down from the upper pasture for milking. After one got pretty old and could barely walk, Uncle Louis came to the house one day with that dog, carrying a 12-gauge shotgun. He said, "Johnny, Lucky can hardly walk anymore and I have to put him away. You can't go with me. But we will make a nice grave for him."

Well, that meant Lucky was going to be shot by Uncle Louis. I was really sad, but that's just the way it was back then. There was no money to put animals away. The barn was always full of kittens and when there was a batch of new babies, Uncle Louis would put them in a sack and take them to Jump Off Joe Lake to drown them.

I had two pet deer, too. We tied red bandannas around their necks, but during one hunting season, one of my deer suddenly disappeared, having been shot. The other got shot the next hunting season, despite the bandanna. At other times I'd have one or two chipmunks, a squirrel, or a snake. I would trap the chipmunks and squirrels in a homemade trap I had made, keep them a while, and then let them go. Once when I was in about fifth grade, I found a mouse nest on the homestead. It held five baby mice about an inch long each. I took them as pets, feeding them with an eye dropper and taking them into school for show-and-tell.

Dad with my new Appaloosa, which he'd bought from the local Indians. That's me on the left.

We also had two horses, though they could really never be ridden. They were too wild. To tame the Appaloosa, Dad hired a local guy—we called them Indians back then—but the horse was still too wild. When I was in third grade, I wrote a school essay about one of these horses:

My New Horse

I have a new horse. Her name is Lady Luck. I can't ride her yet. When she gets bigger I'll ride her to school. When I was taking Lady to water she got away from me. I hopped upon a pile of rocks, then I jumped on her back. I got off her back in a hurry. She isn't broke to ride yet.

So instead, while we lived at the homestead, sometimes after Mass on Sunday I would ride with a local family in their car up to their fish farm above Uncle Frank's place, and they'd let me ride their horse. Its name was Oosey, and it was very gentle. Then I'd stay and have dinner with them before Dad came to bring me home.

Horses made frequent appearances in other schoolwork, too. Another story I wrote—with good handwriting, given my mere eight years of age— was more fanciful than the last:

Three Wishes

One day when I was walking down the road and a flash of light appeared in front of me. Then the light turned into a Fairy Godmother. She said I could have three wishes. I wished first that I had a horse that would buck. I wished next that the world would turn upside down. I wished next that the roots of the trees would grow up in the air. Suddenly I sat up and rubbed my eyes. I dreamed it.

Of course, living a farm life came with many chores, simply part of each family member's duty to the rest. I had to feed the dogs and cats and bring the cows in for milking, with help from the dogs. I loved the animals, though. When I was seven, my Uncle Frank took me to see my first movie, Walt Disney's *Bambi,* at the theater in Chewelah. After that I became more convinced I didn't want to do much hunting. I never saw Uncle Frank shoot a gun, either, or hear about him hunting, probably because he'd served in World War I, "the war to end all wars." Uncle Frank's favorite dog, Tippy, had her right leg accidently sawed off at the mill, but he never shot her as some farmers would have. She had no problem limping along. After seeing *Bambi* and trying to kill the rabbit in the barn, I felt the same way. During hunting season, we would sometimes find a newly born fawn in the woods whose mother had been killed by hunters. They looked just like Bambi. Aunt May would put it in a cardboard box behind the wood stove, and I would feed it milk with a baby bottle.

Once Uncle Louis tried to show me how to castrate a steer, and the lesson included some events he hadn't intended. I watched safely from the fence as he lassoed the steer, but that steer had no intention of being castrated, not without a fight. It dragged Uncle Louis around the corral, with him kicking and swearing comically for about thirty minutes. Finally he was able to jump on the steers' back, force it to the ground, and tie it up. By then his pants were torn and his arms were bleeding. He castrated the steer, poured salt on its wound, and untied it at last. When my uncle got up and walked to me at the fence, I said with a laugh, "Is that the way you do it, Uncle Louis?" He told me to shut up and keep quiet about it. I don't know how he explained his torn clothes and blood.

Matt, my grandfather with his crutches, and one of my dogs

Keeping the wood box filled, and chopping wood and kindling, were also my jobs. As I got older, I was supposed to help with the dishes and other kitchen jobs as well. We always had an old-timer living at the ranch house across the meadow, too, and Mom would send me on errands for them. One of those old timers was Teeny Mally. Another was Matt Peternell, who would cut a piece from his plug of tobacco with his knife and chew it. When Mom wasn't around, he also gave me a small piece to chew, but it made me sick. Matt had a hearing aid with the speaker attached to his front pocket. I got into trouble one day when he came over for breakfast—I stood up close to his chest and yelled into the speaker, "Hello, Matt!" Living in a small farming community meant you helped without expecting to get paid for it.

We also lived brief periods in Spokane for various reasons, such as when Dad came home in April 1943 and was stationed at Fort Wright. Mom also briefly worked at the Bremerton Naval Shipyards with her sister, Frances, in 1942. Just before the end of the war, Dad was stationed for about a year in Texas at Fort Hood, then still known as Camp Hood. Mom and I took the train to get there; she was afraid to fly. We lived in a trailer, and while it wasn't a farm, I did keep pet snails and horned toads in a cigar box in my room. I spent a lot of time at the swimming pool. I also took tap dancing lessons—Mom had bought me tap shoes—and I danced in the officer's club. When I did, the audience threw quarters on the stage for me, and I was hooked on performance for life.

Mom at Camp Hood

I was glad when we returned to Washington, though, even if I might have a smaller audience there. Dad was stationed at Fort Wright near Spokane. We lived in town for two years, and I attended first grade there at Sheridan School after a brief stint at the Irving School. While at Irving, I went home with a friend after school one day without having told my mother I was going to do that. Later that evening, there was a knock on the door of my friend's house. His mother answered to find the police standing there. They were looking for me. Mom and Dad were afraid that I'd been kidnapped. When the police brought me home, I got a licking, and I never did that again, believe me.

After I finished the year at Sheridan School, we moved back to the homestead. For second and third grade, I went to Jump Off's two-room schoolhouse a mile away from our house. My grandfather and his siblings had been among the school's first students when it was built in 1892, and it still had a small barn nearby where students who rode to school kept their horses. My grandpa and my mother had also attended there, and Mom told me a story about when she and her brothers, my uncles Louis, Jake, and

Andrew, had hidden in the barn's hay loft to avoid their male teacher, who was very old and not liked by her brothers. The teacher came looking for them. When he climbed a ladder to see if they were up there, they pushed the ladder over! They apparently got into a lot of trouble. That teacher was long gone by the time I got there, but I walked every day, just like they had. Sometimes a deer would start to cross in front of me and just stop and stare.

Six grades attended the school together, and our teacher, Viola Smith, used a willow switch on us if we misbehaved. I know this for certain because one day, while we were outside playing, I decided to put rocks into the pockets of the teacher's coat, which was hanging in the cloak room. Another student, Danny Banks, saw me do it, and I warned him to stay quiet. But as we came in from recess, Danny said, "Johnny, are you going to tell the teacher you put rocks in her pockets?" This ended with the teacher bending me over and switching me. Obviously I didn't like Danny too much.

Our one-room schoolhouse

During this period, Dad was working at the U.S. Army recruiting office in Spokane, and traveling from the homestead to town for work each day. One day, as soon as he left, Mom said, "Johnny, we are leaving. We are going to pack our bags and we're going to leave."

Only six or seven years old, I said, "Where are we going?" She just replied, "We're leaving." We ended up in Pasco, Washington, motel. It must've been a few days later when Dad showed up, came in, and said, "June, what are you doing?"

She said, "I'm leaving you, John. I'm leaving you."

They got in a big argument, Mom insisting she was not coming back, Dad would say, "Yes, you are coming back. You and Johnny are coming back." This went on for a long time, with me wondering what was going to happen the whole time. Finally Mom gave in and said, "Okay, I will come back." And we went back to the homestead. That was really traumatic. My mother never did tell me why we'd left home or what had prompted her to do that. Too young to understand what their problems were, I was just happy to get back to the familiar homestead I knew. Later my parents still had disagreements, but they never swore or yelled like Aunt May and Uncle Frank did.

My favorite pastime came mostly in the summertime: fishing at Jump Off Joe Lake. When I wasn't in school, I fished every day. The owners of the resort there would let me use a rowboat for free. I can't remember the name of the first owners, but the second owners' names were Van Diesels, then the Kirbys after them. Fishing at the lake prompted me to poetry for another third-grade school assignment:

The Lake
I like to go fishing in the lake
And see the fish swim
They go so fast
They swim right past
But my bait they never take.

One day, Aunt Margaret came fishing with me. Out on the lake, I had to go to the bathroom really badly. She said, "You'll have to pee in the boat," which I did. It was embarrassing. Most of the time, though, I had more fun. When I fished I sometimes caught 20 or 30 bass, sunfish, and perch a day. I also fished in many of the local streams, including the creek at Uncle Frank's cabin. Mom would fry them in a black skillet, and we ate fish all summer.

In the winter, we would go to skate on the lake, which was frozen over. Many others would come and build a nice bonfire on the shore, where we would roast marshmallows. One winter, when I was just learning to skate, I headed towards the resort's first owner going too fast, ran into him, and knocked him over. He took a bad fall, which broke his leg. I felt bad, and Mom was very upset with me.

Uncle Frank, who was married to my Aunt May, had been a very good baseball player in high school, and he gave me his old mitt. Once in a while we played catch together. I also joined the Scouts and did a few campouts. We didn't have any fancy camping gear or equipment—we just concentrated on having fun in the great outdoors. For instance, I have vivid memories of running through the woods, sticking to old Indian and cow trails. When I turned 11, Dad took me to see the 1951 movie about Jim Thorpe, the Indian runner and 1912 Olympic gold medalist. *Jim Thorpe—All-American*, which starred Burt Lancaster, really inspired me. After seeing how fast he could run, I starting running through the woods by myself, experiencing a great sense of freedom.

Other aspects of country life weren't so great. One morning when I was ten years old, I was outside the cottages, waiting for the school bus. My dog came running toward me just as I was to board the bus. He fell dead at my feet. It was awful. I started bawling and knelt down to pet my poor dog. But the typical attitude toward dogs in those days was different— they were more working farm animals than members of the family—and the bus driver wouldn't wait for me to take the dog's body back home, get my mother, or anything else. I had to leave my poor dog's body there alongside the road. I cried all ten miles to school. When I got home that afternoon, I buried my dog myself.

I was as familiar with guns as most farm kids, but I remember once when I was staying at Aunt May's and Uncle Frank's log cabin, Uncle Frank asked me to shoot a wild rabbit that was loose in the barn. He gave me his Remington single-shot .22 to do it. I shot at the rabbit eight or nine times with that rifle but didn't get it, probably because I never really wanted to kill it. It was terrifying to me to see the rabbit running for its life each time I took a shot. After that the only thing I wanted to hunt and kill were ground squirrels, who dug deep holes in the meadow that cows could stumble into, breaking a leg. The government paid a fee for every squirrel tail you turned in, so I'd shoot ground squirrels with the Frizzell brothers that lived near us at the homestead. We would set up on the hill overlooking the meadow. One of us, with binoculars, would spot a gopher and get the four of us all lined up on it. We would fire at the same time. Usually we'd all score a hit and the squirrel would disintegrate in the air.

A scary incident happened one morning, however, when I was going hunting with my uncles Bill, Louis, and Andrew. We had gathered with our rifles and were huddled outside the house, getting instructions from Uncle Louis as to where we should go. My rifle was a .30-30 and I had it in my arms, pointed toward the ground, but it was loaded and unfortunately it had a hair trigger. I mistakenly discharged it right there between us, and it could have killed any one of those guys. If you were hunting with a rifle, you were expected to know its operation, but I learned. After that, I really didn't want to be around guns, but I continued to hunt with my uncles.

With all those aunts and uncles, there was often family drama. I remember one time, after we had a car, when Dad said we were going to Colville to get Uncle Louis and that I could come along. For us, Colville was a long drive, and I didn't understand why we were going. Mom said Uncle Louis was in jail. I didn't know what that meant, so I figured I'd just better be quiet. Dad drove to the courthouse, where the jail was located, and we went inside. Uncle Louis came out of a jail cell and Mom had to sign some papers. Later I asked her why he was in jail. She said he'd gotten into a fight. "Sometimes the sheriff will put you in jail," she said. "Johnny, you keep quiet about this." I was afraid to ask Uncle Louis anything about it.

Another time, there was an issue with guns at the homestead between the adults. My Uncle Louis had been dating a woman by the name of Eloise Bradbury, who had three daughters about my age and whose first husband had died in an accident at the mine. For a time it appeared they might be married, and Eloise loaned my uncle a number of guns that ended up at the homestead.

Then my uncle became involved with a woman named Margaret Jepson and told Eloise that he wasn't going to marry her after all. My mother got wind of all this and warned Louis, but one day here comes Eloise, the rejected girlfriend, storming into the house with all three of her daughters, Jean, Elaine, and Lou Anne. She appeared to have been drinking, and she confronted my mother, demanding her guns. She also wanted Uncle Louis's .30-06 Springfield hunting rifle. Mom kept asking her what she was going to do with the rifle—surely envisioning my uncle being shot. Eloise just kept saying, "Give me the rifle, June." It was scary! Finally my mother turned over the rifle, but she unloaded all the shells from it first.

After she left, Mom told me about an incident with a shotgun kept in Grandma and Grandpa's closet. When she was a teenager, she and my Aunt May were playing with the gun. Aunt May held that 12-gauge shotgun up and pulled the trigger. Back then, guns were kept with rounds in the chamber and ready to fire, so the blast knocked her against the closet wall and blew a hole in the door. Someone pretty easily could have been killed, so they really got into trouble.

Another fight between two women in the family came to blows. One was from my Tomsha lineage and another was a Trampush; two Trampushes had married siblings of my grandpa Jacob. I don't know exactly what the fight was about, but the relatives created a circle in front of the homestead and made the two fight it out. There was screaming, kicking, biting, and swearing until one of them couldn't get up.

Not all of the arguments were that dramatic, but there were plenty of them. My Aunt May and Aunt Fran never got along, though I never understood why. While we were at the homestead, but later on, too, Mom was always the arbiter between them. If our family did something with Aunt Fran, Aunt May wouldn't come, and vice versa.

Aunt May as a World War II WAC

One day, though, Aunt May and Aunt Fran were together at the homestead with Mom, all of us in the living room. Grandpa was sitting out in the yard, reading his Slovenian Bible. I watched him from inside as he got up with his cane and began slowly walking out of the yard. At first, I didn't say anything. Mom and my aunts were talking, but not arguing—yet.

Slowly Grandpa got to the gate and began walking away, very slowly, down the dirt road. I said, "Hey, look. Grandpa is walking down the road."

They all checked out the window. Aunt May said, "I bet he's mad about something and is leaving."

I thought to myself that since he was walking with a cane, he couldn't be going very far. But Aunt Fran said, "Well, May what did you say to him?"

"I never said anything to him to make him mad. What did *you* say to him?" They began to accuse each other of things I knew nothing about, yelling back and forth and swearing terribly.

Mom said, "Johnny, you go ask Grandpa why he is leaving." So I ran down the road and caught up with Grandpa. He said hello, as friendly and nice as always.

I said, "Grandpa why are you leaving? Are you mad about something?"

He replied, "Why would I be mad? I'm just going for a walk."

I explained that his daughters were arguing over why he was leaving.

He said, "You go back and say that Grandpa said, 'Can't I even go for a walk without somebody getting upset?' I'm just enjoying my walk on this great day."

I ran back to the house, and boy, were they still arguing. I told them what he'd said. They wouldn't believe me, except for Mom, who was always trying to mediate their disagreements. But I never saw Aunt May and Aunt Fran together again after that. I always wondered and felt bad about the mysterious disagreements between them, because I loved them both. They were both always good to me and generous with their money, but they called each other terrible names until they died.

Aunt May, Aunt Fran, and Mom while they were still close

With excitement like that, who needed TV? We didn't have a television—not at the homestead, and not later when we lived in the cottages, either—and I didn't have much opportunity to watch it before 1950, when my Aunt Margaret and Uncle Louis bought the area's first black-and-white set. They were newly married and living at the homestead. I watched the Mickey Mouse Club on their TV every week. Later, I would babysit their kids—first my cousin Michael, then Pat, Christy, and Lindy. I'd stay glued to the TV until the "Star Spangled Banner" played at midnight and the station went off the air.

I also spent a lot of time with my Aunt May and Uncle Frank, listening to the radio in their cabin above the homestead. Some of my favorite radio shows were "The Lone Ranger," "The Shadow," "Roy Rogers and Dale Evans," and "Hopalong Cassidy." There was no running water indoors at Uncle Frank's house. My Aunt May, who was a very hard worker, had to carry heavy metal pails to the creek, which was a few hundred feet away, and bring them back to the cabin. There were always wild geese in that creek, and they would chase her. Carrying two pails of water was difficult for Aunt May when she had to get away from the geese at the same time! Several times she got bit on the legs and butt, and she was always black and blue from those bites.

We drank the water she hauled from a ladle in the bucket. One day she was boiling water on the woodstove, and I was sitting on the counter next to her. When she picked up that boiling hot kettle to pour it into another large pot, she slipped. Boiling water landed on my arm. I screamed and screamed. Huge blisters began to erupt. There was no place to take me for first aid, though. Not knowing what to do, she put Vaseline on my burn, which made the pain worse. She held me in her arms, and I thought I'd never stop crying. It was several days before the pain went away, weeks before the blisters were gone, and to this day I still have a scar.

Uncle Frank introduced me to taking a pinch of Copenhagen chewing tobacco, which was different from the tobacco plugs used by some of the old-timers who'd lived with us. My Uncle Louis, on the other hand, smoked cigarettes, and I sometimes helped him roll his supply on the kitchen table, using a cigarette machine and special tobacco. Uncle Frank also introduced me to talking about politics—he was an astute Democrat—and I remember also being with him years later for President Eisenhower's famous 1961 speech warning about the military/industrial complex. We got into a ferocious argument that got hotter with each drink he had.

My own house was constantly full of music. My mother sometimes found it hard to relax and always had to stay busy. Often, she cleaned while Dad played the piano, which he was always doing when he wasn't working. He was a great musician. He'd also learned early that you had to work for a living, and he managed to combine them playing for military bands, but we got plenty of music from him at home, too. He started me early in music, teaching me how to sing, "Now is the Hour," "Slow Boat to China," "I Saw Mommy Kissing Santa Claus," and "Buttons and Bows." His favorite song was, "Oh Canada." We sang it together, so it became my favorite, too. And of course, we all sang at church.

I followed Dad's musical footsteps.

In addition to giving me a love of music, he and everyone around me gave me a strong work ethic. We always had food on the table, nice clothes, a car, and a home, but the fact that we were not rich or even middle class just made me more motivated to succeed. My first job came when I was about nine years old and my Uncle Louis paid me $.50 an hour to watch for fires around the Jump Off Lumber Company, the small sawmill he owned down the road from our homestead. He'd been in the Navy during World War II, and after he got out, he'd made money working in the mines in Alaska and then used the money to buy a basic sawmill from Sears Roebuck. As that became more successful, he built a bigger mill near Valley, Washington, and then a home near the mill. On weekends, I also rode in his logging truck with him and served as a sort of junior choker-setter. We would go into the woods to load logs, and my job was to hook his crane-like system onto one end of a log while my uncle hooked the other. He then lifted and loaded the log. I was paid $.50 a load. I made about ten dollars a month during those odd jobs, which I liked, since I never received an allowance.

I enjoyed spending some of that money on birthday and Christmas gifts for my mother, sometimes putting items on payment plans at the local Kulzer's Mercantile. You didn't have to pay cash there, and even as a little kid I could go into Kulzer's and create an account. There were no credit cards then; it was all about trust. I learned about savings, credit, and time payments at an early age, buying Mom an iron and a pressure cooker, among other gifts. My payments were around ten cents a month. Even years later, when we finally moved to Spokane for me to attend high school, Kulzer's sent a bill to my parents for the amount the family still owed, and they were allowed to pay it off in small monthly payments without paying interest.

I received gifts of my own on special occasions, too, of course. One of my favorite toys was a Marx train set I received for Christmas when I was six. A night or two later, we went to an aunt and uncle's house on Jump Off Joe Lake, and while the adults were drinking beer in the kitchen, I set up the track in their living room, shut out the lights, and raced the train around the oval track for hours. It made me so happy! I would lay down alongside the track with my eye right up next to it and stare down the engine as it zoomed closely past my head.

A much bigger train would soon take me away from the homestead. Dad was reassigned to Offutt Air Force base near Omaha, Nebraska. We moved in mid-1949, and although we'd return to Eastern Washington before too long, the innocence of my earliest days would soon fade—or, in one instance, be taken away by force.

CHAPTER 2: CHANGES, CHURCH SCHOOLS, & CHALLENGES

"The greatest and most important problems of life are fundamentally unsolvable. They can never be solved, but only outgrown."

—*Carl Jung (popular attribution)*

When Dad was reassigned to Offutt Air Force base near Omaha, Nebraska, in mid-1949, he was assigned to the Strategic Air Command (SAC) led by the famous World War II General Curtis E. LeMay. Offutt AFB's legacy includes the construction of the Enola Gay and Bockscar, the planes that dropped Little Boy and Fat Man over Hiroshima and Nagasaki in World War II. Offutt served for over 40 years as the headquarters for SAC, with its associated ground and aerial command centers in case of nuclear war during the Cold War. While we were there, Mom and I would sometimes go watch Dad play in the Air Force band, which performed for the retreat ceremony as well as in the officer's club.

We lived in a three-story apartment building in Bellevue, not far from the base, and I went to fourth grade at a nearby Catholic school, Saint Mary's School. I played in the woods behind the apartment, and by then I was serving as an altar boy on Sundays, too. My sister Juliana, who we called Julie, was born there, so I was no longer an only child. Julie was as bald as an eagle, with absolutely no hair until she was four years old.

While we were in Omaha, my Uncle Louis visited with his new bride, Margaret Jepson, and a new red Dodge they had taken a train to Detroit to pick up. They came to see us on the way back home, before they moved into the homestead. I remember them pulling up in that new car and Margaret jumping out with a cigarette in her hand. She and Uncle Louis smoked Camels when they didn't roll their own (or have me roll them for them).

We had a near-miss with a terrible tornado that came through about a half-mile from our apartment. My mother lit candles and we kneeled and prayed the rosary. It was a terrifying experience.

My Dad retired from the Air Force out of SAC, though he did join the Air Force Reserves. He and Mom said we were going to fly back home to Spokane, but I cried and cried and said, "I don't want to fly." They finally gave in and in 1950 we went by train from Nebraska all the way back to Spokane. That long journey convinced me that train travel was great.

Dad on the piano at the Offutt Air Force base officer's club

When we came home to Eastern Washington, we settled about two miles from the homestead in a cottage near Valley. It was one of a short row of company houses that had been built for a nearby magnesite mine, and it was a small community of its own known officially as "The Cottages." Eloise Bradbury lived at the left end of the row with her three daughters, Jean, Lou Anne, and Elaine. Despite that fraught family history, we managed as neighbors, and Eloise eventually married James Dunlap. Compared to Uncle Louis, I thought he was a real dud, and I always wished Louis had married Eloise because I had a crush on Lou Ann.

Our other cottage neighbors were Betty White and her husband, who drank like fish; then a relative, Grandma Tomsha, and her sons Jake, Leo, and another known as Little Louie. Leo was truly the town drunk, and he spent a lot of time at the Valley Tavern. He sometimes worked for my Uncle Louis and he also dug graves at the cemetery near our church. Leo would be dropped off down the hill every evening, and he'd stumble up the hill to his cottage, singing in Slovenian the whole time. In the winter, when the road was slick, it'd take him hours to get home and we'd sometimes have to go get him. His younger brother, Little Louie, had served in World War II. He had a girlfriend he made out with in a car right next to our house; I sneaked peeks at them every chance I got.

Finally, in the right-most cottage was a World War I vet with a lung missing. His name was Frank Koreas, and he drove a Model T Ford with a canvas top. He also spent every day at the Valley Tavern, from the time it opened to the time it closed. Neighbor kids would pelt him with snowballs in the winter, and I must admit I wasn't an innocent bystander.

For better or worse, it was its own little community, each member with their quirks and weaknesses. The adults gave nicknames to some of our relatives and friends: Little Louie was also known as Sniffer because he sniffed his nose all the time, while Dad went by Jack Black. Similarly, one of the Burya brothers was known as Black Dog; the others were Jack and Joe. Denny Burya, who was my age, lived down the hill from us. Once we were both in high school, everyone knew that he was having sex with Betty White. He eventually ended up having an affair with my Aunt Margaret, too, except that he and Aunt Margaret got married in the end. It was a little Peyton Place, with a lot of infidelity—probably like a lot of places across America.

When we first moved into the cottages, though, Uncle Louis and Margaret were living at the homestead with my grandfather. Mom found out that Grandpa was being treated badly by Margaret. He was incontinent, but Margaret would let him sit in his chair wet and not change him. Mom told me to go ask Margaret why she was so mean to Grandpa. She was irritated by that, of course, and wouldn't really give me an answer.

It probably wasn't a good time, but I used the opportunity to ask her something I'd often wanted to ask but was too scared. My mom and dad never swore, but all my uncles made up for that, and working around them and the sawmill crew didn't help my vocabulary. So I told my Aunt Margaret, "The guys at the mill say a lot of words I don't understand."

She replied, "What don't you understand?"

"Well, there is one word they seem to say all the time: fuck."

The instant I said that, she grabbed me by the neck, took me down to the basement, and washed my mouth out with soap. I screamed and cried the whole time. She told me I'd better never say that word again and told me to go home. Only later did I find out what it meant.

Eventually, Mom had words with Margaret herself. When that didn't have the result she wanted, she made my uncle build a shower onto our cottage, since Grandpa couldn't get into a bath. Then we moved him into the cottage with us. I was glad about that.

In those years, I started being interested in girls. My neighbor in the cottages, Lou Ann Bradbury, was the first girl I ever kissed. We met in the garage next to our house, sat close to each other and talked, including talking about kissing each other for quite a while. Lou Ann said, "Well why don't we kiss? I'll kiss you first, then you kiss me." She kissed me on the cheek, then I kissed her back. That was it. I was terrified. We continued to play softball or hide and seek together with other kids, but we never met alone or kissed again.

I also had a crush on Marcella Van Doren, who was in my class at St. Mary's. The Van Dorens lived near the town of Valley, and my school bus also picked her up on the way to school. We sometimes sat together, and she and I also talked on the phone. Once, when Mom and Dad were attending one of my school functions at St. Mary's, we picked up Marcella in the car. Mom and Dad wanted to stop for a quick beer at the Valley Tavern on the way to the school, and Marcella and I stayed in the car. As we were sitting there, she took me by the hand, looked me in the eye, and said, "I love you."

I was speechless and couldn't wait until my parents came back to the car. Nothing else happened between us. Later, I believe while I was in college, I heard that she had committed suicide. Feeling very bad about that, I called one of her brothers, but as is often the case, he had no idea why she'd taken her life.

Another early girlfriend, Joan Kolbeck, was a year ahead of me at St. Mary's. Compared to Marcella, she was beautiful, and I had a crush on her from the first time I saw her. But like Marcella, she would later die a horrible death. Many of the hotrodders used the road to Waitts Lake, where we swam during the summer, as a race track, particularly one steep downhill stretch. The summer of Joan's senior year at St. Mary's, she was in a car full of teenagers that was being driven by a young driver who'd had a driving while intoxicated (DWI) infraction. The driver was already speeding when he hit the top of the hill, but he kept his foot on the gas. He lost control of the car midway down and went off the road. Joan was killed instantly and many others were injured. It was heartbreaking for the students who knew her, and especially me.

While at St. Mary's, I had male friends, too, mostly from the neighborhood. Joe Burya's family lived down the hill from us by the highway. Their sons, Nickie and Denny, were always jealous of me because I was making my own money and owned the only Red Ryder BB gun in the neighborhood, plus a new three-speed bike that Dad had bought me. Nickie and I once got into a fight in which he knocked my bottom teeth out. But sometimes we got along better. Nickie and Denny's parents drove a Model T with a canvas top, which they parked in front of Ray's Tavern in Valley. Our parents would bring us kids a big bag of chips and we'd sit up there, out in front of the tavern, shoot the bull, and watch people come and go. Right next door to Ray's was the town's only barbershop, where a haircut cost 15 cents. On the other side of Ray's was the post office. Across from Ray's was another tavern, the Valley Tavern, and the town also had two service stations.

Mom and Dad spent quite a bit of time at the taverns with all the locals. Men there were always trying to grab and kiss Mom in the Valley Tavern, many times in front of me, since kids could still go into taverns back then. Friday was the big night at Ray's Tavern, with many of the locals meeting for a few beers. They'd play punch cards, where you could win or lose money, or shuffle board or pool. The only things to eat there were hot Polish sausages, pickled eggs, and potato chips, but I loved the Polish sausages. Uncle Louis would sometimes come and get Mom and tell her she had to get home. There would be a minor tussle between them because she didn't want to go.

My parents also made home brew, and I started enjoying the taste of beer. Mom told me that during Prohibition, Grandpa Tomsha had distilled whiskey and sold it. The federal agents once came to the house after someone turned him in. At first they could not find the whiskey he had hidden there, but later he did spend time in the Colville jail for it.

When we visited my Grandma and Grandpa Black, alcohol could be an issue, too. Dad's parents had retired from their homestead in Gifford to Lewiston, Idaho, in 1944, and we visited them several times at their home at 509 East Snake River Avenue. Grandma Black was a teetotaler, and Mom and Dad couldn't bring beer or liquor into her house. I always noticed how nervous they'd get before making excuses to go get something at the store. They never took me with them, and I'm sure they were stopping to have a beer somewhere. I couldn't go because they were afraid I'd snitch to Grandma.

Grandma Mary and Grandpa John

It was fun for me to visit her, though—even if they didn't have indoor plumbing. Instead, we had a chamber pot that had to be emptied in the morning. At night I'd see Mom trying to sit on the pot in the dark, and sometimes she would miss it and sit on the floor, waking Dad and I up. Grandma Black was very kind, and she never said anything bad about anybody. Very religious, she'd read to me from her prayer book. I'd talk to her about being Catholic, and ask why she wasn't. She'd explain the beliefs of her Assembly of God church, where she'd been attending for many years. But even at my young age, I was trying to convert her.

My grandpa was a bit eccentric, I thought. For instance, every day he'd go to the store, walking about two blocks to buy gum and bring back a loaf of bread. Grandma always had extra bread on hand and said she couldn't stop him. He'd offer me a stick of his gum, which he carried in his pocket. I liked that, but he also kept all of his used gum in a bottle, and when he didn't have some, he'd take out that bottle and chew an old piece.

When I was eight, I wrote Grandma Black a letter:

> Dear Grandma B,
> I wish you wouldn't be sick. How are you getting along now? I wish I could come down and see you soon. How is Grandpa? Does he still walk to town every day? Did you have a nice birthday? Mommie had a very nice birthday. I am going to send you a Valentine. When you get well, I will come and see you. Daddy has the mumps and he looks like a beaver. Grandpa and I play chicken, he always moves so I can jump him. I am studying piano and am on page 6. Dear Grandma, I will pray for you and Grandpa every night.
> Your loving grandson, Johnny. I love you.

One day in 1950, I was walking home for school back home and saw Dad driving our pickup truck toward me. I must have been nine or ten. He stopped to say that Grandpa Black, who was then 90 years old, had died, so he was driving to Lewiston. I asked if I could go with him but wasn't allowed.

Other relatives were important, too. I would go to Ray's Tavern with my Uncle Frank and play pool with him. It was his favorite place. We'd rack the balls and start a pool game, but then he'd go up to the barstools with his friends, and I was just standing there waiting for him to come back. Or he'd leave to go to town's other tavern, right across the street, and it would be hard to corral him. I'd have to go run him down. Sometimes a pool game would take two or three hours.

Alcohol was a very serious problem for Uncle Frank and others you'll meet in my story. He probably had a serious case of post-traumatic stress disorder (PTSD) because of his service in World War I, though of course nobody had a name for it then. Before the war, he'd worked in the area as a logger and at the John Kulzer sawmill south of Valley. In 1917, he enlisted in the U.S. Army and was sent to France that December. He served with the 20th Engineers Company until the end of the war, remaining overseas with the U.S. Army of Occupation until 1919. When he returned to Valley, he again was employed in various logging operations, becoming the sole owner and operator of a sawmill in 1922. Twice he saw his mill destroyed by fire, and after he married my Aunt May, he finally rebuilt it on family land that included a log cabin and a bunk house next to it. When I was younger and we still lived on our family homestead, I often visited them and stayed in the bunkhouse.

Uncle Frank and Aunt May at their cabin

There were many fights between him and Aunt May. One night as I lay awake, they had a terrible fight in the doorway. I didn't understand what it was all about, but I remember Aunt May waving a large wrench in her hand and yelling, "You dirty SOB, I will kill you!"

Uncle Frank yelled back, "May, just listen to me, listen to me." They continued to yell back and forth and finally stopped, to my relief. The many fights I witnessed between them were due to Uncle Frank's drinking. My mother told me that part of the problem was also that Aunt May wanted to have children but Uncle Frank didn't. Another time when I was staying with him, he was shaving with a straight-edged razor in the bathroom. I was watching from the doorway. The bare-bulb light hanging above him was swinging back and forth as he shaved and was talking, and he was getting very irritated. All at once he yelled, "Son of a bitch!" and grabbed the cord and cut it in half with the razor. Sparks flew everywhere, and the razor disintegrated. I said to him, "Uncle Frank, why did you do that?" He just told me to shut up. He was really upset.

Aunt May worked very hard while married to Uncle Frank. At that point, his third, small sawmill was still operating about half a mile upstream from his log cabin. In the morning she would cook breakfast in the bunkhouse on a wood stove and serve up coffee, bacon, and eggs to the sawmill's crew of about ten men. She also packed them lunches. Uncle Frank would have me put about twelve quarts of Rainier beer into the creek by the mill so it would be cold at quitting time. It was my job to make sure each member of the crew got a quart to drink. They were very thirsty and so was I.

They argued a lot, and Aunt May would eventually divorce him. She went on to marry William Superak Sr., an Air Force sergeant and friend of my dad's whom she'd met at the homestead after my dad brought him out there. But I continued to visit Uncle Frank and fish at his place.

I began attending another school by the name of St. Mary's, this one in Chewelah associated with St. Mary of the Rosary church there. Participation in choir was mandatory at St. Mary's, and we practiced twice a week singing in Latin for the following Sunday's Mass. One day, the Sister leading our choir practice asked me and two other boys to go find the Kowalski boys, two Polish brothers who always wore engineer-type overalls and who were so short that everyone was always playing tricks on them. They hadn't shown up in class. We looked in the hallway and down in the basement, and there they were— both hanging by their suspenders from a coat hook, their feet just swinging in the air two feet off the floor. We got them down, and they were mad as hell, but that's the kind of misbehavior we all were involved in.

My own most embarrassing moment came there at school. Every day I took the bus from the cottages to school at Chewelah, and once while on the bus, I had to go to the bathroom. But the whole route was about fifteen miles, and there were several stops on the way to pick up other kids. By the time we got to school I get hold it no longer and, just as the bus arrived at school, I crapped my pants. I couldn't make it to the toilet. So I ran to the rectory where the priest, Father O'Malley, lived. I knocked on the door and I could tell right away I must stink, because he moved backward. "Are you sick?" he asked. I said yes and he took me all the way home, though he rolled down all the windows in the car for the whole hour-long ride.

Like most, the school had fundraisers; I was always the best salesman, and I put those skills to work for myself, too. I sold Christmas cards, going down the listings of the very small Valley phone directory, calling every name. I ordered hybrid worms from a catalog and raised them for fish bait, and then sold them at the local resort, $5 for 1,000 worms. Worms are hermaphrodites, so even one can reproduce, and I raised a lot. I also responded to ads in newspapers and comic books such as the one that got me selling White Cloverine Salve to earn points and premiums. Cloverine Salve was like Vaseline; you could put it on anything. That's how I got a childhood classic of the era: my Red Ryder BB gun.

About that age I also learned to carve wood, whether making little ships or just carving up sticks. It was a big event when you were old enough to have your own pocket knife, and a few years later, my dad gave me his small, ivory-handled pocket knife that he'd received from his own dad. Back in my grandfather's day, all men carried a small pocket knife, often to cut an end off a plug of tobacco for a chew. I didn't use mine for that, but it might be my most treasured possession. I'll pass it on to my son Shane, and hopefully he'll be able to continue the tradition.

As I got older, I also took old clocks apart and tried to put them back together, which was very hard to do. Of course, on a farm where everything is always broken, I'd learned to fix everything, or at least try. I also learned how to make rubberguns from pine wood. If you made it right, you could hit a target fifteen feet away. We would have rubbergun fights. I also built a tree house in the woods near our cottage. It was about seven feet off the ground. It even had a tower, which I entered through a trap door in the ceiling.

One year about then, I ordered fireworks from Portland, Oregon, when it was still legal to ship them through the mail. I had so many that it took me a whole week to shoot off all the fireworks, and spent at least half a day, every day of that week shooting fireworks. At the end of the July 4 celebrations, my ears were ringing and I was nearly deaf. But it had been fun!

I spent a lot of time in sports, too—whether I wanted to or not. Participation in football, basketball, track, and baseball all were mandatory at St. Mary's from the fifth to the eighth grade. I did the 100-yard dash and high jump; played second base on the baseball team; and was a basketball forward. For football, I was third-string quarterback, and I wasn't that great. I dreaded and feared practice because it seemed like every time we had a drill called "run with the ball," a six-foot boy named Gordon was lined up to tackle me. I was short and very skinny, and he was strong. I would be in the line of players to be tackled, and Gordon would be to my right. I was sure he was thinking, "I'm going to kill this twerp." I would look over at him and could see hate and death in his eyes and fire coming out of his ears. He didn't just tackle me; he would literally pick me up and slam me to the ground on my back, knocking the wind out of me. I felt I had been killed. After I bawled for ten minutes, Knecht would run over and ask me if I was all right. I wanted to say, "Oh, father, I'm okay, but I think I'm paralyzed." I'd get up and do the drill again, hopefully drawing some other guy who didn't want to cripple me for life.

For our games, we played these really rough farm-boy schools, including one night game where the guys on the opposing team seemed really big. Our lead quarterback got his leg broken and was hauled off on a stretcher. Then our second string quarterback got hurt and was hauled off the field, although at least he didn't need a stretcher. Father Knecht said to me, "Johnny, can you quarterback this team?"

I replied, "Well, I'll try." But after seeing that carnage, I was pretty scared. The first play I was to pitch the ball out to the left, and just as I tossed it, I was hit by two guys, who knocked the wind out of me. I was on my back sobbing, and Father came and took me off. Needless to say, we lost that game.

When I had to be indoors, I enjoyed reading, but most of my favorite books were outdoorsy and adventurous and filled with animals, too: *Lassie Come Home*, *The Secret of Skull Mountain*, *Tarzan—Forbidden City*, *White Fang* by Jack London, and the Hardy Boys series. Those were all really fun. Having developed reading habits early, even today, when in doubt, I go somewhere quiet with a great book to read.

Often, though, being indoors meant music—playing myself or listening to Dad's. He was a very gentle, kind person, honest and a hard worker. He never raised his voice. He and Mom had arguments, but not like Uncle Frank and Aunt May. Dad probably drank too much, but that was a product of the war and the alcohol culture of the military in general. That alcohol culture began in the Revolutionary War and expanded to America's first president and then through one American war after another, including every war mentioned in this book.

Being a musician also meant he was always surrounded by alcohol. Sometimes he would come home just shit-faced. Occasionally, in the years that we lived at the cottages and later in Spokane, he would bring home World War II veterans that he'd met. They all drank and chain-smoked. One of them, a retired Army Lieutenant known as James W. Lambert, gave Dad a book called *D-Day* written by famous war author John Gunther while the war was still on. Dad later gave it to me. Lambert had been on Omaha Beach on D-Day. Like all the vets I met as a kid, his hands shook as he smoked. One thing about veterans of the two World Wars is that they never really talked about the war, not that I remember. They played cards, shot pool, drank and smoked, and had fun.

Once while we lived in Spokane he brought home not a vet but a paper salesman who was working to get Dad into his company. They'd both been drinking whiskey, and Mom just went nuts. She had 10 or 15 flowerpots on a ledge in the kitchen, and she started throwing those pots. Dad and I went down the stairs to try to escape, and she threw every one of those pots down the stairs at him. She was really mad, and I didn't blame her.

Her drinking wasn't as obvious as my father's. Once I saw her open a cupboard and take a drink from a stubby she had stashed there. I only saw her really sloshed once, though. I must have been nine or ten years old. A butcher knife was lying on the table, and she grabbed it and whipped it around and stuck its point against my chest—not enough to draw blood, but enough to be scary.

"What are you doing, Johnny?" she demanded.

I said, "What are *you* doing?!" That really bugged me. But everybody seemed to drink, from my parents to our relatives, the Stroyans. Nobody thought anything of it.

I'd soon be sucked into that culture of alcohol. Drinking it was as common as drinking a Coke. The culture would be there later at my high school, Gonzaga Prep, then at Gonzaga University, too. The kegs of beer at my GU graduation were supplied by the Jesuits, who loved to drink as much as we did. So it just seemed natural to continue the habit. It was a way to be a big shot in the culture I was growing up in. You'll read about it in my stories that follow: I had bragging rights, so I drank and bragged.

My image of Dad, however, was that he was always happy, regardless of the circumstances, and he's the one who taught me how to have a good time. He never yelled, he never once spanked me, and he never swore. He had a hard time making decisions, however, and he usually said "No," when I wanted to do something. Still, I felt Dad really loved me. Some nights when he had brought someone home and they were in the kitchen drinking beer, he would crack open my bedroom door and tell whoever was visiting to come over. I'd pretend to be asleep. They would look in the crack so the visitor could see me, and Dad would say, "There's my boy, Johnny, asleep. He's a good boy." I guess I made him proud. I felt bad when, on a couple of occasions, Dad said to me, "Johnny, I wish I would have done better." At those times, I'd tell him that I loved him and that he always did the best he could. Dad was a veteran, and like many vets today, he had a tough time transitioning to civilian life.

He did have one quality I didn't like—he let people take advantage of him. He also never believed in buying a new car, but over the years he spent thousands of dollars keeping our old cars running.

He also may have made another mistake when it came to our car— insisting against her better judgment that Mom learn to drive. Probably about nine years old, I was in the backseat of the car for one of her lessons. He took her on a one-lane road to the top of a big hill with a sharp turn at the bottom before it went over a creek. We were in a big, old Terraplane, and Dad had her stop it at the top of the hill, telling her that she had to pump the brakes as we went. Then we started down. I could see she was anxious. The car started picking up speed and she shoved the brake to floor. There was no brake! She panicked and started swerving while Dad's yelling to pump the brake and I thought we were going over the side into a ravine. We would've been killed. By the grace of God she was able to stay on the road and make the turn, cross the creek, and come to a stop. It scared the hell out of Dad and me, and probably her, too—she said she'd never drive again, and she didn't.

Dad shouldn't have tried to teach Mom to drive.

The greatest thing my Dad did with me in those years when we lived at the cottages was to take me to see the Ringling Brothers, Barnum, and Bailey Circus pull into Spokane and unload. We arrived at the station about 5:00 in the morning, and at 6:00, a very long train pulled by a huge steam locomotive pulled in. Out came the elephants and the crew, and they started unloading the train and setting up the big tent. The elephant hauled the huge tent pole erect, and you could see that everyone had a job. The circus was unbelievable, with sword-swallowers, a bearded lady, and other amazing sights. It was an experience I will never forget.

I also had the rare experience of serving as an altar boy at my own parents' wedding. Because my father hadn't been Catholic, they'd been married outside the Catholic Church by a preacher. But in June 1955, when I was fourteen years old, they finally got dispensation from the Pope and were married at St. Joseph's Mission Church as I looked on and helped.

During the summer, Dad would sometimes drive me and other kids to Waitts Lake for swimming. At the Waitts Lake Resort, a floating dock was attached to the main dock by a long chain. You could jump off the end of the main dock and pull yourself along the chain to the floating dock. My teenaged cousin Billy Stroyan was swimming with us one day when I jumped in to grab the chain, but missed it and started to panic. I was screaming, taking in a lot of water, and about to drown, but Billy was a good swimmer. He jumped in and pulled me to the dock. I owe my life to him and from then on, I was careful about how I got to that floating raft.

By far the worst thing that happened to me during those years, though— or for that matter, in my life—was the sexual abuse I suffered in grade school starting in the fifth grade. From 1950 to 1955 I attended St. Mary's School in Chewelah, Washington, entering when I was nine years old. Father Joseph P. Knecht was the pastor of St. Mary's parish as well as the director of the choir and the coach of all our sports teams: basketball, football, track, and baseball. Under Knecht, serving at Mass, singing in the choir, and participating in all sports and Scouting were all mandatory. Other than my parents, he was the major authority figure in my life and in the lives of the other boys who attended St. Mary's. Every Sunday we suited up in our choir robes and sang in Mass, which was all in Latin. This meant also going to weekly choir practice led by Knecht and our music teacher, Sister Aloysius. All of us boys, about twenty of us, were in effect prisoners in a system created and led by Knecht— who was later proven to be a pedophile and sex offender. His name was released publicly by the diocese in January 2004 and many of the abuse acts he committed on us boys were reported in graphic detail in the Spokane *Spokesman Review* newspaper.

We knew long before anyone else did. Knecht abused me, along with numerous other boys, over his 16 years there. An ordained Roman Catholic priest, he'd been part of the local diocese since 1932 and at St. Mary's from 1937 until his death in 1956, just a year after I left St. Mary's at age 14. Until then, I was one of his "honored" students there, which meant I was a target. So were the majority of boys my age in school, though we never shared our stories until we became adults and the abuse in the Catholic Church became public. Boys were sometimes removed from class and sent to Father Knecht at his request. What he did to me and others was that at least once a month and sometimes more, he would grab me, hold my head tight to his face, kiss me and stick his tongue in my ear or mouth, mostly the latter, and fondle my genitals, all while telling me he "loved" me. This all happened on school and church grounds during his official duties. Just imagine—you're an innocent young boy and this grown man, this priest, is French-kissing you, sticking his tongue in and out of your mouth, his saliva acting as a lubricant and shooting out onto your face. He was the parish priest and head pastor, the school principal and athletic coach, and was heavily involved in Scouting and choir at the school, and I was still serving as an altar boy on Sundays, so it was impossible to avoid him.

The assaults could take place in the church rectory and vestibule, the cloak room, and his car, but his favorite place to bring me and others was the boy's locker room in the basement of the school. He would corner me there when he could get me alone. He would take me in his arms and rub his body against mine. It was a sickening, degrading experience and I was afraid to tell anyone, including my parents. I thought something must be wrong with me for the parish priest to want to do these things to me.

I started feeling inadequate, lacking self-confidence and developing a major problem with self-esteem, which haunts me to this day. I could never do enough, play sports hard enough—or, starting in the tenth grade, drink enough. Although I was successful at school and in my career, this abuse would lead me to become an alcoholic with many behavior problems, one of which would be extensive womanizing in my first marriage. I constantly wanted to prove to myself that I was not gay but heterosexual, that I loved girls and women. I had to prove myself in every social and work situation. Becoming an officer in the Army wasn't enough; I had to volunteer for Vietnam service. One graduate degree wasn't enough; I had to get two. I became sexually compulsive and a terrible alcoholic, finally going into treatment after leaving the military and then, a decade later, relapsing again and again. All my life I have been in therapy and counseling, trying to get to the root cause of my terrible feelings of low self-esteem and self-confidence and of my ever-present anger that constantly needs to be controlled.

Only late in 2003, when I and my fellow classmates filed lawsuits against Knecht and other priests in Washington State, as well as against the Corporation of the Catholic Bishop of Spokane, would all of us former students come and meet in the same room. There with attorneys, we told and heard the horror stories of abuse by Knecht that we had never shared or spoken about for 53 years. No longer afraid of Knecht, we shared our terrible secrets and our stories with each other. All agreed that our grades had plummeted because of the abuse.

One classmate was Joe Newbury, who also told his story in the January 21, 2004, edition of the *Spokesman Review* because he wanted to publicly tell his secret. Some of us chose to be referred to as the plaintiff John Doe. In the newspaper article, our classmate Joe, who was then a retired 63-year old school principle, said, "A priest was untouchable." In the article he told how Knecht would fondle his genitals, kiss him, and hug him in 30-minute sessions, abusing him twice a week for two years. Joe also shared that, as the paper reported it, "twice a week, one of the Catholic nuns would remove him from class and send him to Knecht's living quarters, forcing him to take a circuitous route so that he would not be seen. Another classmate said that 'Knecht pinned me against the kitchen sink and scrubbed my penis with a toothbrush until in bled, then kissed and fondled me.'" In the course of the lawsuit Knecht tried to explain this behavior by saying, "I had to touch the boys to see if they were keeping themselves clean and whether their genitals were developing properly."

Neither these men who'd talked to the reporter nor any of us had ever before shared our terrible secrets with each other or with our parents. We tried to bury them while at St. Mary's and then to bury them even deeper later so we could try to go on with our lives.

By December 7, 2004, the sex-abuse claims against the Roman Catholic Diocese of Spokane were reported by the *Spokesman Review* as possibly reaching $75.7 million, a number so large that it drove Bishop William Skylstad to file for bankruptcy protection. On December 6, 2004, the bishop had sent a letter to all of us who were sexually abused by clergy of the Spokane diocese. It stated in part: "The strongest message you have communicated to me is your deep sense of betrayal by a minister of the church, a person who was to witness to Christ. I pray for the day your trust in God and, if possible, the church, is restored."

Even once they knew of his behavior and that of others in the diocese, however, officials failed to warn parents or anyone else. They should've been removed from the ministry and prevented from coming into contact with kids like me, as the diocese later admitted. At the time the abuse happened, there seemed to be no one to tell and no way to stop it. None of us ever talked about what he did at the time, not amongst ourselves or with anyone else.

It probably caused more abuse, domino-fashion, too. When I was in fifth grade, I was riding on the school bus one night with a whole load of kids returning from a sports game. I had to sit on the lap of an eighth-grader named David. I'd fallen asleep, but suddenly I woke up to find his hand stuck in my pants. I didn't know what to do. I wouldn't be surprised, though, to find out that David had been abused by Father Knecht or one of the other priests, too, and I certainly was. I didn't tell my parents for more than 30 years. Mom and Dad were shocked and couldn't understand why I never told them about Father Knecht. But like most victims, I was simply too embarrassed and ashamed.

As students, even when we thought we might get some justice, we didn't. One day our baseball team was coming back from a game, with about 20 players and a few parents on the bus. I had my arm hanging out the window, and Father Knecht was driving the bus down a hill. Suddenly we all looked up to see him draped over the steering wheel, the bus swerving back and forth across the narrow country road. One of parents jumped up and tried to grab the steering wheel, but Father Knecht was heavy and his body pulled the wheel from side to side. The bus shot across ravine, through a barbed wire fence, and into a field before it stopped. It was a moment of terror, because the bus could have flipped, but no one was hurt. An ambulance came to take Father Knecht to the hospital. He'd had a heart attack. I thought to myself, and I bet the other boys felt the same, that maybe he would die as God's way of punishing him for his abuse of all of us. But he survived.

The abuse didn't stop until my family moved to Spokane in 1955 for my first year of high school. Knecht continued to have a hold on all of us, though. In my freshman year at Gonzaga Preparatory School, I earned the role of Shapiro, the mail clerk, in a play called *Stalag 17*. I sent Knecht an invitation to come see a performance and visit our home in Spokane. His two-page, handwritten reply on December 21, 1955, said, in part, "Dear Johnny, The 'gang,' sisters, and Father O' Neil send greetings. Your name comes up often. Give my best to Dad and Mom. Shall stop by some time when in Spokane. A very blessed and merry Christmas to all of you. Yours, Father Knecht." Thank God he never paid us a visit. My parents would never know what had happened with him until decades later.

Although Gonzaga Prep was also a Catholic institution, it didn't seem to be a problem there, but I would carry the impacts for the rest of my life. Decades later, after Knecht's death, I and many other victims would sue and settle with the Spokane Diocese in 2004 in a case naming Knecht and other diocese priests as abusers. The case, which involved us and many other students and schools around the country, received national attention and later prompted several movies. The most recent was a 2015 film called *Spotlight*. But no legal or financial reparations could undo the emotional damage, which destroyed my self-esteem, made it exceedingly difficult to have male friendships, and left me with a suspicion of authority that complicated my later military career. It was also a factor in my later alcoholism. I would forever find forging close bonds, especially with men, difficult. Instead, I turned to women to create a much-needed new sense of myself, as a young man and then as an adult. I realize now that I was searching for love and the closeness and protection I could find in sexual encounters with strong and forgiving women. I recognized that I was forever wounded. I was forever "damaged goods" and couldn't risk or take well to new hurts.

Another blow came when Grandpa Tomsha died at age 78—on my thirteenth birthday. Back then nobody put old people in rest homes; they lived at home. Grandpa was in the shower that day, and I was sitting outside of it, watching him a bit while Mom was in the kitchen. Suddenly I heard a big thump.

I opened the shower and he was slumped down there, unconscious. I yelled for mom, and as she came running as his face slowly turned blue. He was very heavy, but we carried him into bed and Mom called up to Chewelah. But there was no ambulance or mobile medical service back then, and nothing to do. She was screaming into the phone and I was watching his face now turn almost black. Based on her call, the funeral home sent a hearse, but no other help.

There was no wake for Grandpa like there had been for Grandma. Although I'd been very young when she died—just four years old—I remembered the event. That loss was not such a shock. For her wake, they put her in bed at the homestead and the whole family gathered around, praying the rosary with the priest there. All the relatives, and especially the women, were just sobbing.

We all really missed my Tomsha grandparents.

For Grandpa, we held a rosary at Bryan Chapel in Chewelah one evening and a funeral Mass at St. Joseph's Church in Jump Off. Rev. Pius Mutter said the Mass. I served as one of the altar boys at that Mass. Grandpa was survived by a brother and a sister, four sons and three daughters, 12 grandchildren, and several nieces, nephews, and friends. The announcement in the Chewelah paper called him an industrious worker, a capable farmer, and an excellent blacksmith. In fact, Grandpa had helped to build the church in which he was married in 1907 and from which he was buried, right next to Grandma and his mother and father.

My mother was just devasted by both of her parents' deaths. She cried every night for weeks, and she started crying again when she woke up each morning. The whole experience with Grandpa was traumatic for me, too. In his will, Grandpa gave the homestead to Uncle Louis, and he lived there for a while before renting it out and then selling it to my Aunt May. As much as I liked to visit my favorite uncle, the homestead wasn't the same with both my grandparents gone.

About that time, I began talking to my parents about becoming a priest. It'd been in my mind for a while; in fact, I would say Mass at home with apple juice instead of wine, that's how devoted I was. I'd begun learning Latin at St. Mary's, as all the boys were required to sing the Mass in Latin every Sunday morning. I continued to serve Mass at the local church on Sundays. Then the school church in Chewelah begin what they called a mission, where we attended services and a lecture by a visiting priest every week for a month. The priest was from the Maryknoll Fathers and Brothers, an order that solely does missionary work around the world. I'd heard the lectures about the importance of mission work and helping the poor, and the speaker had a major influence on me. So I began planning to enter Gonzaga's Bishop White Seminary after eighth grade.

In the end, I was too scared of leaving home to live at the seminary. And given the abuse I suffered, thank God I didn't. The seminary was were so many of the area's abusive priests had come from, and I'm sure I would've only been abused by the seminarians, too. Instead, completing eighth grade and graduating from St. Mary's was my escape, at last, from Father Knecht.

Whether in church or at home, though, by that time I found some escape in music. I had played around with drums while we still lived in Texas. Later, while attending St. Mary's, I'd taken lessons for the piano and then the guitar and trumpet from a teacher in Chewelah. I'd always wanted to be able to play like my dad. I got pretty good at each and then gave it up, moving on to something else.

I could never really read music, but that didn't stop me from starting to write it as a teenager. I wasn't yet ready to create music that portrayed how I saw my world, but I felt that coming. Music was all around me. The Slovenian culture was a musical one, and everybody in the family but my mother played an instrument. My Aunt Irene was a vaudeville pianist, a genius on the keyboards, and her daughter Beverly was a "torch singer" who sang in clubs. Aunt May had a beautiful accordion she played polkas on, and Grandpa played a smaller accordion, too.

Our family grew again with the birth of Judith, known as Judy, in 1953.

In Lewiston with Grandma Black, Dad, little Judy, and Julie

Not long before Judy was born, my mother wrote me a letter. There was no occasion that prompted it, and I've carried on this tradition by writing inside my books, including everyone's age, the date, and a message. Her letter said:

> Dear Son Johnny:
> You are now 12 years old and have brought us that many years of joy and happiness. Julie is 3 years and 4 mos. old now and we are expecting our third addition to the family Feb. 11th. Mother is 34 years old and Daddy is 49. Today is the inauguration of Pres. Eisenhower. May God bless you and keep you good boy always. Love, Mother.

I have another from the same day from Dad. His reflected his personality and sense of humor:

Dear Johnny,
Don't forget your sharps and flats, as you'll have many
of them from now on. Always play your life in the right
key, and keep in good rhythm with all your fellow men.
Your Daddy.

After Judy's birth, James followed in 1956, though by then I was a teenager. I had fun with James—when he was only three or four years old, I would put a leather cap on him and put him in a cardboard racing car, with no wheels, that I had built. I pulled him through the house, sliding around the corners. Eventually, we also made music together, with Julie and Judy playing piano. Both were fantastic on the keyboards, and James would learn to play the guitar. We were all forever grateful for the gift of music that our parents gave us.

Dad retired from the military not long after Judy was born, but his retirement pay wasn't enough to support our family. So he took various jobs for the local magnesite plant, at Uncle Louis's sawmill, and tending bar at a Chewelah hotel.

My sisters Judy and Julie with my brother James and me

I graduated from St. Mary's School on May 27, 1955. I still have the commencement program. Then we moved to Spokane so I could attend high school there. My high school years started with ninth grade at the Jesuits' Gonzaga Preparatory School in Spokane. I was lucky that my Uncle Bill and Aunt May offered to help out with tuition, which wasn't cheap. We went through some tough financial times otherwise. Dad first tried to make a living selling musical organs in Spokane, and then got a better job managing printing for the Old National Bank in Spokane, although he quit that one, too, after about a year. Though I missed being close to the homestead, I was glad to get away from St. Mary's. There would be no more Father Knechts on my life's horizon, thank God. And the next half-dozen years, high school and college, would be pivotal for my life—especially in regard to music and my future military career.

CHAPTER 3: MAKING MUSIC & RAISING HELL

"Well, go on down to Jackson, go ahead and wreck your health. Go play your hand, you big talkin' man, make a big fool of yourself."

—Johnny Cash, "Jackson"

After the abuse trauma of the previous years, I didn't get very good grades in high school, mostly Cs and Ds. Just about every class was mandatory. We had to take four years of Latin and philosophy. Other required courses included English, math, geometry, accounting, and typing. Accounting was especially tough. The teacher, Mr. McGinn, was tough, too. He had a wooden leg. There were a few of us in his class that he did not like, starting with me and then Pat Rotchford, John Carlson, and Angelo Roman. Rotchford and I were constantly in trouble with McGinn.

Denny Flaherty (who we called Flats) and John Carlson were my main buddies, and of these friends, Pat, Angelo, and Denny have all passed away. If it wasn't for Denny, none of us would have passed the accounting class. McGinn knew we were copying Flat's accounting sheet, but he couldn't prove it, so he harassed us. Pat and I sat way in the back of the class, and when McGinn was pissed, he would come charging down the aisle toward us, yelling, "You copied Flaherty! I know you copied him." We denied everything.

Pat and I got together and planned an attack on him. One day Pat said, "John R., McGinn has a wooden leg, so let's get him all heated up and he'll come charging down our aisle. We'll have a tripwire hooked up between the desks and across the aisle so that when he gets to us, he'll hit the wire and fall over." We had it all worked out like a military operation.

We were in class early, hooked up the wire, sat behind the wire—which you could barely see—and waited for class to start. Sure enough, when class started, as planned, Pat raised his hand and said to McGinn, "Black and I finished our homework."

I performed onstage starting in my freshman year at Prep.

McGinn started yelling, "Yes, and I bet you both copied Flaherty."

Pat yelled, "Prove it."

That did it. McGinn came racing on his one good leg down our aisle, tripped over the wire, and fell flat on his face. The whole class erupted in a cheer.

McGinn threw us out of class, sending us to the vice principle, where we were both hacked. That meant we stepped into the vault and grabbed our ankles, and the Father hacked you right below your buttocks. We both got five hacks. But where there is no pain, there is no gain. We felt vindicated.

I also took drama classes, performed in two plays, and began exploring my interests in new music, like that of pop and film star Ricky Nelson and other greats of that era, Carl Perkins, Roy Orbison, Jerry Lee Lewis, and Elvis. It was at Gonzaga Prep that my interests in both music and a military career really kicked off.

Me with the rest of the cast of Stalag 17

My family had a long tradition of military service, and not just by my father. Uncle Frank J. Burya, my Aunt May's first husband, was in World War I; he served as a private in the U.S. Army somewhere in France with the Seventh Company, 20th Engineers, C Company, Third Battalion of the American Expeditionary Forces. Aunt May, Private Mary T. Burya (later Superak), was in the Women's Army Corp working as a cook and stationed in Fort Des Moines, Iowa. Her second husband, William Superak Sr., had served in the Air Force as a navigator and after the war flew supplies from England to West Berlin in the famous Berlin Airlift. He retired from the Air Force as a chief master sergeant.

My Aunt May and Uncle Louis in their military uniforms

My Uncle Louis Tomsha joined the Navy and served on the battleship U.S.S. Iowa as a machinist mate 2 during World War II. The Iowa took President Roosevelt to the Tehran Conference, a four-day meeting that started on November 28, 1943. It included Prime Minister Winston Churchill of Britain and the Soviet leader Joseph Stalin. It was the first meeting between the "Big Three" Allied leaders.

My Uncle Jake had also been a Navy man during the war, serving on the island of Tinian in the Eastern Pacific as a Seabee building airplane runways. Other family members served in the Korean War, as well as conflicts to come.

Uncle Frank during World War I

So I'd long expected that I'd probably follow in their footsteps, and perhaps even play in a military band like my dad. By age 16, I was writing my own songs. I'd never heard of a course you could take to learn how, although I suppose they exist. I just sat down one day, inspired by a girl, and wrote my first song. My method was usually to write the lyrics first, and then the music, although sometimes I did it the other way around. I'd work out the melody in my mind as I played the keyboards, then write the chords down for the lyrics as I completed the song. I never used sheet music. I wrote many songs that never got recorded, but some of my early songs I would rerelease many years later, in 2018, on an album called *Back in Time*. It included "People Talk" (originally written in 1958), "Down the Devil's Road" (1962), "Rio Town" (1962), and "Sunday of My Mind" (1977).

I didn't wait that long to record anything, though, or rely on anyone else to do it. Spokane had a great recording studio, so I began recording there. I paid for all my sessions with money I'd earned and always worked toward achieving the highest sound quality I could. Eventually I would buy a Sony four-track recorder and start recording my own songs.

I started performing in the cafeteria at Gonzaga Prep, too. I had a guitar player, bass and drums, and I played piano. I'd perform "Honeycomb," a 1957 hit sung by Jimmie Rodgers that includes these lyrics:

> Oh, Honeycomb, won't you be my baby?
> Well, Honeycomb, be my own,
> Got a hank o' hair and a piece o' bone
> And made a walkin' talkin' Honeycomb.
> Well, Honeycomb, won't you be my baby?
> Well, Honeycomb, be my own,
> What a darn good life
> When you got a wife like Honeycomb.

I also played Rickey Nelson tunes like "Waitin' in School." Later I would only record my own songs.

In high school, I played some golf and I fished. I still visited Uncle Frank, even after we moved to Spokane. I fished at his place, and he told me I could bring friends to a good spot for it, the beaver dam on his property.

It was a good spot for other things, too. Our Gonzaga Prep class of 1958 was the last that was all boys, but at a school social I had met this Marycliff girl, Karen. She was a really cute blond who liked to drink beer. I told her about the beaver dam and how neat it would be to go up there and just drink beer and sit around and talk. She thought it would be fun, too, so I gave Mom and Dad some cock-and-bull story about taking the car to visit my friend John Carlson for the day. I put a washtub in the trunk, dropped in a case of beer, and filled it with ice. I picked up Karen from her house and we headed to the beaver damn below Uncle Frank's place. It was at least an hour's drive. I found the cutoff logging road that led to the beaver dam, drove to the end of the road, and we laid out a blanket. For some reason we didn't make out at all, but just talked and drank beer. After about six hours, we got back in the car and I took Karen home. How I made it I don't know, as we had finished the whole case of beer. It was a rather odd date, but there were no guns involved this time or anyone around to bother us.

Later, I'd take reporters I worked with at the *Spokesman Review* up to fish at Uncle Frank's place, too. Uncle Frank loved the company, and he was good to me. He also enjoyed the country tricks I played on some of those reporters, who slept in sleeping bags by the fireplace on the living room floor. A new reporter came with us on one trip, and after he was asleep I went out to the creek, caught a water snake, came back inside, raised the flap on his sleeping bag, and threw the snake in. The reaction was like a small explosion as he felt the snake on his legs or near his crotch. He jumped out of the bag fully awake and swearing.

In most of my spare time, though, I worked. I earned money doing a little bit of everything, including night watchman duty at Inland Motor Freight. A fellow Gonzaga Prep student who had the job before me showed me the ropes. This all-night job required walking the premises and clocking in at each of several stations to prove it. He figured out how to manually advance the check-in clock to rig the system, because the alternative was not getting all our homework done in time for class at 8:00 a.m. All of this went against what we were learning in ethics, of course.

I also worked part time for my Uncle Charlie Coppula, my Aunt Fran's second husband. He was a lawyer and a bookie. I'd go to his office after school and take phone calls from people calling to bet on games. I also worked as a golf caddy, taking the bus from school to the Downriver Golf Course twice a week. Again I applied the John R. Black Principle of Buying Things on Time, as I had at Kulzer's Mercantile with gifts for my mom. The golf pro, Joe Dunnigan, sold me a basic set of new clubs, and I paid him 90 cents a month. Not a bad deal! Plus I ate at the clubhouse for free when I caddied.

The school principle gave me permission to leave early to caddy, as I had to earn money to cover some of my tuition. (Luckily Aunt May and Uncle Bill very generously covered the rest of my tuition, because my parents couldn't.) I rode the city busy to the golf course. I also shined shoes at the "shoe hospital" in downtown Spokane, and I spent a whole summer working for Nick Skok, a farmer adjacent to our family's homestead.

Nick and his brother, Pete, lived at the farm, which had been inherited by Nick. He raised dairy and beef cattle and grew and sold hay. Work on the farm started early, at 5:00 a.m. on six days a week. The brothers would cook a big breakfast and then we worked until 6:00 p.m., finishing by milking the cows. Never having milked a cow before, I started off on the wrong foot. Nick explained that it was necessary to clip the hairy part of their tails so the cows wouldn't swish them and interfere with the milking. Not paying that much attention to how he did that, I clipped the first cow's tail at the fleshy upper part of the tail. The cow bawled in pain and broke through the stall, causing the other cows to stampede, or at least attempt to. After the ass-chewing I got from Nick, I paid more attention. I was paid room, board, and the use of their old car on Sundays, and at the end of summer I was paid $300.00. Later Aunt May related that Nick said he "lost money on Johnny." I later figured that I earned $25.00 a week for 60 hours of work a week, so I knew I would never become a rich farmer.

When all else failed, I worked distributing handbills for a penny each. My experiences would be even more diverse and interesting later—but first we moved to Idaho.

After I finished tenth grade, Dad left his Old National Bank job and took one as a salesman for Blake, Moffitt, and Towne, a paper company in Lewiston. We moved there. My Grandpa Black had already passed on by then, and breast cancer would take my grandmother while we were there. I started eleventh grade at Lewiston High School. While attending there, I briefly met the girl who would later become my wife, Paula Harootunian. She attended Lewiston High School with me, but we didn't socialize. For one thing, she was a year ahead of me in school, but perhaps more important, she had a boyfriend.

I had an innovative streak, though. We had a big house and yard, and I decided to host a party without telling my parents. I printed up posters for the John R. Black Booze Rally, advertising that beer and steaks would be provided. I put the posters all around school, including the hallways. Then I recruited a couple of my buddies to help get steaks at Safeway and meet me in the store's parking lot. When we got there, I handed each of them an empty paper grocery sack.

I said, "Look, I don't have the money, so we are going to just walk into Safeway, go to the meat department, fill our bags up with steaks, and walk out the front door." They didn't think it was a great idea, but I convinced them it would work. I assured them, "I'll repay Safeway later."

So the four of us walked in, filled our sacks, and walked right past the checker's stand and out the door. About 50 students showed up at the party, a couple with guitars, and it was a blast. The steaks were great. I saw Paula there briefly; in the middle of the party, she pulled up in her car and jumped out, madder than hell at some guy. She ran him down, tore the shirt off his back, and took off, peeling out of the drive way, as my mother watched in shock from the porch. My mother was already ready to kill me, as the neighbors were starting to complain about the noise.

A few days later, Mom wondered where I'd gotten the money to buy all those steaks, and I explained what I'd done. I was put on restriction for a couple of weeks. I built up enough courage to go meet with the store manager and beg his forgiveness. He was so impressed by my honesty that he told me I didn't have to pay for what I had stolen. Relieved, I swore I'd never pull a stunt like that again. Later the school principal called me in and chewed me out for advertising my party on posters at school, and he gave me punitive duty mopping floors with the school janitor. So that was another of life's lessons for me. However, my school buddies said I'd had one of the best parties they'd ever been to, with everything free.

Cruising in downtown Lewiston, just like as in the movie *Grease* with John Travolta, was the cool thing to do. All the guys had ducktail haircuts, wore jeans, and always had a comb stuck in their right rear pockets. Unlike me and a few others who were less cool, many had a pack of Camel cigarettes rolled up on their left shirt sleeves and lit up at every school break. Most of the cars owned by students had their frames lowered with custom wheels—attention-getters if you wanted to pick up girls. I tried to lower our family car over time so my Dad wouldn't notice, but that ultimately didn't work; the frame kept getting lower and lower until he really didn't have to step up to get in. The gig was up when Dad took the car into a body shop to figure out what was wrong and they told him what had happened. One night I had also removed the Plymouth emblem on the hood, which just wasn't cool. A buddy helped me fill in the hole with solder. For this stunt I was grounded, period.

In another adventure, a bunch of my friends heard that a traveling hypnotist was going to perform at the historic Liberty Theater in town. We all decided to go, as did many from our high school class. The promotional brochure promoted "a new sensation," talking about arms going limp, weightlessness, the gentle lull of a hypnotic trance, and that when you came out of the trance your grades would improve. So the scuttlebutt was that as many of us as possible should try to be hypnotized, both to experience it and maybe to get our pictures in the paper.

But the guys were concerned that they were going to get an erection while on stage in a trance. That would be embarrassing. At the theater, we all tried to sit as close to the stage as we could, about four rows back. The theater was packed. It was like a high school pep rally scene, with everyone screaming and yelling and coming unglued—another scene of my life that resembled the movie Grease, where Sid Caesar as Coach Calhoun got up and cheered the student body on to win the next football game.

The hypnotist explained what he did, saying that hypnosis would take us to a deeper subconscious level that sometimes ends in behavioral changes for the better. Everybody was screaming, "I want to be picked!" A chant broke out in the theater: "We want to be hypnotized, we want to be hypnotized."

I told myself I could use this, too.

"Let's have some volunteers," said the hypnotist.

Immediately everyone was in a panic to get onto the stage as if it were a fire drill. People started crawling and jumping to get onto the stage. My buddies and I were right there with them.

The hypnotist started by picking a girl my age. He went through his routine, staring into her eyes as she looked out into the audience. Suddenly she fell backwards to lay on the stage.

There was a hushed silence. She started moaning as if in pain.

The hypnotist said, "Don't worry, some of you will moan. That means you are in a deep trance, and whatever is bothering you wants to leave your body."

I thought, "Why not? I've got a lot of stuff that wants to leave, too." I was lined up with ten others and he started his routine on us as a group.

The hypnotist said, "I am going to slowly put you into a trance as deep as I possibly can." That was scary. Suddenly I realized I was lying on my back with the others. The hypnotist was running around the stage getting more people to line up. I now felt like I was in a trance, and as I lay there I realized I couldn't make contact with the outside world but felt trapped within my body.

The next thing I remember hearing was, "This kid is in a deep trance. We've got to get him outside."

"I can't get him awake," said somebody else.

I remember being carried out of the theater to the sidewalk outside, with the hypnotist yelling, "This kid is out of it!" Slowly I came out of the trance, got up, walked around, and asked one of my buddies to drive me home. The strange feeling that my body had been taken over slowly left, but the experience had no impact in keeping me out of trouble in the future. My grades certainly didn't improve, either.

Since I had too much time on my hands and needed money, I answered a newspaper ad calling for teenagers to deliver cheap costume jewelry to residences. The company worked temporarily from the Lewis and Clark Hotel, which I could see from our house in Lewiston. (Later, Paula and I would spend our honeymoon night in this hotel.) Operators manned a bank of phones in a scheme connected to magazine subscriptions, and my jewelry deliveries were part of that.

Then a greater opportunity came along at a newly formed television station, KLEW. Since I had been shooting a lot of family movies, I just boldly walked in their front door and told them they could hire me as an intern and that I wanted to make a career in television and production. When they asked me what experience I had, I told them I'd been making home movies and that I was very creative. They hired me. First I worked as a news assistant and cameraman. I was also an assistant to the reporter covering the famous Lewiston Roundup rodeo and the Joie Chitwood Thrill Show with stunt drivers, who appeared as part of the rodeo events.

Back then there was no such thing as a video camera; everything was black and white 16 mm film. The special events reporter would bring me along to the Roundup. We'd shoot film of the stunts and rodeo events and then come back to the station and develop it in the darkroom. That evening it would be on the news.

I was so fascinated with the new movie cameras that I went to the local camera store and managed to convince the owner to let me borrow and test one of the new cameras. Impressed that I was working with KLEW, he let me borrow a camera for a couple of days.

My work at the Roundup almost turned into my own version of "joining the circus." The Joie Chitwood drivers drove Ford cars, leaping from platform to platform like Evil Knievel did on motorcycles. In fact, Knievel credited Joie as his inspiration. After seeing them at the Roundup, I went back and got an after-school and weekend job washing cars for Joie, earning real money. He told me, "Kid, you do a good job. Go tell your mom you can travel with my group and wash cars. I'll double what I'm paying you now." I thought it was a great idea! But Mom didn't, even though I begged and pleaded.

Washing cars for famous stunt drivers went to my head. One evening I took our only family car out for a spin to meet friends at the local hamburger joint. Afterward, I hurried back home, taking a shortcut on a dirt road because it was getting late. As I went around a sharp corner, the car slid sideways and slammed against a curb. The two right wheels were bent, which didn't make for a pleasant drive home. My dad asked what had happened and I lied, making up a story about being chased by a bunch of drunk teenagers who drove me off the road. To top it off, I said they wore masks. Dad came back after getting it fixed and said the repairman told him that if he believed that story, he'd believe anything. Obviously, I was grounded—no car for two months, as I was still under suspension for souping up the Plymouth.

My mother didn't like the house Dad had picked out in Lewiston. She was a country girl, and what Dad had for us was a three-story mansion overlooking the Snake River. So we moved before Christmas to a place she liked better in Clarkston. I had to switch schools and attend Clarkston High School, just across the Snake River.

Our Clarkston High math teacher was a real problem. He expected us to be instant mathematicians, and he didn't really like a few of us in his class as we generally misbehaved. He would call us out and then give us extra homework. That pretty much grinded away on us, so three of us decided to make our presence known while trying to stay out of trouble. So for Halloween, a few of us who'd gone afoul of his extra homework rule got together and put a plan in place.

The math teacher lived down the street from my house. We figured that the many trick-or-treaters coming to his house would give us protective cover. (Definitely twisted thinking.) The plan was for the three of us to get a large Mason jar and urinate in it, filling it to the brim. Then we'd hang out undetected. When the coast was clear, we'd draw straws. The two losers would take the full jar up to the door and lean it against the door so that when the door opened, the urine would go gushing inside. Of course, they had to knock first and run.

We executed the plan flawlessly and could hear him cussing a blue streak as the urine unleased itself into his entryway. His yelling up and down the street was something like, "You little dirty sneaking bastards, I know who you are, you are going to get it." But we were long gone—we thought.

The following math classes were tougher, however, and the homework increased. We knew he knew, but we swore a blood oath that we wouldn't squeal on each other no matter how bad the pressure or increased homework.

He got us in the end, though, as all three of us got Ds in the class.

Although school changed when we moved, I kept working at the jobs I already had. My main job at KLEW was running a camera for the evening news and other shows, but I also convinced the producer I could write commercials. I'll never forget writing one script for Safeway's Chinese Chop Suey. You could never do this now, but I asked one of the news employees who looked Asian to wear a Chinese coolie hat and a robe and sit behind this table with the chop suey we were selling for Safeway. I had him talk in a stereotypical accent: "Ah so," that kind of thing. It was so funny, and it sold a lot of chicken chow mein. The producer was happy, so I continued to think up innovative ways to improve the introduction to the news cast and the weather report.

At 17, it felt like a big deal to be responsible for operating the camera for many different types of shows, particularly when they involved celebrities. KLEW was the only TV station in Lewiston, and its management was hungry for success. Getting and pleasing sponsors was important to have the revenue stream for operational expenses, let alone profit. I was once told to be ready to operate the camera when Tex Ritter's wife came to town.

Along with Gene Autry, Roy Rogers, and Ken Maynard, Tex Ritter was one of the most popular of America's singing movie cowboys. Dorothy Fay, his wife, was an actress mainly known for her appearances in westerns, including several with Tex. She was the mother of television actor John Ritter and the paternal grandmother of his son, actor Jason Ritter.

She was also a knockout. When I was introduced to her she said, "Young man, you are so young!" I told her I was 17, and she replied, "I'm sure you'll do great in this business." For me this was another experience akin to the movie, "The Graduate."

On this job I would learn early, at age 17, that innovative ideas require enough testing to avoid failure. After the Booze Rally steak heist, I had two great innovations that initially worked, and then one failed, getting me fired. The first was the introduction of the news anchor from a black screen to the anchor's head shot. The station's current way of doing this was sloppy, so at home I went to the garage and built a wood frame larger than the head shot, then added a sliding wood piece. The sliding piece displayed the printed titles of the newscast, such as the anchor's name, and I'd slide that piece out and behind it would be the head shot—the transition was then seamless. The anchor loved it.

Similarly, for the weatherman I built a large weather map and put it on hinges. With that, I could go to a shot of him and he'd say, "Here is a breakdown of the news." Then the weather map would swing out next to him, for another seamless transition. It worked great. My downfall was not keeping the sliding piece for the news anchor's introduction greased and tested ahead of the news. One day I went to slide the piece and it stuck. As a result, the anchor was talking behind the frame and I was forced to lift it up over his head for the camera to capture his entire head shot. After the newscast, he blew his stack and fired me in front of the crew. I started sobbing. The weatherman, a guy named Jerry, agreed to take me home to Clarkston. I sobbed all the way, but I had learned my lesson: test an innovation multiple times.

I then saw an ad in the paper for an assistant cameraman for a crew filming a documentary about Hells Canyon on the Snake River. When I called about that job, the guy who answered asked, "Are you a girl?" because my voice wasn't deep, but I'd worked with cameras before, and I got the job. It was a week-long trip, two days to reach the head of the canyon on jet boats.

I also took an odd job in the *Clarkston Herald's* photo section. But I just didn't always work while we were in Idaho. One night I went to the local skating rink, where Gene Vincent and His Blue Caps were performing. Back then big-name rock and roll bands traveled the country by bus putting on shows, and it was a great way for me to learn more about popular music. I was five feet from the stage when Vincent sang his 1956 top-ten hit, "Be-Bop-A-Lula," a significant example of rockabilly. Vincent was named to both the Rock & Roll Hall of Fame and the Rockabilly Hall of Fame.

Mom wasn't very happy away from her family, however, so we weren't in Lewiston and Clarkston very long. Dad had joined the Air Force Reserves and would retire from there as a master sergeant in 1960, but reserve pay wasn't enough to pay bills. My Uncle Bill helped him study for the U.S. Post Office test, and Dad managed to get a good, steady job at the post office back in Spokane. I was glad to finish high school somewhere that felt more like home.

With the experience I had acquired working at KLEW-TV and the *Clarkston Herald*, I wanted to continue in the news and TV field. My mind starting churning over how to get in the front door in Spokane and call attention to my creativity without going through a tedious application process. I was energized when I read a *Reader's Digest* article about a teenager who'd used a homing pigeon to land an interview and a job. It was simple but effective. The kid had found a homing pigeon owner, rented a pigeon with a cage, put a message in the capsule on the pigeon's leg, and delivered the bird, its cage, and instructions to the place where he wanted to work. Basically the instructions were to reply to the message in the capsule with the answer written on a small piece of paper, insert it into the capsule, and turn the pigeon loose.

I did more research. Learning that pigeons had been used very effectively as military messengers in World Wars I and II, thanks to their homing ability, speed, and altitude. So I rented a pigeon and showed up at the desk of the secretary of the president of KHQ-TV wearing my traditional white shirt and tie. I told the secretary who I was, put the cage on her desk, and gave her instructions for her boss to follow. About three hours later, I got a phone call from the pigeon owner: The pigeon had returned and the note in the capsule said for me to contact the president for an interview.

I got an appointment to meet with the president. When I arranged it, the secretary said the president had been very impressed with my innovation and would promise an interview but not a job yet.

I went to the interview, a bit worried that my approach would be seen as a stunt rather an example of a young genius innovator at work. The interview was great, but the president said that although he was very impressed with the pigeon approach, he had no positions open for someone my age. As I left his office, the secretary handed me the empty cage. She repeated that I had really impressed the president.

I worked a lot elsewhere. I sold Fuller Brushes as what they called a "stripper," who called back on the houses where no one had answered for the regular salesman. I had a sample suitcase, which had legs that snapped open into a stand. I wore a white shirt with tie and slacks, so was pretty dapper looking. It also helped that we were taught to snap open the case just as the door opened, putting the legs into the door jamb so the person answering couldn't shut the door. Once I was invited in by this woman who was about 40, sloshed and with a drink in her hand. She called me Johnny, said, "You are sure cute," and offered to get me a drink. I knew I needed to bail out of there soon because she was up to no good—it was like a scene from *The Graduate*. She bought several brushes, so I made the sale, but only after I was forced to sit on the couch next to her and hold her hand. "What a sharp young teenager will do to earn a buck," I thought to myself.

With distractions like that, maybe it's no surprise that I had trouble at Gonzaga Prep with my grades, particularly in Latin. Fortunately for me, my favorite teacher, Mr. Small, had me meet with him two or three times a week after school. (The Jesuits in process to become priests were called "mister" rather than Father. They were brilliant and working on their second graduate degrees.) Mr. Small helped me improve my grades. But the first time I applied to Gonzaga University, I wasn't accepted because my grade point average still was only 1.1. I'd built up a fantastic résumé, however, learning a lot of great skills, particularly how to sell myself and the product that went with it.

Dear John,
　　Well, Buddy, I see that you
made the finals in the Elocution
contest but didn't grab off the
laurels. What is going on here!.
I don't trust those judges. Saw
the picture of the old ham in
the Gonzagan which I received
recently. Congratulations on the
recent "You Can't Take it With
You". I hear that it was a great
or good success. What is this of
you feeding your thumbs to the
big snake? At least you didn't
have Rich Perry and Mauro pest-
ering you. How is Angie doing? I
see that he grabbed off a part
in the "12 Happy Men". I saw the
movie by the way and can see tha
play would have tremendous potential. But without you pacing
the boards, Mr Goebel is liable
to have a flop on his hands. I's
everything going will with you
in your senior year? Where is th
picture you promised me? Say a
prayer for all of us. Hello to
your Mother and Dad. God bless
you now, Johnny.
　　　　　Mr. Small, SJ

Mr. J.R. Black
1202 E. 12th
Spokane, Washington

A postcard from Mr. Small after he was reassigned to California

Another problem was that I was drinking too much. Like a lot of high school students, I'd started drinking my first year at Gonzaga Prep. I'd always been around alcohol; all the men in the family knocked back shots of whiskey before Thanksgiving dinner, for instance. Like my Uncle Frank, my dad drank more regularly. In Spokane, my friends and I, including Denny Flaherty, John Carlson, Tim Hopkins, and Pat Rotchford, would go to Idaho, where the drinking age was lower. We got fake I.D.s and we'd wear suits, fill our coats up with Rainier beer stubbies, and go into clubs in Idaho. Usually we'd get in and a waitress would come and we'd order a round of beers. But after drinking those slowly, we'd put the beers in our pockets on the table, hoping the waitress wouldn't notice or assume another waitress had done the serving.

We went every Friday night with Denny, although some nights, it was just me. One night that I didn't go, he was hit in a cross-walk by a Cadillac doing about 90 miles an hour. He was in traction and hospitalized for months, and we'd go visit him at Sacred Heart Hospital. His dad was a doctor, and Denny had his dad bring a fridge into his room; when we got there, he'd be in bed drinking beer. We'd go to visit Denny just to have a Coors. The nurses weren't very happy about five guys sitting around drinking after school with Denny, who was in traction and also drinking a beer. Those were the days.

Or sometimes we'd go to the Spokane Valley to dance with the farm girls, and we'd always make sure we'd had enough to drink beforehand. This was a routine event, maybe once month. John would often stay out in the car drinking, and a number of times when we went to leave, we'd find that he'd been in a fight and gotten a couple of black eyes. But at least Denny and I had a lot of fun dancing with the girls.

Gonzaga Prep went to the state basketball championships my junior year, too. Union Pacific put extra cars on the train to get all the students to Seattle for the final games. You can imagine a train full of students, and of course everyone's drinking beer. We got to the old Seattle Union Station downtown and someone said, "Let's check into the Olympic Hotel." We sent one guy in to get a room and all the rest of us, about ten of us, came up the fire escape. It was really wild, and things started getting really out of hand. You could jump in bed with a girl from Richmond for 50 cents; they had it all set up. Guys were lined up down the hallway until the police came and broke it up. Luckily, I chose not to take part.

At one point Tim Hopkins said, "Come with me, John R."

"What are you doing?" I asked. He had a handful of water balloons and a can of shaving cream. He led me down the stairs and onto the overhang of the roof of the Olympic Hotel. There he filled the water balloons with shaving cream.

"Wait until the people start getting out of their cars, and while the doorman helps them with luggage, we'll let them have it," he said. "We won't have a lot of time to get away."

So again it was Tim leading me into trouble. That trouble came when we nailed two women wearing fur coats. The hotel doorman called the police. Luckily they caught Tim, not me.

At another point, all ten of us were in a hotel room, drinking beer, when Pat appeared on the fire escape in his jockey shorts, wanting in. We couldn't figure out how he got there in his jockey shorts. We weren't going to let him in, either, so he just broke the glass, jumped through, and came in anyway. Later, I'd gone downstairs, where Tim was unscrewing this statue that sat at the bottom of stairs. It was maybe two feet high, and he took it out into the middle of the intersection and sat it there. Then he said, "Come on, John R., I'm collecting gas caps." He had a big sack, like a gunny sack, and he went up and down the road unscrewing gas caps and dropping them in his sack. I said, "I'll do a few, but then you're on your own, because I think you're going to end up in jail." And he did, again.

I went once to the basketball game, but a lot of guys didn't even go. The hotel called the police a couple of times. I don't know how I survived all that, to tell the truth.

My senior portrait

Nonetheless, I managed to graduate from Gonzaga Prep on May 30, 1958. The graduation party was like something out of National Lampoon. It was a wild party at Pat Rotchford's house, which was on Hayden Lake next to Bing Crosby's. The Rotchfords were friends of the Crosby family. We all showed up at Pat's, and there must have been 20 guys and maybe 10 or 15 girls from Marycliff, the local Catholic high school for girls. Everyone was celebrating together, and most of the girls were naked. At the time, I didn't realize what fun that could've been! Pat (who has since passed away, along with my friends Tim and Denny) was a really wild guy, and he was wearing nothing but his jockey shorts and a bowler hat.

Pat had a case of beer, and he got me to go for a canoe ride with him. We paddled quite a way out onto the lake and then he asked me if I knew how to swim very well. No, I didn't! But that didn't stop him—he tipped the canoe over. I had on all my clothes and barely made it to shore.

A real character, Pat decided to join the Navy. He was assigned to a ship posted offshore in Korea. He ended up marrying a Korean girl there. When he brought her home on leave, his parents were aghast. They weren't going to have a Korean in the family. They arranged for Pat to divorce his wife and sent her back to Korea. It's pretty clear what that says about Pat's family, but I'm not sure what that says about Pat or his relationships with either his parents or his bride.

Despite distractions, I graduated from Gonzaga Prep.

Tim was another wild friend with us at that graduation party. He climbed up the water tower next to Pat's house, taking a bunch of Rainier quarts with him, and was dropping bottles down on the cars parked below. He also turned off the wheel for the water supply for about half the houses on the lake. The sheriff finally showed up and everybody took off. Tim, John, Pat, Bruce Hopkins (Tim's brother), and I jumped in the Hopkins' new Plymouth convertible, with Bruce, who didn't drink that much, driving. Somebody said, "Let's all go to Wallace (Idaho), to the Luxe." I didn't know what they were talking about, but the Luxe was a whorehouse, just like the Canyon Ranch in Las Vegas.

When we got there, we climbed a long line of stairs and these women came out, one of them a pretty young blonde but most of them about 50 years old. It was easier to get admitted to the whorehouse than to the clubs in Coeur d'Alene. Pat Rotchford picked the blonde and Tim the next-best-looking one. I picked one woman who could've been my mother.

To make a long story short, I never lost my virginity on that trip! As I remember, John and Bruce did not partake, either. They stayed in the lobby, nursing a beer, smoking, and looking cool.

A peek into a room at the Luxe

Nonetheless, I'd managed to not only get my high school diploma but to survive the celebrations. In college, although I still had fun, I'd become much more focused on music and my eventual career.

CHAPTER 4: CHOOSING LIFE PATHS

"What was a normal goal for the young man becomes a neurotic hindrance to the old."

—Carl Jung

I attended my first year of college at what was then called Eastern Washington College of Education in Cheney, not far from Spokane. I realized I'd been raising too much hell and needed to settle down, so I took Reserve Officer Training Corps (ROTC) courses and got a job making deliveries for the Star Leather Company, where my aunt Fran worked as a bookkeeper.

Working at Star Leather taught me a lot about how a company should be run. The owner was known as Apple, and he was short and smart. Aunt Fran had recommended he hire me, as I overheard her say one day, "Apple, that Johnny is a smart kid, he goes to Gonzaga Prep." My direct boss was Wilfred, who taught me management while I stocked shelves and made deliveries to suppliers. He was a taskmaster. There were no coffee breaks for anybody, and I brought my own lunch. Sometimes I wouldn't have the money for bus fare and would borrow the 10 cents to get home from someone else waiting for the bus.

Harold was the delivery driver. I didn't have a license to drive yet, but I'd sit next him in the car and when we stopped, I ran the supplies into the shoe stores. I didn't like the way Harold talked about our former President Roosevelt, who'd died more than a dozen years back. Harold would get started on a tirade and his favorite words would be, "That President

Roosevelt was a no-good dirty-rotten SOB." He'd say that right out of the blue. I'd make the mistake of asking him why, and he'd just keep going on his tirade.

I still got into some trouble with friends, though. Once I took a number of friends up to our homestead, which at the time was owned by Uncle Louis but being rented to someone else living there. We had guns with us, about four rifles, a 12-guage shotgun, and my uncle's pistol, as well as alcohol—we always traveled with a case of Rainier quarts—and we got into a real fire-fight with live bullets. I tried to orchestrate it like a combat scene in a film shoot, sending two of the guys up the hill in the orchard to get behind the rocks. I thought then we'd shoot at the rocks, so not to worry, but that wasn't very successful. I stayed below with Tim Hopkins with two rifles and a pistol. When the other two got into position, Tim and I opened fire.

The guys behind the rocks didn't follow the script; they stated shooting over our heads, which upset the renters across the meadow. Not to be outdone, we fired back. Finally, I told everyone to stop firing and get into the house, but unfortunately it didn't stop there. We grabbed some cold beers out of the refrigerator and started shooting flies off the ceiling, creating a cloud of smoke in the house. Tim and I locked the kitchen door, but by then the other guys were upset and rammed the door with a log that had been outside. It blew the door off the hinges and onto the kitchen floor.

This commotion only ended when I saw my Uncle Louis's red Dodge speeding toward the homestead. The renters had called him. He got out and ran to the bunkhouse. I told my friends to relax and to prop the door up against the wall. Louis came up to the door and knocked on it. It fell over into the kitchen. He came into the smoky living room, saw the bullet holes in the ceiling and shell casings on the floor and yelled, "What the hell is going on?"

It didn't help when I replied, "Well, Uncle Louis, these are my GU buddies, and we are just having a few beers." To show what a great guy Uncle Louis was, later, when I got back from my first Vietnam deployment, he pulled me aside and said, "Johnny, I wanted to tell you that I should not have chewed you out in front of your friends that time you were at the homestead." I told him to forget it and said, "Thanks for being a great uncle."

While I was at Eastern, I raised my G.P.A. to 2.5 and was admitted to Gonzaga University for the following year. I was proud of that, and even prouder when I made the dean's honor roll after my first year there. I thought that was pretty darn good, coming from a homestead, and even though I had an alcohol problem, I was overcoming it.

That summer after my first year of college marked a milestone in my music career—my first recording. I met a girl named Mary Jo Jepson, who was the niece of my Aunt Margaret by marriage. She was visiting from California, staying with Uncle Louis and Aunt Margaret. I asked her out.

Though I'd had a girlfriend in eighth grade, this was my first official date where I got to drive rather than having to ride with parents. We went to dinner and a church social on a Saturday night, and I fell in love. I wrote her a song, my first real rock-and-roll song. I pulled together a drummer and bass player, booked a session at Sound Recording Company in Spokane, and cut my first vinyl recording, a 78 RPM titled "Mary Jo," on August 27, 1959. It cost me $20.80. I handled the keyboards with some backup vocals by my sister, Julie.

On my second date with Mary Jo the following weekend, I played the record for her. The lyrics begin:

> "I'm sure they were watching as we romanced;
> The dreamy touch of your face in mine
> Made me see love's only sign—
> I knew I'd fell in love.
> Oh Mary Jo, oh oh,
> I love you so."

She was speechless. She went on to Whitworth College and we corresponded with each other that fall until the distance finally made the relationship fizzle.

Still, that song lit a fire under my recording career. I started to think about writing topical tunes, something current or of local interest. I formed the John R. Trio with several fellow students: Jerry Harr on the banjo, George Votava on the guitar, and me handling keyboards and vocals. We played music in a style between country and the rock and roll of that era. My idols back then were Buddy Holly, Jerry Lee Lewis, Ricky Nelson, and Elvis, and I called my first crude attempts rockabilly. My rockabilly began sounding more folksy, as Jerry played banjo and George the guitar. We played around town, including at Gonzaga University socials, where we started developing a sound like the Kingston Trio's.

The John R. Trio

Even in high school, I'd been working to peddle my own music to record companies — Am-Par Record Corporation in New York, Liberty Records in Los Angeles, and RCA and Mercury Records, to name a few. I also had photos taken to provide to artist and repertoire (A&R) companies in Seattle that were asking for them. I was collecting rejection slips, but I also had a number of artist and repertoire (A&R) representatives visit me from Seattle to meet me and listen to my music. They were the ones who could sign me to a label. That didn't happen, but they did give me suggestions.

A publicity photo taken for a Seattle artists & repertoire (A&R) company

When I'd started at Gonzaga University, I'd also connected with Mike Pugh, a student a couple of years ahead of me and a founding member of the Chad Mitchell Trio. This Spokane folk group had gained some fame starting in 1959 with a performance at Carnegie Hall backing Harry Belafonte. Mike gave me some tips for developing my style.

In the meantime, I had college and work to keep me busy. While at Gonzaga University, I had a good job as a copyboy at the *Spokesman Review* newspaper. I wore a white shirt and tie, and I ran errands for reporters, picking up research materials from the library. I also worked for the editorial staff. At that time, we produced eight editions a day. The earliest edition went to the subscribers who were the farthest away, and the last, local edition contained the latest news and went out about midnight. Some reporters and the crime desk worked until 10:00 or 11:00 p.m. to get stories in that last edition. All evening, my job was to get each edition as it came off and hand it to the editors for markup.

While working there, I also became a stringer for the Associated Press (AP). The AP had an office in the *Spokesman Review's* building, so if I saw or heard about an accident or something else they might be interested in, I let them know. They followed up and gave me a check each month for whatever information I'd provided.

All my work helped me to have a savings account at the bank. At that time, our family's used car had broken down, as usual, so I went to the local car dealer and put down $80 on a foreign car that had been newly introduced in the U.S., an Opel. That left me with $10 in my bank account, and I made the monthly car payments myself. Unfortunately, later I would be taking my sisters downtown and singing away behind the wheel, and I rear-ended another car. There was considerable damage. When I told my mother, she was so upset, she sobbed. I did manage to pay for the repairs, though.

Another thing I spent my *Spokesman Review* earnings on was the crush I had on this famous reporter, Dorothy Rochon Powers. She was one of the town's most beloved reporters and would later run for Congress. Dorothy's sensitivity to the suffering and vulnerability of others guided her writing throughout her four decades at the paper. Although she was 20 years older than me, I wasn't deterred. She had great legs and wore low-cut dresses. I sat three rows up from her in the newsroom, and I worked from 6 p.m. to midnight, six days a week, so I had a lot of time to get to know her. With a wink and a smile, she would send me to the *Spokesman Review* library in the same building to research various articles she was writing. I frequently had dreams about marrying her. When she was working on a story with a short deadline, she'd put her right leg out to the side, which caused her dress to inch up way above her knee. That view left me speechless.

Her birthday was coming up, so I took some of the money I'd saved to Nordstrom's and bought her a pair of knee-length pink panties, kind of like pantaloons. I asked her when she'd be home so I could bring her gift by. When I arrived, her husband wasn't there, but she was putting on makeup in the bathroom before going out with him. She said, "Johnny, please come right in. Why are you here?" I said, "Dorothy, it's your birthday, and I've brought you a birthday present." She finished her makeup and then opened the gift, held it out, and exclaimed, "Oh Johnny, I just love them. I'll wear them tonight!" Then she grabbed me and gave me a great kiss on the cheek. Needless to say, after that I had many dreams of her wearing her sexy panties. I never saw her again after I left that job, although I would have liked to. She passed away on October 18, 2014, at age 93, though she's still in my dreams.

Not everything that happened to me at the *Spokesman-Review* was pleasant. It would never happen today, but I had a run-in with one of the editors who was really crabby. There were a number of news and city desk editors, and I'd sit behind them in the evenings, running errands for them and waiting for them to hand me copy. I took orders from them all. One night he wanted me to go get something for him, and I told him I couldn't right then. I had another assignment.

He said, "That's the last straw. Every time I want something from you, you won't do it." Really mad, he grabbed me by the neck and shook me, calling me a son-of-a-bitch. He nearly strangled me; it was so hard to breath that I was terrified. All the other editors just sat there, watching.

I really liked editor Ken Grippen, though. Like a military man, he had polished Florsheim shoes, starched shirts, cool ties, and cuff links. He's the one who got me into wearing Florsheim shoes. Like most of the rest of them, he smoked. It all looked like a movie: *All the President's Men.*

My shift ended at midnight. I'd catch the 12:30 a.m. bus to go home and study. The whole family would be asleep, the house quiet. I'd get my books and a cup of coffee and sit at the heat vent behind our sofa and lounge chair. Warm there, I'd do homework or get ready for the next day's classes until 2:00 or 2:30 in the morning. Since I usually had early classes, it made for short nights.

While I worked at the *Spokesman-Review,* John F. Kennedy came to Spokane to speak as part of his 1960 presidential campaign. Kennedy was in a tough battle with Richard M. Nixon that would go down to the wire, and Spokane was seen as a key battleground for the state's electoral votes. He ultimately made four different campaign trips to the city, his last just two days before the election. One of those events was at Gonzaga itself, but I also went to one of his rallies at the Lincoln Monument downtown, which was just down the street from the newspaper building on the corner. I stood about 50 feet away from him and Washington Senator Henry "Scoop" Jackson, and I was mesmerized by his words.

When the election happened on November 8, Kennedy eked out a victory by a very slim margin. He took the oath of office as the nation's 35th president in January of 1961, and of course, he'd be killed in Dallas less than two years later. As it turned out, that date would also be important to me for another reason.

I covered Kennedy's visit to Spokane.
(Photo reprinted with permission of the Spokesman-Review)

After Kennedy's visit, I got together with my future wife. Paula Anne Harootunian, who I'd known briefly in Lewiston, had come to Gonzaga a year ahead of me. In addition to being a champion swimmer and tennis player, she was very beautiful, smart, and loved to party. She'd been raised mostly by her mother, who had come to the United States from Northern Germany through Ellis Island, like my great-grandparents. When Paula and her sister, Susie, were toddlers their father, a lieutenant colonel in the Air Force, was killed while flying maneuvers in the Californian desert in preparation for combat in 1941. After that loss, her mother moved to Lewiston and had to raise her family on less than $200 a month. She eventually became a nurse and bought a house and a car, but it had to be a difficult childhood. Paula and Susie were able to go to college primarily because the military covered most of their tuition, since her father had been killed on active duty.

After my first date with Paula, I wrote a song called "A Girl Named Paula." I put together a group of friends from ROTC and we sang it at the university's St. Patrick's Day convocation talent show in 1961, billed as John R. and the Five Gentlemen. It brought down the house—in fact, we won the contest.

The Trio had plenty of gigs, including at the Gonzaga cafeteria and student union building, the COG. We also were invited to perform at a major GU assembly. Oscar Brand, a Canadian-American folk singer, was famous back then. He performed some songs considered inappropriate by some, but not by George and I. We decided we'd sing "Follow the Man." The lyrics included, "My husband's a mason, a mason, a mason, my husband's a mason is he. All day he lays bricks, he lays bricks, he lays bricks, at night he comes home and drinks tea." When we rehearsed the song, Jerry said, "Did you guys clear the lyrics with Father Lyons?" Father Lyons was the school's dean of men and the censor.

We told Jerry we had, but we hadn't. We thought they'd get through the censor. When we sang the song at the assembly, the students went nuts, laughing, yelling, and applauding. We were a hit—but not with Father Lyons. The three of us were asked to come to his office. When we reported there, Lyons yelled, "You're all expelled! The song you sang is about nothing but fucking!" When the dean of men and a priest was using the F-word, we knew he was really upset and that we were in trouble.

After about an hour, he finally backed down and said we could avoid being expelled if we published a retraction in the school newspaper and promised we would never sing that song, or anything like it, again. We agreed. Afterwards, Jerry was upset that we'd lied to him, but at least we were all still in school.

Our trio also had gigs at a March of Dimes event and at the non-commissioned officers' (NCO) club at Fairchild Air Force Base in early 1962. One Christmas Eve, I planned to record a new song and my dad was selling Lowry organs at the time. We hauled a Lowry organ up the stairs to the studio for that song, which was called "The End." Unfortunately, that's one recording I've lost, but I still have the lyrics:

> "The wrinkles on my brow keep increasing, one by one.
> As I grow older, my step gets weaker, and I know my
>   days are done.
> Maybe I need someone to talk to when the winter winds
>   blow,
> Maybe I need someone to love me, oh I don't know."

The Trio

After years of trying, the John R. Trio signed a contract with B-G-L Recording Company on March 14, 1962. The contract called for us to record 12 songs, and for the first time, the cost of all those sessions was covered. Jerry, George, and I added John Malone on bass and a drummer whose name I can't recall. We used the studio in Spokane to record five original songs I had written and that we'd been performing around town: "Sheila," "Henry's Body Is Buried," "The Alligator Man," "Down the Devil's Road," and "Rio Town." I'd written "Sheila" about a girl I had a crush on, Sheila Whetstone.

"Sheila" and "Rio Town" first were released on B-G-L's Gemco label as a 45 single that got considerable airplay in the Pacific Northwest and down the West Coast. "Rio Town" was a classic folk song:

Rio Town
Copyright 1962, words and music by John R. Black

Well I wanted to roam many years ago
So I left the north that I loved so
And I traveled down to Rio Town
Well I packed my bags and I followed the sound
Hitchin' my way to Rio Town
Met a girl and looked around
Sunnin' myself in Rio Town

Down in Rio town, Oh oh Rio Town
Where the girls dance all around
Where the food is cooked outside
Where you can buy a donkey ride
Where it rains but once a day
Flowers bloomin' thick as hay
Down in Rio Town, so I left one sunny day
I was tired any way headin' back to northern land
Eatin' chicken from the fryin' pan
Goodbye Rio Town shall we head north babe
Ya man, how about Montana
Well how about Washington
It's world's fair time
Spokane, Seattle here we come

Ed Costello, the entertainment editor at the *Spokesman Review*, wrote a great piece for us in the April 8, 1962, issue. Under the headline, "Record Is Cut by Gonzagans," he said, "The trio was born at GU, where the inspiration of Bing Crosby and the Chad Mitchell Trio apparently is a match for the more bookish Jesuits."

Following the release of the 45, the *Review* also published another story about our album contract, and we performed "Henry's Body Is Buried" live on a local KHQ-TV charity telethon hosted by Raymond Burr. Burr was a Canadian and American actor known for his title roles in the TV drama Perry Mason and Ironsides. As MC, he introduced us. It was great. I later included his introduction on my Armed Forces Network album for the song, "Henry's Body Is Buried." Burr says, "That's what they say."

As a result of our TV appearance, we were called by the military club at Fairchild Air Force Base near Spokane and asked to perform there. Again, however, we were all drinking before our performance and we flubbed it pretty badly. We were not asked back. That was a lesson in the importance of moderation—one that would be hard for me to learn. Lurking in the back of my mind, always, was Father Knecht telling me that I wasn't good enough.

I had plenty of more ordinary college fun, too, though. Sometimes when spring break came, we'd wonder what to do. One year I had an ROTC buddy who was living in the same apartment complex as Paula, who I'd been dating. His name was Troy, and like her he was a year ahead of me. Troy owned a Harley-Davidson motorcycle, so I suggested that we go to Reed College in Portland and hang out with some of the students and professors there. Reed was a very left-wing college, with known Communists teaching and attending there. The scuttlebutt around Gonzaga, which I continued to deny, was that I had attempted to join Fidel Castro while attending my junior year at

Gonzaga Prep. I had indeed been gone from school that year, because my family had moved to Lewiston and Clarkston.

The rumor had one fact at its heart, though: While at Prep, I had assembled a scrapbook about Fidel's thinking, which sounded interesting to me. I documented in my scrapbook how Castro was said to be in Cuba's Sierra Maestra Mountains, preparing to take over Cuba by revolution. This mountain range runs near the coast of southeast Cuba. Since Cuba's press was censored, Castro had contacted foreign media to spread his message; he became a celebrity after being interviewed by Herbert Matthews, a journalist from *The New York Times*. Reporters from CBS and *Paris Match* soon followed. Matthews had been directed by the U.S. State Department to brief the new ambassador to Cuba, Earl E. T. Smith, and pushed for ending the provision of any military equipment or arms to the government of the current Cuban president, Fulgenico Batista. Batista was viewed as a dictator who cared little about the people of Cuba.

Castro in the Sierra Maestra. My interest in him started a persistent rumor.
(Photo: Pictorial Press Ltd/Alamy Stock Photo)

So when we got the idea to go to Reed, I asked Troy how far it was. He said, "I travel 80 m.p.h. on my bike, so it's a piece of cake. It's 353 miles, so normally would take five hours and 12 minutes, but I can make it in three hours."

I told Troy, "Okay, when are we leaving?"

As the story around town went, I left home and headed for Cuba with a rifle broken down to fit into a large suitcase and leaving a detailed note about my plans. Because of that note, my parents reported me to the FBI, whose agents apprehended me in Denver, Colorado at the bus station and returned me to my parents. This never happened! But good stories linger—I recently attended my 60th class reunion at Gonzaga Prep, where several classmates wanted details about my alleged attempt to join Castro in the Sierra Maestra mountains.

The truth is that Troy said we'd leave for Reed on Friday and come back on Tuesday, which gave us three full days at the college. We planned to attend a few classes and hang out at the local bar. Troy's estimate was right; with me riding behind him on his Harley and the speedometer stuck at 80 or more, we were sitting at a bar near Reed at 3 p.m. that Friday.

By early evening, I was sitting next to a Jewish girl, or at least that's what she told me. As she lit another cigarette, she also said, "I think I really like you." By late evening she had propositioned me to go to bed with her. As we were deeply involved in a debate about what Communism really was, I said, "Well, okay, but let's talk some more first."

We did talk a lot more, and by morning I found myself waking up with her next to me. I hoped I was still near Reed College. I had no idea what had happened to Troy, but I figured at least I had a place to sleep until Tuesday. After this girl and I had breakfast, she said we'd go to another bar where a group of students would be meeting, and she would introduce me. So that night, the political conversation that had started on Friday continued. Troy finally joined us. He'd gassed his motorcycle and found someplace to sleep.

I couldn't believe how exciting our conversation had been. We debated the good and bad points of Lenin, Castro, and Communism. At some point I hinted that I had attempted to join Castro while at Prep, and the other students went wild. "You're a real revolutionary!" they said. I couldn't deny it later, because the sudden notoriety had gone to my head.

Sunday blew on past, too, and my Jewish girl said she would take me with her to class, introduce me, and try to get a debate started there as well. She said that professor had Communist leanings. I couldn't wait.

By then, Troy was getting antsy and wanted to leave early Tuesday morning. So we went to class on Monday, the Jewish girl and I both hung over. I really thought I was falling in love again with her. We debated whether communism has far more advantages than capitalism, such as the ideas of people being treated equally no matter what their occupation or type of higher education, and that every citizen in a communist regime can keep a job. We noted that in capitalism, everyone is treated differently by class, and many lose their jobs due to various reasons, including competition, which doesn't exist in communism. As a result, maybe there was less of a daily struggle between people for jobs and raises. (Back then I was naive.)

The debate was turned upside down, however, when I said that I knew exactly what communism was from my Jesuit teacher, Father Leo J. Robinson. He was head of the sociology department at Gonzaga University and, as a Jesuit, he defined communism as a debased society based on a materialistic interpretation of everything. All hell broke loose after I made that statement.

We debated back and forth until lunchtime, then my Jewish girlfriend decided we must all go to the bar for a few beers. We all continued to debate and drink beer until late in the evening, and again we went back to her apartment.

Tuesday came early, with the sound of Troy's Harley starting up outside the window. I threw my clothes on and said goodbye to my new friend, who I never saw again. Troy and I made it home in a little over three hours, never stopping except for fuel. It was a memorable trip I have never forgotten.

Another fun adventure came when I went with a buddy of mine, Bill Stowe, to Butte, Montana. Beverly Fanning, one of my cousins, had an old boyfriend tending bar in Butte. Chris invited me to come for spring break. I called up Bill, who lived on nearby hill south of me, and told him about the invitation.

"Let's go by freight train," I said. "We can just hop a freight." He agreed, so we did some research and thought we had found a Union Pacific freight train leaving the trainyards in Spokane and headed toward Butte. Our parents knew what we were doing. In fact, Bill's mom dropped us off in the trainyard near evening. We carried sleeping bags and some food plus a fifth of Jim Beam. By the time we found what we thought was the right car, it was getting dark, so we jumped aboard, rolled out our sleeping bags, and proceeded to make a dent in the bottle. We figured we'd be in Butte by early morning.

We both went to sleep, waking up and going back to sleep each time the train started and stopped, hooking and unhooking cars. At last it seemed we were rolling toward Butte and we dropped more soundly into sleep.

Early the next morning, we heard CLANK! Then another clank. The train came to a halt. It must be Butte! We rolled up our bags, jumped out, looked around—and realized we were still in Spokane.

To save face, we took a taxi to the Greyhound bus depot and caught a bus to Butte. When we arrived, we checked in with Chris at the tavern where he tended bar. Glad to see us, he gave us keys to one of his rooms upstairs. We almost never left our room except to go to the bar downstairs every evening to dance with local girls.

Then one day Chris took us out to lunch. "Wait until you see this," he promised, as we were approached by a waiter, an older guy wearing an apron. Chris told us he was the restaurant's owner. The guy came over and asked what we wanted. Bill and I asked for hot dogs, the specialty of the house.

"How about this one?" The owner reached under his apron, pulled out a small cloth penis, and whacked it on the table.

"Or do you want this size?" he added. He reached deep into the apron this time, pulled out a red, 12" penis, and struck that one on the end of the table, too!

We all laughed and ordered the foot-long. It was delicious.

Bill and I continued to party every night and probably could have gotten engaged by the week's end, but our stay was cut short. At our room's window, which looked out over the parking lot below, were loose bricks. One evening before bed we opened that window and two bricks fell on the hood of a car below. Deciding it was time to leave, we hastily packed and headed to the bus depot for an uneventful ride home. Later, Chris told us it was good we left when we did, as a couple of guys were looking for us. They didn't appreciate the dents in the hood of their car.

Back home, I realized that my absences from Spokane during this break and my trip to Reed College sparked rumors that I'd actually left for Cuba. That story of my attempt to reach Cuba still dogs me today, and as the famous Dr. Bernard Fall said about the Pentagon, "A denial is an affirmation." You decide. A book that my brother James and sister Julie put together for my 65th birthday includes these entries:

> "You told mom and dad that you wanted to join the Cuban revolution in the late 1950s on the side of Castro. You apparently then hitched a ride on a freight train out of Spokane, heading south. I cannot remember the rest—did you ever fire a shot?"

> "John R. provided a lot of excitement for us kids. I remember when he and his friends hopped a freight train. He felt he was needed in Cuba for the Castro revolution. He also worked at the *Spokesman Review* and became the Boy Wonder there. They liked him quite a bit and he met some interesting people."

Finally, the hot topic of conversation at my 60-year class reunion for Gonzaga Prep in 2019 was, "Okay, John R., come clean on Cuba. We know you tried to join Castro and were stopped by the FBI."

What I didn't want to tell my former classmates is that I really wanted to join Castro. As a young teenager at Prep who would have left home and washed cars for Joie Chitwood or motorcycles for Evel Kneivel, joining Castro in the Sierra Maestra mountains would have been icing on the cake. Before the media began changing the image of Castro from a man, a rebel, a hero to a hardline Communist, he sparked the desire in me to be part of a movement overthrowing Cuban President Fulgenico Batista, a terrible dictator. However, Castro became a dictator worse than Batista, impoverishing his country and people.

Amid such intrigues, things were good with Paula, too. For another spring break, about a year before I graduated, Paula invited me down to Lewiston, her home town, to meet her mom. George came with me, and we took the one-car train that ran from Spokane to Lewiston. It took about three hours, and I brought a bottle of Johnny Walker Red with me. George kept holding up a newspaper we had purchased so the other occupants couldn't see the bottle. By the time we got to Lewiston, he and I had finished it. You could smell it everywhere in the car. Paula met us at the train station, where we just about fell off the train. When we got to her house, her mom wasn't home yet from work, so I went in the living room and laid down on the floor. We were really shitfaced. George was throwing up in the backyard just as Paula's mom drove in and saw him.

Her mother, Magda, came in, saw me on the floor, and asked Paula, "What the hell is going on?" Paula said, "Well, I invited my boyfriend to visit." George stayed overnight, while I stayed about five days. It's a wonder Paula's mom did not throw us out.

I majored in sociology at Gonzaga, with a minor in philosophy, pretty sure I wanted to become a criminologist. Books written by the wardens of the Sing Sing and Alcatraz prisons had fascinated me. I was even awarded a graduate fellowship in criminology at Washington State University. But while at Gonzaga University, I attended ROTC summer camp. I was thinking about making the military my career, taking my commission, and joining the Army. I was encouraged by my Dad, my uncles, and Aunt May, who had all served in World War II.

On Feb 17, 1961, I received a letter from our professor of military science, who was a lieutenant colonel in the infantry. He singled out me and others, called "top five-percenters," because of our "achievements and fine personal qualities" to go into the advanced ROTC program. I got another letter of distinction on September 21, 1962, and was on the dean's honor roll at Gonzaga. By then I'd seen the classic movie, *Lawrence of Arabia*, which came out that year and starred Peter O'Toole. I also read T.E. Lawrence's book, *Seven Pillars of Wisdom*, which is one of my favorites. I really admired him. He was an officer in the British Army during World War I who led the revolt of the Arabs against the Turks. He united the Arabs and led guerrilla raids against the Turks, losing only four men. He was also was an enigma, which I found fascinating.

So when I graduated from Gonzaga in 1963, I became a distinguished military graduate. Prior to commissioning, we got to state our preferences for which Army branch we were interested in, which would give our training and career service. We had three choices. My first choice was the infantry, then armor, with artillery as number three. These three are the combat arms that do the main fighting. They're supported by the other branches, such as the Corps of Engineers, Signal Corps, Finance, and so on. By the time I graduated, I'd gotten my first choice and been selected for appointment as an infantry officer in the regular Army, per a letter from the Pentagon on December 14, 1962.

My ROTC class; I'm the one in glasses with my hands clasped.

A strange thing happened not long before I graduated, one that would later haunt me. Paula and I were still dating, and unbeknownst to me, she got pregnant. I was clueless that she had a baby; she never told me. Later on my kids would say, 'How could that be?" She had gotten really big and nobody really said anything, even her friends. I just never really paid attention. We even went to a military ball and danced at that time, with her very pregnant, and I don't know to this day why I didn't see it or why we didn't talk about it. I still remember dancing with her by the ROTC staff at the ball, and I can imagine they were thinking, "What the hell?"

She had graduated the previous year, 1962, with a psychology degree. She was living alone in an apartment and working at Eastern State Hospital. Toward the end of January 1963, I called her apartment, and there was no answer for a couple of days. So I said to one of her friends, Jeannie, "Let's meet over at her apartment." We were worried. We went inside, and there was an ironing board there and a Dr. Spock book, *Dr. Spock's Baby and Child Care*. We thought, "That's really strange," but went home.

When I got a phone call from Paula later, I asked her where she had been. She made up some story about being with her mother, and I believed her. No one thought anything of it. As it turned out, she'd had the baby on January 30, checking into the hospital under an assumed name and then leaving again. The hospital had put the baby up for adoption. It would be several years before we tried to find this child. At first we were unsuccessful, but eventually we were able to reunite the family.

I probably should have known she was going to get pregnant. Back then, it was a sin for a Catholic to practice birth control. If you were married the rhythm method was the only option, and you were certainly not supposed to have sex out of marriage. Of course, that didn't stop us. Every time I went to confession, I confessed to having sex with Paula, and every time the priest would say, "Oh my, my. You have to use condoms or you have to abstain."

It seemed impossible for Paula and I not to have sex, and she didn't like condoms. Yet an abortion was out of the question. Back then, abortion clinics didn't even exist; you had your baby and put it up for adoption. So I think we both knew that eventually she would get pregnant.

When she did, though, I didn't know it—or I blocked the reality out of my mind, realizing I could do nothing to change anything. I graduated from Gonzaga with Paula and her mother there to help celebrate. Her mom said, "What's going to happen with Paula? Are you going to marry her?" Paula was kind of anxious about it, so I asked her, and we made plans.

I was commissioned as a second lieutenant in the infantry, and they gave me a May date ahead of that year's class from West Point as a way to give me some help and put me a little ahead for the next promotion. So I was assigned right away to Fort Lewis, Washington. I spent May and June of 1963 on active duty there, running a rifle training range. Then I moved to Fort Benning, Georgia, for the Infantry Officer Basic Training course and Army Airborne training. I had to take a taxi to downtown Columbus, Georgia, to the tailor shop where I had to buy my uniforms. Here I am, this white kid with no real experience with anyone at school who hadn't been white. So when I got out of the taxi, I looked up and down the street at all the black faces and thought, "So *this* is the South!"

I reflected on our homestead, where we lived near an African-American family that had moved to the country from the city. My uncles would help them when they asked for help with farm machinery or had questions about farming. I never heard my family or any of our neighbors say anything negative about them; they were accepted into the community with everyone else.

My dad had sometimes made anti-Semitic comments, however. Such prejudice was more common back then, but that always bothered me, and I cringed when I heard racist comments. Maybe it's no coincidence that I later spent large chunks of my career in equal employment and race relations roles.

During my early Army training, Paula and I were so broke that I made sure I always had the number of a payphone near our house. She and I would write letters and set a time when I'd call the payphone and she'd go to answer it. That's how broke we were: We couldn't even afford to make a telephone call on a payphone.

As a regular Army officer and distinguished military graduate, I was scheduled for several weeks of infantry school followed by three weeks of Airborne training and finally eight weeks of Ranger school. While at infantry school, I once went with a group of fellow officer infantry students to a famous strip club in Atlanta. We wanted to see their six-foot stripper who danced with a boa constrictor wrapped around her. She used it in her striptease. We also couldn't believe that she wore pasties over her nipples, with little chains on each one, and she was able to throw one to the left and one to the right at the same time. Those and the snake were the main attraction.

Airborne training included ground week, tower week, and then jump week, where we would make five jumps from a C47 at 1,000 feet. During ground week, our oversized company of 800 students did the Airborne shuffle for five miles. Periodically, for no reason except that you were an officer, the drill instructors (DIs) would drop you for fifty pushups. Tower week was the toughest, though. The DIs targeted officers there, too. They controlled when and how we dropped from what is called the "swing landing trainer," they would not drop us so we landed feet first. Instead they dropped us when our bodies were horizontal to the ground—that's when it hurt. There was always a student breaking a leg or arm during that week.

After graduating from the Infantry and Airborne schools, I got deathly ill with what they called the "Benning Crud" and was cut from Ranger School. That was a big disappointment at the start of my Army career. (Later I would apply for Ranger and Special Forces out of Germany.) At last, in November, I received orders to U.S. Army Europe in Augsburg, Germany, to join the second battalion of the 34th Infantry there. The Cold War was on, it was the age of Kennedy's Camelot, and I was ready to serve.

Paula and I married just before I was scheduled to depart, on November 23, 1963—the day after JFK's assassination. In fact, we were married in Lewiston, and I was checking on her at the hairdresser when I saw Walter Cronkite on the salon's TV, announcing that the president had been shot. It was a shock, particularly after I'd seen him in Spokane.

Paula and I married in 1963.

Paula and I as newlyweds and with her mother, Magda

I was happy to be getting married and starting a new life, but now no one was looking forward to a bright future. The assassination caused intense mourning in the country and even put a damper on our wedding. The Pentagon, thinking that perhaps this was a Russian plot to take over the country, put all the Armed Forces on alert throughout the world, and Kennedy's untimely death left my generation with a lot of questions about the Cold War as it proceeded. If he'd lived, would that war and the arms race have come to a close sooner? Would we have wasted so many lives and so much time in Vietnam? It's hard to know, and Kennedy had actually increased the number of U.S. advisors in Vietnam from around 1,500 to more than 16,000 by the time of his death. His administration also took part in planning the coup that overthrew South Vietnamese President Ngo Dinh Diem. And the fact was, Lyndon B. Johnson had become president in his place and my road through Vietnam, at least the first time, was already set.

The wedding party

Prepared to leave for Europe, we didn't have a honeymoon in the traditional sense, if you don't count what the Army supplied. We spent that first night in the Lewis and Clark Hotel in Lewiston, watched television, ordered a steak dinner from room service, and made love. Then we went to Spokane for painful farewells. It was a sobering experience to leave home with my new wife, and My mom, dad, Julie, Judy, and James plus Paula's mom, Magda, sent us off at Spokane International Airport, then a simple wood building.

Once in Seattle, we boarded a Boeing 707 and were invited to first class since we were honeymooners. I was served a big martini. We reached New York, where we stayed at the Waldorf Hotel, called home, and burst into tears. The flight from there to Stuttgart, Germany, was in a four-engine prop plane, in a storm, with water leaking from the ceiling all the way. When we arrived in Stuttgart, a sergeant helped us get on the train to Augsburg. Paula was throwing up with morning sickness. I reported for duty to the Executive Officer, Major Weldon C. Honeycutt, who later as a lieutenant colonel would lead the infamous May 1969 direct assault on Hill 937, also known as Hamburger Hill, in Vietnam. (The battle resulted in over 400 U.S. casualties and caused outrage in U.S.) He told me that my unit was in Berlin and that I needed to proceed there immediately.

I said, "My wife is sick in the officer's transient billets."

He said, "Lieutenant, get your ass on the train. If the Army wanted you to have a wife, they would have issued you one."

Needless to say, I got on the train. The other wives left behind took care of Paula.

While I was stationed in Germany that first time for the Army, I was also in an Allied Command Europe mobile force (AMF), first with the Second Battalion, 34th Infantry and then with the First Battalion, 19th Infantry. When I arrived, the Second Battalion had just gotten the assignment to relieve the battalion then in Berlin, so I rode the troop train to Berlin by myself to catch up with them. This was before the Berlin Wall came down, and each of the "four powers"—the United States, France, England, and Russia—occupied Berlin and had a force at the wall, each in its own sector. We guarded our side of the wall, and many times there would be an East German who attempted to escape. We'd help them to the extent we could, but most of the time they got shot in the area filled with mines and barbed wire. It happened a lot. Sometimes American servicemen would be shot on either side of the wall, usually on our side. I knew a major who was simply shot in the head while in his Army sedan on the East German side.

The Berlin Wall DMZ

We'd also drive in sedans, fully armed and in our uniforms, on what was called a G2 intelligence tour to the Russian sector (and they could come into our sector, too). We could drive right up to the other bases and park there. Other times, tanks would roll right up to the Berlin Wall gate.

After 90 days in Berlin, our U.S. Army Mechanized Infantry Battalion of about 800 men returned to Augsburg. We went through East Germany. It was still deep winter, and we were all locked and loaded with live ammo. We stood alongside our vehicles for more than four hours, in snow up to our knees, while the Russians inspected the whole convoy. There was a lot of tension with the Russians, who were not in any hurry to get us moving, and both sides had live ammo.

Back in Augsburg, I was reunited with Paula. One of my jobs there was to lead the 24th Infantry's Entertainment Group, which had been known as the Soldier's Chorus until the previous year. Not long after arriving, I wrote a song and performed it for the two-star general at a party on base. Later, I was told that the lieutenant in charge of the Entertainment Division was leaving and the general wanted me to head it up in his place. About two dozen men were involved, many of them with professional music and acting credentials. My company commander told me taking the assignment could negatively impact my career.

"You're a regular Army officer," he said. "Leading a music group is not going to look good on your record." My battalion commander, however, who was one level up, said, "The general wants you to do this. You have no choice."

We toured for two years, sometimes performing every day. One of our shows was a 45-minute comedy musical revue called "Cross the Pond," which was based on the idea of talent show winners competing on the Ed Sullivan television show. As I told one newspaper reporter, the production was a departure from the USO variety programs and other shows from the United States. It was conceived, written, and performed entirely by the members of the division. We played for over 45,000 service members in that time. We also performed in German for the local communities and also went to Munich to record a radio broadcast for the Armed Forces Network. It was a really big deal. I had writers creating new songs for us, and our radio recording was broadcast on Radio Free Europe behind the Iron Curtain on April 1, 1964. It was high-quality work.

One day a representative from the Army's Criminal Investigation Division (CID) came to me and told me that three of the musicians were homosexuals who were going to be discharged. I was surprised; it had never been an issue to me and since I was new to the Army, that was my first experience with the Army's policy then. I had to replace them.

I also formed my second trio, a folk group called the Forgers, with two particularly talented members of that Entertainment Group, private first class Michael Bump and private first class William "Bill" Barringer, who had acted in films and on TV back home. We played on the Armed Forces Network and also had our music broadcast behind the Iron Curtain by U.S. Army

Europe in 1964 and 1965. We rerecorded my songs "Rio Town," "Sheila," "Henry's Body Is Buried," and "The Alligator Man," for that broadcast, along with playing eleven other songs. We also rerecorded several songs I'd originally recorded on four-track tape while at Gonzaga at the home of the colonel in charge of my school ROTC program who was also a guitar player. Those songs were "Don't You Grieve After Me," "There's Whiskey In The Jar," and "When Johnny Comes Marching Home."

The Forgers

After the entertainment group assignment, I was told I had to get back on my career track and was assigned as a platoon leader to the First Battalion, 19th Infantry, 24th Infantry Division. After I reported I noticed a familiar face among my soldiers. A platoon has about forty soldiers assigned—three rifle squads and one weapons squad. The newly assigned private first class I recognized was a kid who'd lived next to my family after we moved from the cottages to Spokane so I could attend Gonzaga Prep. Much bigger and older than me, a skinny runt, he had bullied and harassed me unmercifully.

There in formation, I looked him in the eye. He shrank like wallflower. I could have made his life miserable but I was his leader and I was not about to take revenge.

While in my new assignment, our battalion was deployed on a joint forces operation as a member of the Allied Command Europe Mobile Force (AMF), a small NATO quick-reaction force with headquarters at Heidelberg, Germany. The U.S. unit was our First Battalion, 19th Infantry. The AMF was commanded by a British brigadier general, and we flew our whole battalion, 800 men, on a ten-hour flight from Fürstenfeldbruck, Germany, to Diyarbakir, Turkey, for operations there. That was interesting stuff. Our colonel, Lieutenant Colonel Hammonds, was a good guy, but he was something else. The first day were there in Turkey we were putting up all the tents, and he stepped out and said, "Everybody keep a hand on your weapon or some Arab's going to steal it!" Well, we were in Turkey! There were no Arabs there.

U.S. Army General Lyman Lemnitzer, who was and Supreme Allied Commander Europe of NATO, attended the exercises we did on the plains of Diyarbakir. While in Turkey, when we weren't doing exercises, we'd always go to the British officers' mess tent because they had the best gin and tonics. Other nations represented were Italy and Belgium.

Turkish mud

One night I practically drowned. Warrant Officer Musgrave and I shared a tent, which meant we each had an Army cot, with an air mattress on that, and then a sleeping bag that we crawled into on top. It had been raining, raining all night. I woke up at one point because it felt like my air mattress was moving. We were floating! We stepped off our cots in our underwear into water up to our waists. The tent had four feet of water in it! It was a muddy, mucky mess until we finally flew out of there in the C-130s.

I had another adventure aboard a French duty train from Strasburg. I could catch it in Augsburg and ride it to West Berlin, or vice versa. I liked to ride it; the train had a good French breakfast, a croissant and good coffee. I was riding back home in uniform once and the gendarmes serving as guards on the train saw me. In broken English they invited me to their car, where they broke open champagne and we talked about the Vietnam War. I told them that if I had a choice, an opportunity to do things again, I'd want to be a Frenchman. We drank all the way to Strasburg.

Another train trip ended when I got off the platform and couldn't recall where I'd parked before I had left. It was five or six in the morning, so I left my luggage and walked around the corner to look for my car. When I got back, my luggage was gone.

"What the hell happened to my luggage?" I wondered. Then I saw a door opening at an apartment nearby. A lady stepped out and waved me over. When I got to her doorstep, there was my luggage sitting inside. She'd brought it inside, she said, because she didn't want anyone (else) to take it.

Paula and Shane

My first son, Shane, was born in August 1964, and Heidi followed about a year later. Both gave me and Paula great joy; it was a happy time. As the kids got older, we had great fun going on trips around Europe. My mother visited us there when Shane was born, and my mother-in-law came when

Heidi was born. During Mom's visit, we were traveling with her for the first time, staying in various hotels in Germany. It was hilarious—and terrible!—when my mother thought a bidet was also the toilet and did her business in it.

Mom with Heidi and Shane

Often, I would leave work on Friday and we would drive to Berchtesgaden in the Bavarian Alps to ski. One year, during my second deployment to Germany in the 1970s, we did a trip to Sweden. We left on a Friday with all the kids in the back seat, sound asleep. I was very sleepy, too, so I pulled our VW camper off the road and fell asleep. I woke up two hours later and realized that if I didn't get moving, we would miss the ferry we needed to take from Germany to Malmo, Sweden. Luckily, we made it and stayed two weeks in Sweden. Eventually, we got to travel not only to Berlin to see the Berlin Wall as a family but also to Switzerland, Austria, France, Italy, Yugoslavia, and Turkey.

Paula, Shane, and Heidi

In addition to lots of happy family time, though, I also had my first affair in those years. In 1965, my Entertainment Group did a show in Munich during Fasching, a big celebration equivalent to Germany's Mardi Gras or Carnival season. We were all invited to party with our German hosts. I danced there with a woman named Christine, and we started a brief relationship. We made love that night. I had a chance to see her in Munich again later, and once time in the middle of winter I drove to Munich in the middle of a snowstorm to see her, telling Paula we had a show there.

Alcohol didn't help. I knew I had a serious drinking problem. I'd wake up many mornings with the shakes. After the relationship ended, I never saw Christine again, but I did unexpectedly hear from her. The mail came in the morning to our quarters. Suffering from a terrible hangover from the previous night, I had the shakes then. Paula and I were on the porch, waiting for the mail, our neighbor was near us on her own porch. The mailman came with the mail, which included a small package addressed to me. Paula opened the other mail as I opened my package.

It was a small baby doll. The return address was Christine's. I quickly covered it up, starting to shake. I figured the baby doll was a signal from Christine: "John, I had a baby by you."

Our neighbor said, "What's wrong, John?" Paula covered for me, saying something about the tough schedule I had.

It was a shocking message. Would I have fathered two babies outside of my marriage? But I didn't stop drinking.

Paula's mother, Magda, came for a visit, and one night I came home intoxicated and yelling. Paula wouldn't let me into the apartment, and rightly so. I went across the street to the basketball court and slept on the pavement. When I woke, it was daylight.

I went back to the apartment, where Paula let me in. Magda told Paula she should pack up and come home, but she didn't. After that incident and others, I told Paula I needed to get into a treatment program in Augsburg. I was badly in need of help. To my surprise, she talked me out of it. When I said I was going to stop drinking, she said, "No, you aren't. It'd ruin your career."

It was true that we were invited to many cocktail parties, and drinking and partying went on in the stairwell about every weekend. But I wish I had resisted and gone into treatment. In the long term, it would have probably saved our marriage.

Shane torments Heidi while Magda looks on

I was stationed in Europe that first time for more than three years before we returned to the U.S. in the summer of 1966. By then, the Gulf of Tonkin incident had taken place in Vietnam, and the war had ramped up significantly. A lot of officers were being assigned to Vietnam, and I felt that I needed to volunteer to go, too, and sooner rather than later. I told Paula and then applied for eight weeks of Ranger school, since I'd missed it before. I also applied for the Special Forces. She was not excited. That would mean months of schooling for me, home for a 30-day leave, and then a whole year in Vietnam.

Meanwhile, John F. Kennedy had put on a big push for advisors for the South Vietnamese, regular Army Infantry guys like me. So the Pentagon came back to me and said that instead of what I'd requested, they were going to send me to Civil Affairs Advisory Training and then to the Defense Language Institute to study Vietnamese before sending me to Vietnam. As it turned out, I'd still be gone from home the same length of time as if I'd gone the Ranger and Special Forces route.

Paula was pregnant with Ben when we flew back to the United States. The preparation for my first deployment to Vietnam was about to begin.

CHAPTER 5: MY FIRST VIETNAM OPERATIONS

"Fix your eyes on the greatness of Athens as you have it before you day by day, fall in love with her, and when you feel her great, remember that this greatness was won by men with courage, with knowledge of their duty, and with a sense of honor in action."

—*Thucydides, Funeral Oration of Pericles*

"In peace, sons bury fathers, but in war fathers bury sons."

—*Herodotus, The Histories*

On April 5, 1966, I'd received orders in Germany to report to Fort Gordon, Georgia, on July 24 to attend a six-week U.S. Army Civil Affairs Advisory Course for Vietnam before proceeding to the Presidio of Monterey by September 11 to attend the Defense Language Institute. There, I'd take a short, 12-week Vietnamese language training course before being assigned to the United States Army Military Assistance Command.

When I pinned on my Second Lieutenant bars, I succumbed to the pitch of an insurance salesman who'd visited me prior to my first assignment. I bought too much life insurance, so I was nearly broke, but I had my family covered if I was killed in Vietnam.

So I was trying always to pinch pennies, so to speak. Once back in the United States, I decided to catch a military hop out of McChord Air Force Base near Seattle. I was lucky and got on a C119 heading to Augusta, Georgia, which was near Fort Gordon, then the home of the Civil Affairs School.

On the way we hit terrible weather, and our flight put down at Fort Polk, Louisiana. After the hair-raising turbulence, I told the crew I was going to get a civilian flight to Augusta.

I finally was on a civilian airline, a Douglas DC3, which was a converted C47. On the way to Augusta we again had terrible turbulence. My seat was near the door. The plane pitched and bounced every which way, with no flight attendant in sight. The red baked hills of Georgia were right below us and passengers were getting sick.

Just then the cockpit door opened and a flight attendant who was dressed to kill in her airline colors but barely able to stand up as she balanced a tray of Coca Colas. She began serving Cokes for those who could drink it. It was an exciting way to start my Civil Affairs Training—the beginning of my training in revolutionary development.

I was billeted at the Bon Air Retirement Home in Augusta. The Army was short on room space because it was prioritizing getting advisors through Civil Affairs Advisory Training and on to Vietnam. Our classroom was across the street from the retirement home. Many of us there at Civil Affairs school would continue immediately on to language school. While I was in Georgia, Paula and the kids went to stay with her mother in Lewiston, Idaho, until I finished Civil Affairs training, when I'd drive across the country, pick them up, and head south to Monterey.

My fellow students and I were all temporarily single guys billeted with a lot of rich Southern women, many of whom were widows. Other women came from around town to dance with guys headed to war. They loved dancing. Every weekend there was a big dance that we students were invited to. Between dances we were kept busy with homework. My buddy during the course was a Marine Corps colonel on his way back to South Vietnam to be part of the new Civil Operations and Revolutionary Support structure being put in place. He was single, and we often had a beer together in his room as he dressed in civvies to head out on a date. We had great short conversations, as he thought it was pretty cool that my Dad had been a Marine stationed in Peking in 1925.

As students we had to perform a civic action survey for the Province of Go Cong in the Republic of South Vietnam, which was interesting given that I'd soon be assigned there. We had to cover the situation, mission, execution, and administrative pieces of the puzzle which included convincing the people in the province that the existing government supported their wishes and needs for development. We had to determine the best way of the winning popular support of the people to simultaneously strengthen the nation, enhance the image of the Army of the Republic of South Vietnam in the eyes of the population, and demonstrate that the military was up to the task of protecting the population so they could live normal, productive lives. The assumptions were that the government of the Republic would remain favorably disposed toward its current concept and progress of civic action. Also—and this was a big one—that the government would continue to fulfill the necessary requirements to be eligible for U.S. aid and assistance *and* that the assistance would continue.

It all sounds familiar to the present status of our nation's foreign aid programs. My personal two cents about the situation we faced in 1966 was that the world was being driven by the doctrine of dialectical materialism as espoused by Marx, Engels, Lenin, Stalin, and Mao's Tung. I wrote that this doctrine tended to neglect human nature and the standards of values in vogue. Russia was trying to evolve with the times because it had a little economic rent it could collect from China, but on the other hand, it was still looking for a good source of economic rent—that is, industry—over production of consumables or more property.

I put together a diagram for my paper to partially indicate the massive, devious, world-based plan of Communism we were facing in South Vietnam. I argued, "This student strongly feels that one must always maintain the lasting imprint in one's subconscious, never forgetting the tremendous philosophical, ideological, and psychological impact this form of power has in its inner core." I maintained this train of thought later in South Vietnam with a Communist sympathizer and had earlier at Reed College in Portland, a hotbed of liberalism. However, I was about to encounter lectures and detailed reality presented by my training and my own boots on the ground as an infantry officer in Vietnam combat, where I would recognize the folly of my thinking.

At Civil Affairs school, one of my instructors was Dr. Bernard Fall, a reporter, historian, and the author of *Street Without Joy* and six other books on Vietnam. He'd been a teen in World War II, with both of his parents working in the underground and killed by the Nazis. After escaping, he eventually became the preeminent authority on Indochina. He'd been there five times since 1953 and had interviewed Ho Chi Minh, and by 1961 he'd concluded that the U.S. military tactics weren't likely to work. By the time I learned from him, sitting in presentations where he showed slides he'd just reviewed with the Pentagon, he felt the South Vietnamese were losing. This was 1966, remember, and the recognized expert on Indochina, Dr. Fall, had already said we were losing. He showed us slide after slide of facts and data about the drastic situation there, which were different from the Army's glowing briefings. Those of us in his class sat in awe as he told us that 80 percent of the ground in South Vietnam was infiltrated by the Viet Cong, an estimate the Pentagon denied. Fall pointed out to us that a denial by the Pentagon was as good as an affirmation that something was happening. After this course, I continued to follow Dr. Fall, reading all of his books and eventually creating a musical tribute to him and his wife, Dorothy.

Bernard Fall in Vietnam

Dr. Fall's books are legends; it's too bad they were only studied by lower-ranking military officers. Retired U.S. General Colin Powell said, "We probably all should have studied Bernard Fall a lot longer and with greater intensity, especially people in high policy positions, because he made it clear and we should have realized that it was a war as much about nationalism and self- determination within this one country than it was about the ideology of communism or the worldwide Communist conspiracy."

General Westmoreland kept several of Dr. Falls' books at his bedside in Saigon, but as he said in his memoir, *A Soldier Reports*, "I usually was too tired in late evening to give the books more than occasional attention."

In his book *In Retrospect: The Tragedy and Lessons of Vietnam*, Robert McNamara, former U.S. secretary of defense under President Lyndon Johnson, said there were no experts on Vietnam in this country to which he could turn for information. McNamara, a finance whiz from Ford, created the body count metric for Vietnam. He could speak about the statistical correlation between U.S. bombs dropped on North Vietnam and Vietnamese supplies brought down to the South, but he didn't understand the basics of Ho Chi Minh's nationalism and that the way out of Vietnam was only a Dr. Fall book away. McNamara used faulty data that measured the wrong things—body count.

McNamara's own whiz kid was Alain C. Enthoven, a professor of public policy at Stanford University. In their book *Critical Condition: How Health Care in America Became Big Business & Bad Medicine,* authors Donald L. Barlett and James B. Steele call Enthoven "the person generally credited with spawning the idea that competition would be the salvation of American health care... a technocrat with a coldly analytical belief in the power of computers to solve public problems." Enthoven headed up systems analysis for McNamara and is credited by Barlett and Steele for "devising the infamous body count, the controversial program that purported to measure the progress of the war by tabulating the number of enemy dead..." They suggest that applying quantitative methods to complex human endeavors, including war, "was, in the words of one military historian, 'the height of arrogance.'" I'd also call it stupid.

Colin Powell went on his first tour to Vietnam in 1963. I followed in 1967. In Powell's 1995 book, *My American Journey,* he references body counts:

> The first confirmed kill produced a boost in morale among the ARVN. The numbers game, later termed the "body count," had not yet come into use. But the Vietnamese had already figured out what the Americans wanted to hear. They were forever "proving" kills to me by a patch of blood leading from an abandoned weapon or other circumstantial evidence. Not good enough, I told them. I became a referee in a grisly game, and a VC KIA (Viet Cong Killed in Action) required a VC body. No body, no credit.

Later in the book Powell continues on the topic of body counts:

> Dark episodes like My Lai resulted, in part, because of the military's obsession with another semi-fiction, the "body count," that grisly yardstick produced by the Vietnam War... Counting bodies became a macabre statistical competition. Companies were measured against companies, battalions against battalions, brigades against brigades. Good commanders scored high body counts. And good commanders got promoted. If your competition was inflating the counts, could you afford not to?

Later in my career I would study waste and its implications in any type of organization, and combined with my study of war, I found it very interesting that Ho Chi Minh's understanding was surprisingly parallel to those of Taiichi

Ohno and Henry Ford. In 1952 Ho Chi Minh issued a paper titled, "To Practice Thrift and Oppose Embezzlement, Waste, and Bureaucracy." He said: "Waste takes on many forms: Waste of labour—because of lack of a sense of responsibility or bad organization, a large number of people are assigned to a job which can be done by a few... Waste of public property assumes many forms, such as Army men who do not take good care of their weapons, equipment, and the booty captured." He continues in great detail, addressing the many forms of waste he considered enemies of the people, the army, and the government.

But much of that understanding was still in my future. After learning from Dr. Fall and Civil Affairs school, I moved on to 12 weeks of language school. I left Fort Gordon at 11:00 a.m. on a Wednesday, driving our Volkswagen square-back, which we'd shipped from Germany, pedal to the floor from Georgia all the way to Lewiston, 2,381 miles away, arriving that Saturday. You make good time when you average 80 miles an hour! In Lewiston I rented a 4x4 U-Haul, loaded it with two baby beds and essentials, and with my family on board and Paula pregnant, we arrived in Monterey, California, another 962 miles, the following Monday.

Jazz pianist Dave Brubeck was appearing that the Monterey Jazz festival that September. His hit album, "Time Out," had been recorded when I was still in college and had been the first jazz album to sell a million copies.

When we arrived at our hotel, I went inside and the guy at the desk said no kids or animals were allowed. I got a room anyway and snuck the family up the back stairs. The kids had to keep quiet, which wasn't easy for toddlers. That was really a trip.

Language school was fun. The first day of class, the language instructor started speaking Vietnamese, and every student was given a tape recorder, 20 words to learn each night, and a dialogue to learn that we had to perform with another student the next day. If you didn't pass the class, you still went to Vietnam! Everyone in the class was headed there. So I learned as much as I could.

It wasn't always easy to concentrate on my homework, though, which I had every night in our hotel. To complicate matters, Ben was born in California that October, the day before Halloween. Shane slept in a regular bed, but both Ben and Heidi would rock in their baby beds, making a loud squeaky sound like the floor was caving in. This was in a hotel that theoretically didn't allow kids, remember. One night after we had put the kids down, there was a huge pounding sound from the unit below. When the kids stopped rocking, the pounding would stop. I told Paula to ignore it.

Ben, in the middle, completed our family

The next night and the next night the pounding started again, and it seemed to be getting louder each night. That third night, I went down to the hotel room below, knocked on the door, and was meant by a hostile, angry woman—the wife of another military officer. I told her that I was there on TDY (temporary duty), that we had two small kids with another on the way, and that we couldn't stop them from rocking their beds. I mentioned that I was on my way to Vietnam and that we were doing the best we could under the circumstances.

She was raving, "You don't know what you are putting us through! It sounds like the ceiling is going to come crashing down, right into our bedroom below you!" I tried to reason with her, but she wouldn't listen and slammed the door in my face. So the nightly pounding continued.

I told Paula I was going to explain the situation to the commandant of the school, a U.S. Army colonel who was a Vietnam vet. When I went to see him, he said he would bring both me and the Air Force lieutenant living with his wife in the place below us into his office for a chat. We both showed up, and the colonel explained to the lieutenant—who hadn't been to Vietnam and wasn't going to go—that I *was* going to Vietnam. He asked the lieutenant to explain why his wife was beating on her ceiling with a broom handle, then he said, "Infantry officers have a 25 percent chance of not coming home. If you continue to beat on the ceiling between your quarters and Captain

Black's, you will be removed from the course your attending here and I'll see that there is a letter put into your personnel file explaining this situation as well." The Colonel added, "Do you understand, lieutenant? Am I clear?" The lieutenant said he understood. I went home and told Paula what had happened. She was relieved, and I told Shane and Heidi to rock away at night, and they did. There were no more poundings from the below.

Still, trying to make ends meet and take care of your family while getting ready to go into a war zone, where 500 Americans were dying a day, was stressful. It was stressful for Paula and for me, who in the back of my mind wasn't sure I was coming back. It affected the kids, too, regardless of how old they were.

Then, just before the end of the year, I got my orders for Vietnam, as expected. My mother was visiting, and I put her, the kids, and Paula on a flight home to Spokane while I drove our car and trailer home and then found our family a place to live on 36th Avenue. I had 30 days of leave, and during that time I worked part time doing stocking in a liquor store in Spokane. Everybody working in that store was drinking on the job from a bottle they kept stashed on the shelf. I watched them take shots during the day. Then I left my family in January 1967 for a year-long deployment.

Leaving home was very emotional. The closer we got to date I was leaving, the more uptight we all got. It was then that I finally learned from Paula about our first baby. Those last 30 days were hard. I said goodbye to everybody, who was sobbing and crying. Shane was two, Heidi was 15 months old, and Ben was a newborn, two months old. My little brother James was only about ten. I thought to myself, "You're leaving everybody, but how could you also leave your only little brother?"

At that time, the evening news showed heavy losses each day in Vietnam; it was unbelievable. By the end of 1966, when I arrived in Saigon, there were 385,000 U.S. soldiers in South Vietnam plus an additional 60,000 sailors stationed offshore. Five hundred and eleven U.S. soldiers were dying a month, and over the next year that would rise to 929 each month. More than 6,000 Americans had already been killed with 30,000 wounded. An estimated 61,000 Viet Cong had also been killed, while their troops then numbered over 280,000.

So I never really expected to make it home alive. And yet my greatest fear was that I would not return, leaving Paula and my little kids fatherless. This was a very sad and stressful time to be gone for a year, and I didn't want to imagine Paula having to make a living by herself, just like her mother had when her husband was killed in a plane crash when Paula was still young.

When it came to the dangers of flying, I'd also experienced something of a prelude to my Vietnam tours when I was 17. My rich Aunt Fran had invited Mom and me to accompany her on a flight from a Seattle airfield to Jackpot,

Nevada. The plan was to leave Friday after I got out of school at Gonzaga Prep and come back late Sunday night.

We met up with Aunt Fran at a small airfield outside of Spokane. There it was—a two engine vintage bomber that definitely was old, something like the C47 and other aircraft I would later fly in in Vietnam. At first, it looked like we would be the only passengers, but then four more showed up. All appeared to be intoxicated. Aunt Fran always carried a small flask in her purse, too, and every once in a while she would take a drink. Everybody was smoking except Mom and me.

When the pilot said it was time to take off and for us to get in and take a seat, Mom and I took a seat near the front. Aunt Fran was right behind us. The pilot—on his own, without a copilot— started the left engine, then the right one. Both belched flames and brief bursts of smoke—not a reassuring start. Mom reached into her purse and pulled out her rosary, just as I would do later when flying to Vietnam. To this day, I carry my rosary in my brief case, along with a small plastic statue of Jesus on the Cross from my grandmother's casket. I also picked up the strange habit of turning my watch backwards on my wrist prior to takeoff while quickly making an act of contrition. For me this little ritual provides a reassurance that the plane will not crash, or if it does that I'll go straight to heaven.

When we finally took off from Spokane, the pilot told us as we climbed that we were going to fly at about 10,000 feet of altitude. It was a clear day, and the wheat fields of the Palouse country below us were reassuring. An hour into the flight, it looked like everyone was asleep except me, the pilot, and Mom.

Suddenly the right engine began sputtering, with oil spraying out. The pilot muttered, "Son of a bitch, I told that maintenance guy to check the oil leak." He uttered several other expletives as we appeared to lose altitude. Mom appeared to be scared stiff.

As the left wing dipped, the pilot yelled, "Don't worry folks, everything is under control." The right engine continued to sputter and we continued to lose altitude. Everyone now was awake.

Finally, at about 3,000 feet, the pilot said, "Attention, everyone! It looks like I am going to have to land in a wheat field. Make sure your seatbelts are on tight." I could see clearly ahead out the front of the cockpit. The pilot was maneuvering the airplane toward one of the fields ahead of us. Mom and I both were praying the rosary out loud. The passengers in back look horrified; one yelled, "God dammit, I knew we shouldn't have taken this damn trip!" Two women were screaming, "We are going to die, oh my God, we are going to die." One guy told them to shut up. Another woman in back was drinking out of her flask, and so was Aunt Fran.

I, too, figured we were going to die, although the pilot was yelling, "We are going to make it, we are going to make it. Everybody just hang on, hang on." We were now at 1000 feet and dropping quickly toward the wheat field ahead.

The pilot screamed, "Everybody bend over and grab your legs and hang on!"

A guy in back of me yelled, "Grab your legs, bullshit! Grab your ass!" I closed my eyes and prayed along with Mom. When I opened my eyes, there we were with the pilot maneuvering as the plane came in with wheels down. BUMP! We landed safely, coming to a smooth stop.

Everybody cheered and clapped and thanked the pilot. When we were all out of the plane, he said we all had three choices: Stay with him and hope he can get the engine repaired, hitch a ride on the road to Jackpot on our own, or wait until he could call for transportation. He made it clear, however, that his airline would not reimburse anyone for expenses or transportation. We were really on our own.

Mom and Aunt Fran decided to get up to the road about a half mile away, where they would try to hitch a ride. We had packed light, but it was still tough hauling our luggage. We made it up to the road and got a ride, luckily one that went all the way to Jackpot.

The next day, Aunt Fran told us she had chartered a small, one-engine plane to fly us back to Spokane on Sunday. Mom said, "Are you sure it's going to be safe?" Aunt Fran said, "Yes, I hope so. I don't want to take a bus home, so we have no choice."

Mom told me she was really worried about flying back in a small plane after our crash landing, but Aunt Fran was paying for everything, so we had no choice but to follow along with her. When Sunday came, Mom and I were nervous. The sky was dark, with thunder clouds forming.

We took a taxi to the local airport, checked in, and went to the plane, a single engine Cessna. The pilot wore a business hat. Aunt Fran sat in the co-pilot's seat, with and Mom and I behind.

"We are going to be flying over the mountains, and there are storm clouds looming," said the pilot. At that ominous comment, Mom and I pulled out our rosaries right from the start. My cross was in my pocket. We taxied out to the runway, the pilot revved the engine, and we took off.

I could hear Mom's voice: "Hail Mary, full of grace, the Lord is with thee." I prayed under my breath, Aunt Fran sipped from her flask, and our plane slowly climbed toward the black clouds ahead. The plane shook in a little turbulence—and then more. The sun was blacked out by the huge thunderstorm. The pilot turned to Aunt Fran and said, "I'm not going on. There is no way we can safely fly through those clouds."

He turned the plane around and we headed back, landing safely as Mom finished up her rosary. When we landed, Aunt Fran agreed to take the bus back to Spokane, and Mom and I thanked God under our breath.

We enjoyed a peaceful ride home, sleeping most of the way. I promised myself then that I'd never ride in another airplane. Little did I know what my future held. Now I was on my way in a plane once again, this time not into a thunderstorm but a war zone.

The gut-wrenching goodbyes took place at the Spokane International Airport. Everyone was crying. I couldn't hold back, either. Once I boarded the Alaska Airlines flight and took my seat next to an older woman, I briefly controlled my emotions but then broke out into tears. She asked why I was crying, and I told her I was just leaving my family on the way to Vietnam.

My flight took me to San Francisco on my way to Travis Air Force Base in California. In San Francisco, I walked into a bar to order a beer. I'd just turned 26, but I looked young and had to show my ID.

At that time the military was chartering flights to Vietnam with World Airways and Flying Tiger airways. In fact, a couple of years previously, my friend Tim Hopkins had been on a Boeing 707 World Airways flight that disappeared into the Pacific Ocean, killing a full load of new Army soldiers headed to Vietnam, including him. My charter was a Boeing 707 that had engine trouble, so we stopped in Manilla in the Philippines. I was a captain then, and I was sitting next to a Special Forces sergeant on his fourth tour, if you can imagine that. When we landed in Manilla, I said, "Let's go downtown and get a San Miguel beer."

He agreed, so we were downtown, on the patio of the Hilton hotel, when we look up to see this 707 flying overhead. That was our flight! They'd taken off again without us. We went back to the airport, where I went to Thai Airways and got us a ticket to Saigon and flew in there.

When we arrived on January 9 in Saigon (now known as Ho Chi Minh City), we reported to Koelper Compound, which was where advisors were briefed before being assigned to a Military Assistance Command Vietnam (MACV) advisory unit. We really got reamed out for being AWOL (absent without leave), but we just said, "What are you going to do?" We were already in Vietnam, how much worse could it get?

*Downtown Saigon in 1967 from the roof of the Rex Hotel, where I later stayed
with my son Shane when I went back to Saigon with him in 1999.*

We were there in Saigon for briefings for two weeks. While there, I took
a picture from the rooftop of the bar of the famous Rex Hotel. I would revisit
this hotel many times during my two tours of duty in South Vietnam. The
Rex is where the war's infamous military press briefings known as the "five
o'clock follies" took place. AP correspondent and Saigon bureau chief
Richard Pyle called these briefings "the longest-playing tragicomedy in
Southeast Asia's theater of the absurd." The credibility gap between the truth
as journalists saw it on the ground and the official reports presented to them
at the briefings sometimes prompted either cynical jokes or shouting
matches. Barry Zorthian, a U.S. diplomat who for several years led those
briefings as public affairs officer, later said, "In Vietnam, we reached a stage
where the government's word was to be questioned until proven true,
whereas in the past it had been the government's word is valid until proven
to be wrong."

My briefings in Saigon were meant to prepare me to be a province senior
advisor for a regional/popular force (RF/PF) training center. The briefings
were a firehose of information—including graphic, color photos of the body
parts of soldiers diagnosed with syphilis and gonorrhea, as well as the dangers
of fraternizing with Vietnamese women who could be Viet Cong agents. For
those of us headed to the Mekong Delta—a region of more than 15,600
square miles in southwestern Vietnam— the briefer covered the fact we
might be working with the U.S. Navy Swift boats, which had been used as
coastal patrol craft in Vietnam starting in 1965 to stop seaborne supplies on

their way to the Viet Cong and the North Vietnamese army in South Vietnam. If you were being assigned further north, you learned to be wary of the underground tunnels everywhere, which were used a lot in the development of boobytraps. We were briefed on the dangers of stepping on *punju* sticks buried in the ground and the use by the Viet Cong of trip wires and explosives. These trip wires could activate many things, from a simple grenade to stranger things like scorpions and dangerous snakes falling onto the soldiers who activated the wire.

We were also briefed on the situation in South Vietnam and the role of the RF/PF. During the Vietnam War, the South Vietnamese regional forces were Army of the Republic of Vietnam (ARVN) militia. Recruited locally, initially for as province and village defense, they fell into two broad groups: regional forces and the more local-level popular forces. (The RF/PFs were called Ruff-Puffs by American forces). In 1964, the regional forces were integrated into the ARVN and placed under the command of the Joint General Staff. The RF/PF units were militia men who also worked part or full-time elsewhere. With mostly obsolete equipment, they served as a front-line defense. When the U.S. intervened, they first were relegated more to guard and security duty and then later, with better training and management, they carried out wider operations while the ARVN's regular forces were deployed. The RF/PF force gradually grew to nearly a quarter of a million men.

After briefings, we were sent to MACV supply at Ton Son Nhut airbase to get our gear. Officers got the standard issue: fatigues, boots, backpack, steel pot, pistol belt, compass, mess kit, frag vest, knife with sheaf, M1 carbine, .45, first aid packet, a 10-pound flak jacket, and much more. The most useful item for the monsoon season was a poncho.

I collected all my gear, weapons, and ammunition and got it all packed to carry south. The next day I said goodbye to Saigon and was taken to Tan Son Nhut for a flight.

During wartime, flights were in and out all the time. I flew down to My Tho, which was headquarters for my tactical zone, Four (IV) Corps, the most southern of the four regions and the area of the Mekong Delta. Each had a senior advisor, a full colonel. I reported in there, got briefed, and then waited about a week and a half. There were a number of operations in the region with Viet Cong guerillas, and our sleeping quarters were just a big room of stacked bunks, even for officers. I went to the post exchange (PX), got a can of Muriel cigars, and shared them with the guy in the bunk below mine, Captain Hardy W. Peeples, who was a Ranger advisor. We talked about our families. He was looking forward to meeting his wife in Hawaii for R&R in a few weeks.

I was glad I didn't get assigned to that team, because those guys had a short lifespan. In fact, a few weeks later the chaplain came to the province where I'd been assigned, Go Cong Province, and told us that Captain Peeples had been blown up by a Viet Cong landmine while riding in his jeep on an operation.

I thought to myself, "What did I get myself into?" In our briefing at My Tho, they tossed out a lot of numbers. There were currently 485,000 American soldiers in South Vietnam, plus ARVN as well as troops from South Korea, Thailand, Australia, the Philippines, and New Zealand, all totaling 1,343,000. The same story kept repeating itself: "We were winning the war." "It's getting better." "We are killing more Viet Cong than they are killing us." I was in a daze, but then I heard, "Okay, Captain Black, you're flying into Go Cong Province. Get all your stuff."

A helicopter was coming for me. I rode the chopper to this dirt airstrip. As we're landing, I look down the strip to the garbage dump at the end of it and see an old jeep sitting there among the sandbags. We were advisors, so we didn't get the new stuff. I see a staff sergeant sitting there wearing a brown beret. I get my stuff off the chopper and he comes to greet me, saying, "My name's Sergeant A.C. Cunningham." He would be my non-commissioned officer (NCO). I could tell he'd been drinking.

He added, "I'm going to take you to meet the sergeant major of the RF/PF training center." The acronym stood for Regional Force/Popular Force (RF/PF), and I'm thinking of a nice, air-conditioned building. We get in the jeep, pass the garbage dump, and finally make it to the building. It turned out it was this mud fort, and we go into a room made of mud that has a table in the center of it. The sergeant major, who's been napping, comes out and brings the beer and tall glasses. We have a few beers before he takes me to meet the lieutenant colonel and shows me my "room." It's really just an open villa with about 10 advisors in it, nothing fancy. That's where I ended up. If you watch war movies, you think choppers are always landing through gunfire and it's always like that, but this place was more like everybody was sleepy.

When I got there, the political and military situation in Go Cong (GC) was that the province was the second most pacified province in Vietnam. But there was a truce between the government of Vietnam and the Viet Cong. The truce existed because the province chief was a political appointee of Nguyễn Cao Kỳ, the prime minister of South Vietnam. The province chief was corrupt and had succeeded in duping the Americans during his tenure. In Go Cong you could travel the roads without fear, circle low in aircraft over the VC havens without drawing fire, and go on operations without results.

Operation Phoenix

It sounds like the consequences of a sound program in revolutionary development, but it wasn't. In 1967, the VC collected about 250,000 Vietnamese dollars (about $25,000) in taxes from the people in GC. Every month the Special Joint Report went out to MACV headquarters and General Westmoreland, and the report's the facts and figures ultimately went to Washington, with Secretary of Defense Robert McNamara and President Lyndon Johnson always painting a pretty rosy picture. Those of us in Vietnam and the military generally viewed the report with skepticism. Every month province senior advisors in the country had to submit a detailed report of progress called a Hamlet Evaluation Survey (HES) to Westmoreland. The bottom line was that if you didn't show progress in what you reported, then you were not going to receive a good efficiency report. I wrote a funny song I called "HES" that all of us in Go Cong sang in the bar.

Those of us in Go Cong Province were a country team made up of various military and civilian representatives, all focused on the mission of neutralizing and eliminating the Viet Cong infrastructure (VCI). But we were also helping the Vietnamese people build better lives with specific civic-action projects for the populace of the province. Those efforts ranged from a Spanish medical team that worked in the local hospital, rotating every 18 months, to advising locals on the right fertilizers for raising better crops and pigs. In addition, we built schools, stocked fish ponds, built village wells, and encouraged village self-help projects that were decided on and carried out by the local villagers, who were getting their first practical experience in "rice-roots" democracy.

This program, called Civil Operations and Revolutionary Support (CORDS), was designed in 1966 by Robert W. "Blowtorch Bob" Komer, who was a member of the U.S. National Security Council and later became an ambassador to Turkey. He believed that LBJ's goal of peace in Vietnam would require not only weakening the insurgency and its numbers directly but by eliminating the insurgent force's support and infrastructure in the rural civilian population. That meant increasing security for civilians and winning over their sympathy, both for the South Vietnamese government and our forces. Komer emphasized that this strategy had to be widely applied to turn things around. That was the concept behind CORDS, which was implemented starting in 1967 under the military's command structure but with the involvement of the South Vietnamese civilian authorities. This had the crucial advantage of bringing massive financial resources to civilian projects that would not otherwise have happened without the military's involvement.

Under CORDS I was rated by the military deputy senior advisor and endorsed by a civilian, the province's senior advisor. CORDS was eventually implemented in all 44 South Vietnamese provinces, each with a native province chief supported by an American province senior advisor. The advisor's staff was also divided into a civilian part—which supervised area and community development—and a military part, which handled security issues. In the opinion of many of us junior officers, it worked. It was not a burn-down-the-village strategy but rather one to "win the hearts and minds of the people."

Armed VC in the province amounted to 300 to 400 men in tactical groups no larger than a squad (10 men) or platoon (40 men). The province chief's force consisted of about 4,000 men, all outfitted with U.S. Military Assistance Program equipment and all capable of destroying the enemy. However, they were not effectively used. We had a ratio of friendly forces to Viet Cong forces of about 15 to one. The books say that 12 to 1 or even 10 to 1 should be sufficient to defeat insurgents. On a larger scale in the Delta, 147,500 friendly forces faced a VC force of about 80,000. That's not counting one brigade of the Ninth Infantry Division (some 3,000 men), that was also operating in the Delta.

Komer's initial pacification program evolved into a more tough-minded project called Operation Phoenix, which was implemented in each province, including ours. Conceived by the White House and supported by the CIA, the Phoenix program's prime objective was to gather information on the

VCI. That intel was then used to target and neutralize VCI members. Phoenix operations involved local militia members and police, instead of military forces, as the main operational arm. In our province, the local Central Intelligence Agency (CIA) operative used *Biêt Kích*, a special forces group of former Viet Cong that had come over to the South Vietnamese side, essentially defecting, which was called *chiêu hoi*. Getting paid to join our side, they were part of Komer's Operation Phoenix. As an infantry commando squad, they wore what looked like black pajamas. Sometimes I would be assigned to participate on an operation with them. (I did not wear black pajamas, though.)

For example, one operation led by a CIA operative required the unit I was with to be transported by boat to a location identified as controlled by VC, with the village chief confirmed as a communist. We traveled for several nights. The method of operation was to focus on the identification and elimination of VC infrastructure, not burning down villages.

Between my arrival on January 27 and October 5, I went on 11 operations. I've described how reluctant I was to kill an animal while hunting, and as an infantry officer carrying a rifle in Vietnam, I never once fired my rifle in combat or used it to kill an enemy soldier. I wasn't a pacifist, but I was an advisor, and my job was simply to advise my counterpart. I only had to fire a weapon to protect myself or my radio operator, or if the unit I was with engaged in a firefight, of course. On one operation, my company and I were almost destroyed swimming to cross a canal. The company I was advising was taking our gear across on jury-rigged bamboo rafts. Halfway across, we came under friendly fire by U.S. Navy Swift Boats that mistook us for Viet Cong. It was easy to do, since except for me and my radio operator, my *Biêt Kích* company was in their "black pajamas." The event brought back my near-drowning experience when I was a kid at Waitts Lake. I was finally able to make contact by radio and get a cease fire before anyone was killed.

I only went on one operation that included the Ninth Infantry Division. That was interesting, as my Ninth Division counterpart carried about a 50-pound pack, while I wore a helmet and carried a first aid pack, an ammo pouch, and two canteens of water along with my M16. The operation reported 19 killed in action with 200 prisoners captured.

I went on 11 operations during my first Vietnam tour.

On this first tour as an infantry captain in combat, I soon realized that we'd had great training at Infantry School at Fort Benning, but we weren't prepared for all sorts of contingencies. That included how the Vietnamese soldiers we were advising were committed—or not committed—to the Geneva Convention rules of combat. The convention is shorthand for a series of international treaties on the treatment of civilians, prisoners of war (POWs) and soldiers who were outside the fight or otherwise rendered incapable of fighting. The treaties have been designed to protect wounded and sick soldiers, whether friends or enemies.

One operation I'd call hairy and interesting was with my radio operator Jim Rode, an eighteen-year-old infantry soldier. The unit I was advising was a company of RF/PF soldiers, the province chief's own small but effective army. My counterpart was an RF/PF infantry lieutenant. We were spread out in a line formation and connected with other RF/PF units on each side, who were also being advised by other infantry captains from Go Cong Province. We were all moving toward a tree line about 500 meters in front of us, where we suspected the enemy was located. We were moving slowly, the entire line being directed from the command chopper, which was 1000 feet above us and continuously circling the battlefield. The chopper contained the province chief, his S3 (operations officer), our province senior advisor, and our own S3, Major Bill Pooley, who has since passed away.

As my company begin moving through a graveyard full of tombstones, all hell broke loose. We came under fire and hit the deck. My radio operator dropped behind a tombstone for cover and I dropped behind another a few feet away, stretching our radio cable to the max. I made sure we both had thick tombstones to hide behind until we figured out what the hell was going on. I immediately radioed the S3 that we had made contact and would send him a situation report (SITREP) ASAP.

To my left, RF/PF soldiers were firing grenade launchers toward targets they'd identified. While all U.S. forces had the latest weaponry, Westmoreland's policy was not to man the RF/PF with the latest launchers to help make sure they didn't fall into the hands of the VC. The latest launchers were M79 grenade launchers, a single-shot, shoulder-fired, break-action grenade launcher that fires a 40 x 46 mm grenade with very little recoil. It was very effective at close range; if you were good, you could drop a round onto enemy positions with enough accuracy to hit a 50-gallon barrel at 300 yards. Instead, my RF/PF soldiers were firing grenades off M1 rifles from World War II.

As their grenades went off in front of us, I was hearing some pretty raunchy Vietnamese cussing—*du ma may*, which meant fuck your mother; *da ma* or motherfucker; and *du ma thang sau nay*, or "this motherfucking ugly guy." I decided I'd better get us closer to the action.

I told Jim, "We are moving out. Follow me." In combat situations, you prepare as much as possible for the unexpected, but I wasn't prepared for what I came upon. The RF/PF had killed several Viet Cong. They had been under water, breathing through reeds, when we'd surprised them. They were all wasted.

I reported all killed in action, "enemy KIA." An RF/PF soldier came up to me with a small plastic food bag, which appeared to contain pieces of meat. He offered me a piece and said in Vietnamese that it was liver; if I ate it, I would be strong. I said, "No, I will not eat it," also in Vietnamese. The soldiers were all were excited, eating the liver and laughing at me, taunting me to eat it. In fact, they had cut open a couple of the dead Viet Cong and cut out their livers—definitely cannibalism.

This was nothing like what had happened in World War II. The most well-known example from that war must be the incident on Chichijima Island, where the Japanese flak had shot down four U.S. Navy TBM Avenger bombers. Nine pilots had parachuted out. Eight of them landed on Chichijima, where they were captured, beheaded, gutted and prepared for food, served up like sushi for the Japanese officers. The ninth, a certain Lieutenant Junior Grade G.H.W. Bush from the U.S.S. San Jacinto, drifted off to sea, where he was rescued by the submarine U.S.S. Finback.

The case I observed in Vietnam was obviously a violation of the Geneva Convention Code of Conduct. I reported the incident up my chain of command and had my counterpart do the same. In the meantime, the operation continued on toward the tree line, then we filed our after-action reports and debriefed our S3. I ended the day at the team club, glad we'd completed another successful operation. My efficiency report for this period said, "He displayed military competency and courage under enemy fire." I thought to myself, "What was the other option? Retreat?"

During the eleven operations I went on during this tour, the unit killed at least one Viet Cong soldier on every one, 19 on the largest, and a total of 88. In all of South Vietnam, however, during the four years between 1968 and 1972, the Phoenix program neutralized 81,740 suspects, of whom 26,369 were killed. As a result, the program managed to quite successfully destroy the VCI in many important areas. The CIA also claimed that Phoenix enabled them to know about the structure and identity of VCI in every province of South Vietnam.

After leaving the Pentagon and in the clear light of hindsight, however, Komer waxed bittersweet about Vietnam. "I would have done a lot of things differently and been more cautious about getting us involved," he said. He called the war "a strategic disaster which cost us 58,000 lives and a half trillion dollars."

I grew to really respect the RF/PF and the *Biêt Kích* forces, who earned their status as special forces operatives. The RF/PF fought a major share of the war at the rice-roots level. They comprised about 50 percent of Republic of Vietnam Armed Forces (RVNAF). Popular Forces were in all but one of the country's 237 districts. Regional Forces were in all but five. By contrast, the Army of the Republic of Vietnam (ARVN) had troops in about half the districts. More than 3,000 PF platoons and 1,700 squads defended villages and hamlets, guarded key installations, and provided security for officials. Better than 800 RF companies performed the same types of duties at the district level. Their mission, though, was the conduct of combat operations. These soldiers I advised accounted for more VC kills than the ARVN, both in Go Cong Province and in all of Vietnam. Their bravery was legendary in Vietnam.

Army Second Lieutenant Kelly, me, my radio operator Bill Robinson (in plaid), John Fuller, and a Navy intel officer (who is probably giving all us Army guys the finger), with Jim Lacy in front. After the Viet Cong Tet Offensive attacks launched in January of 1968, Kelly would become paralyzed from the waist down when his jeep overturned during a mortar attack in Go Cong Province.

Isolated units of the PF, with an automatic rifle as their heaviest weapons, had repelled 97 percent of VC assaults received. The RF light infantry company had about 130 men, and their heavy weapons were 60 mm mortars. The policy was not to arm the RF/PF with anything heavier, so they carried carbines, while my radio operator and I carried M1 carbines. The Viet Cong were more heavily armed.

The PF also had the lowest pay scale in the Vietnamese forces. A PF private with a wife and two children was paid $18.20 (1,820 piasters) a month, compared with the 3,690 piasters in pay and allowances an ARVN private in the Delta received in the same circumstances. Families lived with the PF, sharing their fortified positions and building their makeshift homes alongside. During attacks, the women passed ammunition, operated radios, and if necessary, took up weapons.

On September 19, 1967, I was with some of the advisors when we were approached by volunteers with the International Voluntary Services, a nonprofit organization working there in agriculture, education, and community development. They had the opportunity of living closely with the Vietnamese people over extended periods of time. They wanted us to join them in signing a letter to President Johnson that said, "We have been able to watch and share their suffering since as early as 1958. What we have heard of the effects of the war in Vietnam compels us to make this statement. The problems which the Vietnamese face are too little understood and their voices have been muffled for too long. It is not enough to rely on statistics to describe their daily concern. It is to you, Mr. President, that we address ourselves."

The five-page document addressed their view of the atrocities of the war: free strike zones, the refugees, the spraying of herbicide on crops, the napalm. They acknowledged that Viet Cong terrorism was real, but so were the innocent victims of U.S. bombing, strafing, and shelling: every victim, the dead, the bereaved, and the deprived.

Their petition was well documented, but we in the military would not—and could not—sign, even though we agreed with many of their conclusions and recommendations. Our concerns had to be taken up with our chain of command instead.

Later, on October 3, 1967, I attended a meeting in Can Tho with my counterpart, Captain Tuong, commander of the local military police force and also commandant of the RF/PF training center. Basically I witnessed a good old Army "ass chewing" of Captain Tuong by Lieutenant Colonel Trung-ta Dinh, chief of staff for IV Corps. He said to Captain Tuong, "There are about 2,200 to 2,500 PF troops in GC Province, and only 1,000 have been trained. Why is this so?"

Captain Tuong said he could not answer the question and was obviously afraid to say why. The answer was that the province chief, a man by the name of Xuan, did not care whether they were trained or not. Captain Tuong and I had done everything except build it with our own hands but the province chief ignored us and had done the same to my predecessor, Captain Shaw. The fact that the province chief had no interest in the individual combat, small unit training of his soldiers was reported in the Special Joint Report up the chain of command.

At the conclusion of our meeting we had a beer together and Captain Tuong said, "We have been fighting since 1945. We have now had 23 years of fighting and the Vietnamese cannot take much more. The Vietnamese cannot understand why we will not cross the DMZ and fight the Northerners on their own soil, and we cannot understand why the Americans will not go with us to Hanoi." In my report to my province senior advisor, I added the following information reported by Captain Tuong: "There is no progress in Go Cong and Vietnam. The Americans are very sincere and the Vietnamese like the Americans. The French were not sincere and did not know anything of true desire except the feeling of a colonial power." My conversation with Captain Tuong had continued, with him repeating, "Only by the Americans crossing the DMZ can we win the war."

Captain Tuong in Can Tho

At times, while on an operation or flying in a chopper, I reflected that I didn't mind giving my life for my country, but I worried about what would happen to my wife and kids left behind. Paula and I were basically broke, living paycheck to paycheck. My dad had loaned me $800.00 when I left home on our first assignment to Germany. My base monthly pay was $583.00, plus foreign duty pay of $30.00 and combat pay of $65.00 a month. We did get a subsistence and housing allowance, another $173, but that was it—and from that, more than $500 was deducted to cover insurance, taxes, and a $10,000 Gonzaga student loan I was paying off. That loan amount in 1967, a year with an inflation rate over 3 percent, was equivalent in purchasing power to more than $75,000 in 2018. I finally paid off that student loan in 1975.

Before then, money was tight. In 1967, I received $90 in cash monthly from my paycheck to buy personal items like toiletries and personal items like cigars and beverages. The other $234.00 went in a check to Paula and the kids. The average monthly rent that year was more than half that, and the average new car would have cost an entire year's take-home pay. My income as an officer was hardly fat and sassy, and I was pretty worried about my family's financial condition if something happened to me.

A 1967 pay stub

Nearly 60,000 men did die, and there are no nonbelievers in foxholes. You know that it is up to you to use the training and skills you've been taught to increase your chances of survival. That said, I prayed a few rosaries while in Vietnam.

We all managed to have some good times while there, too, and those off-hours include some of my enduring memories.

CHAPTER 6: VIETNAM ENTERTAINMENTS

"Anyone who wants to save their life must lose it. Anyone who loses their life will find it. What gain is there if you win the whole world and lose your very self? What can you offer in exchange for your one life?"

—Matthew 16:25-26

During my first Vietnam deployment, the awareness that I might get killed made me think of the baby that Paula and I had out of wedlock. I decided right away that I had to do something about finding this child, and then Paula could take over if I did get killed. So I wrote Paula and went to explain my situation to Major Shaw, the deputy senior advisor. He listened and said he wanted me to see the Military Assistance Command adjutant general in Saigon, Colonel Robert E. Lynch. So on February 3, I went to Saigon and met with Colonel Lynch, explaining that I wanted to go home and find out if I could adopt my son or daughter. (I didn't even know the baby's gender.) Colonel Lynch was very understanding and said that I needed to get home, so he'd give me a 30-day compassionate leave. I could hardly believe how understanding everyone was, even in the middle of a big war.

I got home on February 10. Paula and I got together to figure out how we could track down the baby. We spent a month looking but couldn't find the child; adoption agencies wouldn't release records back then. We did find her later, but not for many years. On March 11, I headed back to Vietnam, and within a week I was on another operation there. Later Colonel Lynch would recommend that I teach at West Point. I was very grateful to be nominated, but other circumstances prevented it.

In the meantime, I'd learned that in February, Dr. Fall was killed by a booby trap while on an operation with the Marines on the "Street Without Joy" in the northern part of South Vietnam.

We took fire on our operations, but it wasn't that bad compared to what was experienced by the regular Army units. It made life interesting. We had to make our own entertainment otherwise. I'd go to A.C.'s hooch for cocktails. He had a bucket that we'd put ice into, pour in Trader Vic's mai-tai mix, and add some 150-proof medical alcohol. Those were our martinis.

Sometimes we just weren't thinking. We got briefed one late night about 11 p.m. by Major Bill Pooley, our S3, Operations. George Egner and I were teamed up. We would cross the line of departure (LD) about 0600, the beginning of morning nautical twilight. We each carried carbines and a .45, and for this operation we figured we needed the Browning Automatic Rifle (BAR), too. The BAR was used by the French and by South Vietnamese soldiers as well as some U.S. units.

We drove over to the headquarters compound to get breakfast before we went. George parked right below the Province Advisor's window with the loaded BAR resting on the top of the windshield. George pulled the hammer back and let it go. It let off a burst right above the lieutenant colonel's window. If he'd been in his room, standing up to dress, he could have been killed.

I said, "Jesus Christ, don't you know if you pull the hammer back it is going to fire?" Luckily for us, the colonel was not in his room. He was in another building getting briefed, so he didn't even know what had happened. We decided to hell with breakfast, and we left. When others asked us about hearing the BAR fired, we said we'd just been testing it prior to the operation. We both learned a lesson.

I loved non-commissioned officers (NCOs), and working with them was one of my jobs as administrative officer there. The province senior advisor didn't like A.C., mainly because every time he saw A.C., he was drunk. But I loved A.C., who was great. He was on his third tour already but he put in an extension. The colonel said, "I am not approving that." He told me to write it up as denied. I did that, and he put his stamp on it. But I also wrote up an approval that I didn't tell the colonel about, switched the stamp to that one and sent it in. So when the approval came back, the colonel saw that and said, "What the hell is happening with the Army? This guy got it!"

I just said, "You must be disappointed."

He told me to call Saigon about it, and I said I'd try. But we were on the South China Sea. You couldn't just call Saigon. You couldn't call anybody. But A.C. was a good soldier, and he was so happy. He'd never done anything wrong; the colonel just didn't like him. Sometimes you do what's better for the soldier, not the Army. That's what I did.

One of my friends, Carl D. Robinson, was a former *Time* magazine reporter and was then in international development in the province. I was invited one night to Carl's new house along with George Egner, a captain from West Point who was one of my buddies. Newly built, the house was plush by our standards, and he even had a houseboy and a new air conditioner.

We were drinking, as usual. Lyndon B. Johnson was on the cover of a 1967 issue of *Time* magazine that Carl had at the house; Johnson had been named *Time's* Man of the Year. In the article about him, Time called him, "an immensely complex, contradictory, and downright unpleasant man." It went on to say, "He never managed to attract the insulating layer of royalty that a Roosevelt or a Truman could fall back on. Consequently, when things began to go wrong, he had few defenders and all too many critics." LBJ and McNamara were two peas in a pod, and *Time* had no compliments for McNamara, either: "The Vietnam War with which he will forever be linked was caused not by inadequate skills or a lack of diligence, but by his failure to question that which his boundless intelligence and diligence caused him to believe."

That night, I picked up the magazine, ripped LBJ's cover off, and pasted it on the wall, which had just been nicely plastered.

"Too bad we don't have a copy of McNamara's issue," I said. "Hey George, I bet you can't put a hole in each of LBJ's eyes." We always carried our .45s in our back pockets, locked and loaded. You could put on civilian clothes to walk around the town in the evening; it was a pretty sleepy place. But we always carried our weapons in case we ran into trouble.

"What are you talking about?" Carl said.

I said, "Calm down, Carl, we're just going to take a couple of shots." We all ducked around the doorway and I started out, sticking my .45 around the door and pulling off about three rounds. They bounced off the plaster and zinged all around the room. The houseboy ran out of the house screaming and took off down the street.

Then George took a couple of shots, I took a couple more, and then Carl said, "You guys get the hell out of here! Look at my walls!"

Since we had to leave, we both emptied our clips except for a couple of rounds that we emptied instead into Carl's new air conditioner. The 45 rounds that ricocheted around the room were sobering; it was the closest I ever got to friendly fire. LBJ was all shot up, and so was the air conditioner. Carl was really upset.

"Don't be a sore ass, Carl," said George. "Lighten up."

That did it. He threw us both out and it would be a month before we got invited back.

A friend of mine, Army Warrant Officer Gary Varner, flew in an L-19 Bird Dog every day to check enemy activity. He was the first pilot I flew with on that duty. Later, after he came home, he wrote, "I never realized how much beer I drank every night." It was often a six-pack each or more. Varnum was replaced by an Air Force captain who drank a fifth a night. His hands shook every morning, and one day that seemed to catch up with him. He went to the airfield for a flight over the province but forgot to gas up his plane, an L-19 Bird Dog.

How could a trained Air Force pilot flying in Vietnam in 1967 forget to make sure his airplane was fueled before taking off on a mission? Well, the military had given Cessna a challenge: The plane had to be capable of taking off and landing over a 50-foot obstacle in less than 600 feet at its maximum allowable gross weight. The plane that resulted from these specs, Cessna's Model 305, became known as the L-19 Bird Dog. During the Vietnam War it was used mostly for reconnaissance, finding targets or adjusting artillery, escorting convoys, and providing forward air control for tactical aircraft such as bombers It would later be renamed the O-1, with the O standing for observation, until the Army officially retired it in 1974.

The Bird Dog was aptly named. I flew a number of those flights over Go Cong seated in the rear observation seat. If you were flying slowly over the province, it was easier for the passenger to search for and locate enemy ground positions. When we found the enemy— we hoped that was who it was, but in free-fire zones we usually knew who it was—the passenger would radio in that position to bring in artillery fire, for example. As a result, when the VC spotted a Bird Dog flying low overhead, they might expect that something might soon happen. The plane was vulnerable to ground fire, but the VC would not always take a shot because then they'd definitely be revealing their position. A Bird Dog passenger in another province who came into the country about the time I did took a round in his seat but was able to recover.

Luckily I didn't get in that seat one early morning with this particular Air Force pilot, who was stone cold drunk. I said, "I'm getting out here and will take your picture as you take off." A movie clip of that takeoff would have shown a very brief taxi and takeoff but a great image of what followed. When he got to the end of the runway, the engine quit and the plane took a nosedive right into the swamp.

I helped the pilot out of the cockpit, as I recall, and when he started to walk away, I said, "What are you doing?"

"I'm going back to bed," he told me, and he walked back to the billets. When he woke up he was told he was relieved of duty as soon as his Seagram's hangover wore off.

What happens when you forget to fuel the plane

And yet plenty of pilots flew through hangovers (and worse) and never crashed, only to be followed by someone new and inexperienced who did. John Paul Vann's chopper pilot, Warrant Officer Bob Richards, was another Seagram's drinker who held his alcohol and flew straight regardless of the weather or circumstances. (You'll read more about Bob in Chapter 7.) In my opinion, he was a hero who safely flew Vann into hairy places.

He wasn't the only one. One night at the team house, Gary climbed to the top of a glass Chinese cabinet and took a dare from the Airborne dudes, who dared him to jump from the top of the cabinet. He did it, but brought the cabinet with him. We thought he'd earned his first purple heart for the cut on his arm, which came from flying glass not bullets.

So where did all this drinking come from? There was plenty of it in the Revolutionary War, then more of it after Washington became the country's first president. I just finished reading David McCullough's *The Pioneers: The Heroic Story of the Settlers Who Brought the American Ideal West.* According to McCullough, Charles Dickens spoke about the country's alcohol culture when he arrived in America in 1842. Dickens was then the author of a half-dozen novels that were immensely popular in England. He noted that Americans seemed all alike, with no diversity of character, no conversation, no laughter, cheerfulness, or society, except in spitting around the stove when a meal was over. Other said that alcohol was consumed "to the most frightful excess." McCullough quotes a Philadelphia clergyman who disapproved of riverboats, complaining, "Usually on board these western steamboats whisky is used just as freely as water. All drink. The pilot—the engineer—the fireman—all drink. The whisky bottle is passed around several times a day and then the dinner table is loaded with decanters." It all sounds familiar to me because to a certain degree that culture hasn't changed much, except now there is more of it.

Perhaps ironically, in June 1967 I wrote my sister Julie, who had recently graduated from high school. One of the things I advised her was, "Take it for what it is worth, it is very wise to watch your drinking. It is all right to do it socially and at home and to a limited degree at parties—but other than that watch it—you can get yourself in trouble. I'm not lecturing you, this is just from your brother to his sister." I was concerned about her being with someone who might drink and drive into a deadly accident, "a good way to end up on a slab at the morgue." I didn't even know if she *was* drinking, and here I was, every night a little inebriated, usually with A.C. Cunningham.

A lot of times, though, we were bored. It was a big night in the Delta when A.C. brought porn videos from Singapore after having R&R in Korea, where his wife was located. On video night, the whole team made popcorn and watched them together. One of the movies was similar to the scene in *The Godfather* where Michael Corleone is in Cuba at a club; the main attraction was a woman having sex with a German shepherd. A.C.'s movies were definitely X-rated.

The CIA compound where I met operatives Stewart and, later, Stan. My main reason for visiting was to get a Johnnie Walker Red Label scotch served in a large beer glass over ice.

Another big Sunday event at team headquarters was when we fed a rabbit to the 20-foot python that was kept in a cage in front of team headquarters. Finally A.C. and I periodically went to the cock fights. It was a big event—

really interesting, like horse racing, with the roosters wearing these spurs. I never bet on these fights, but A.C. might have.

When there wasn't anything as interesting as that to enjoy, we had M79 grenade launchers to play with. A.C. and I would whip up a batch of our special martinis and then I'd spend a couple of hours watching him defuse and take apart the big, round M79 grenade rounds to make ashtrays out of the brass bottoms. I told A.C., "One of these nights you're going to slip up and blow up the whole back end of the house! Then we are toast." After a couple of our special martinis, though, we weren't worried.

Fun with live explosives

We did create a few other explosions after he and I took on the duty of getting rid of live landmines. A.C. and I would ride motorbikes to go see a CIA operative I knew by the name of Stewart who had invited me on a couple of Phoenix operations. We were at the CIA compound one day, drinking Jack Daniels Red on ice. I knew that mines the Viet Cong had put down on the road were collected and stored in a shed under the CIA's management, so I asked Stewart, "Why do you store the mines in the shed?"

"Because I can't ever find anyone to disarm them and blow them up," he replied. I volunteered A.C. and I on the spot, and it became one of our monthly jobs.

The firing mechanisms on some of the mines were held together with rusty safety pins. We'd pick up mines from the shed, loading up our Jeep full of those mines or piling them on a trailer we towed behind it, and drive out of town. There, sometimes with an audience of our advisees, the Vietnamese Regional Force/Popular Force soldiers, we'd pile the mines up, put C4 around them, and blow them up. There'd be a hole left that we could stand in, and we kept aiming to create bigger holes, stacking the mines in a pile and then detonating them with a claymore. At any time during the process, we could've been blown sky high, but A.C. and I just downed a couple of our infamous martinis beforehand. It was something exciting to do on our days off, whenever we got them, which was not usually very often. Sometimes we were also called on to detonate mines found buried in the street. Fortunately A.C. was a demolitions expert, which is why I'm still here with all body parts intact.

Preparing C4 to blow up landmines

Later we might be at the province senior advisor's staff meeting and as people talked about the day, someone would say, "Anybody know what the explosion was out there earlier today?"

I'd be quiet. "No sir, no idea what that was!" I never 'fessed up.

The bottom line was that I felt at ease hanging out with A.C., learning from him, dealing with road mines, and going on operations. He told me later that I didn't realize it but he had saved my life a couple of times. "You know Captain," he said. "At first I thought you were just a young buck smart-ass officer, but then I changed my mind about you when you put your life in my hands and didn't know it."

In the hole left after landmine destruction

Helping to dig up and blow up mines, watch my sergeant take M79 grenade rounds apart to make ashtrays, and a whole list of other oddball, dangerous, and questionable duties in combat were all pretty mild, though, compared to something my Air Force sergeant and I experienced once when we stayed overnight at the Dong Khanh Hotel in Saigon. We had come up from our province with other advisors on a booze, beer, food, and "pussy" run. (The James Bond character Pussy Galore had been immortalized in the 1964 film, *Goldfinger*.) As an advisory team, we were not supplied by the U.S. Army like the other infantry units were; we had to get our own. Plus the edict from the province senior advisor was, "There will be no fornicating in the Division Tactical Zone (DTA)," and he meant it. So we would put together a very small armed convoy, a couple of trucks and jeeps, to ride in and to haul our supplies home. About ten of us went this particular time.

When we checked in to the hotel, the idea was to get to the bar, which was at the top floor of the hotel, as quickly as possible. The bars were at the top to help prevent the Viet Cong from lobbing a grenade into the middle of our social networking. Of course, the bar was more than a bar, and beautiful Saigon gals were there too to "entertain" the troops.

We crossed the Mekong River on our way to Saigon.

But before we could get there, it took us a while to check our ammunition, rifles, pistols, and hand grenades at the front desk, especially since the hotel clerk was shaking as he handled and stored our little arsenal. Once those administrative details were taken care of and our hotel rooms were assigned, the second order of business was to hit the bar. The group of us decided to order enough beer for the whole evening, so we ordered five cases to be delivered. The barkeep stacked them all in the middle of our table and we started enjoying ourselves. A couple of captains from Westmoreland's headquarters joined us.

As the evening got later, the Air Force sergeant and I, who were rooming together, decided we would have some company. We invited a couple of women from the bar to spend the night with us. The Vietnamese women were beautiful dressed in their *áo dài*, the national garment—quite stunning, tempting, and alluring for a GI far from home. They came to our room and we started to *really* enjoy the evening, but that was soon broken up by an obviously drunken GI in the hotel's upper stairway. He lobbed a grenade down the stairs and it exploded in the stairwell outside our room. Our room had a glass wall that shattered, spraying glass all over the room and our bodies. My sergeant and I agreed this was a message from God and we ended the party, realizing that we couldn't even claim our injuries as combat related. Our bronze stars would have to wait.

That wasn't my only brush with a non-combat injury. My friend Carl Robinson had a Vietnamese girlfriend, Kim Dung, and sometimes we got ourselves a car and visited his girlfriend, who lived 10 miles down the road. One day he and I were drinking Johnnie Walker Red Label scotch with a CIA chief for the province named Stuart who also had a local girlfriend. Stuart had access to mopeds, so we all got on them at 3:00 a.m. and went down the road through friendly checkpoints toward Stuart's girlfriend's house. We could've been shot at any of the checkpoints as we barreled through them, or hit a road mine at any time, but it was exciting.

There was always a "pucker factor" when driving on Delta roads.

The girlfriend's house was locked, and she said, "You can't come in!" Stuart was ready to leave, but I said, "Hey, I can break the door down." I hit it with my shoulder and busted the door, but I also broke a couple of ribs. I was all black and blue, and I got bandaged up. When I saw my wife on R&R not long afterward, she wanted to know what had happened, and I had to make up a war story to tell her.

At Vung Tau Resort with Kim and Carl, who were soon to be
married, as well as our driver

A.C. was married to a Korean gal; I think he was the only guy I ever knew who went on R&R to Korea. But Paula and I met in Hawaii that summer. I had 7 days of R&R, which was really great. I'd been able to talk to her and the kids on the phone, with the kids usually crying, but now I got a visit. I flew to the islands on a PanAm 747 holding 400 GIs who hadn't seen their wives in six months or a year. Just seeing the wide-eyed stewardesses was kind of crazy, and they probably got way more attention from their passengers than they might have liked. Once Paula and I both arrived in Hawaii, we went to Duke Kahanamoku's club in Waikiki.

Kahanamoku was a five-time Olympic medalist in swimming between the 1912 and 1924 Olympics. He also turned surfing into a mainstream international sport before becoming an actor, law enforcement officer, and businessman. While we were in his club, we listened to Don Ho sing "Tiny Bubbles," which was on the charts for a year in 1966. Our table was right near his piano and I put many dollar bills in the jar to hear "Tiny Bubbles."

I looked over at the bar to see this captain I'd sat beside on the plane, alone. So I went to talk to him and ask him, "How's it going?"

He said, "Pretty bad. My wife had a letter for me at the hotel saying she's divorcing me and wasn't coming." That happened to a number of guys—getting home to a divorce. Not great at all.

Just as Paula and I were leaving the club, the Duke himself was standing out front beside his gold Cadillac, which the valet had just brought around front. You couldn't miss him; he was over 6 feet tall with solid white hair, a beautiful Hawaiian shirt, and very tan Hawaiian skin. Before he got into his car, Duke turned and waved at everyone in the club through the large front window. Paula and I couldn't believe it, Do Ho and the Duke both—and we were there.

Life in the Delta was always exciting, too. One late afternoon, Carl and I had been in Saigon and were hitching a ride with an Air America flight to get back to Go Cong Province. Air America was an American passenger and cargo airline covertly owned and operated by the U.S. government from 1950 to 1976. It was used as a dummy corporation for CIA operations in Indochina. The pilots were fantastic and fun to fly with. Whenever we went to Saigon, we would always try to go to the Air America restaurant near Tan Son Nhut Airport. You could always get a good steak there.

On this trip back, it was getting close to dark and the pilot was on a milk run flying a Curtis C46 Commando, a twin-engine prop plane that I liked to fly in. (Another great aircraft that was perfect for the Delta was the Pilatus PC-6 Porter, which only needed 100 feet of runway. When we were being shot at, that was what we advisors preferred to have pick us up!) This pilot would make the great Delta circle flying out of Saigon heading south, stopping at My Tho and then dropping us off at Go Cong's dirt airstrip, which was also used as a garbage dump by the Vietnamese. It could be a bit touchy flying into Go Cong; there were sometimes mopeds and bicycles clogging the airstrip.

Carl and I made sure we had picked up a pint of bourbon, as we knew it would be a hairy ride in the dark. Most isolated airstrips such as that one in Go Cong had no runway lights. As a result, the pilot would first fly over the runway at about 100 feet of altitude with his landing lights on to check for people or any obstacles. Then he'd come around and touch down.

By the time we got to My Tho that night we had nearly finished the bottle, and we didn't care if the pilot landed on somebody's roof as long as we got down. We approached Go Cong in the dark and the pilot did his usual 100-foot pass, but at first he couldn't go back and land because the runway wasn't clear. Finally we touched down; the pilot kept the engine running and we jumped out of the plane. The only bad thing was that by then the bottle was empty.

Another Delta experience I had that was more hairy involved another workhorse, the single-engine, high wing, propeller-driven DHC-3 or Otter operated by the U.S. Army in Vietnam. This was a very dependable aircraft that we often used to fly out of Go Cong and to transport supplies from Saigon to Go Cong. I was sent on a mission to restock our mess hall. Advisory teams did not have a supply chain supporting them—or at least ours didn't. In addition, we had discovered that some of the mess hall workers, particularly the women who served our meals, were Viet Cong agents. So the first sergeant collected money through alcohol sales—the beer was not free—and we used that for funds. I was assigned an additional duty as mess officer. A restocking trip meant packing an overnight bag, strapping on my .45, and getting a ride to Saigon by air. Once there, I would go to the commissary and buy canned groceries based on a list the mess sergeant had given me. He would've gone himself, but he was too shaken up—he'd just received a letter from his wife telling him he was being divorced. I volunteered to go in his place.

Getting to the commissary in Saigon was no problem. Then I had to line up an Otter to fly me and our groceries back to Go Cong. I arranged it, making sure the Otter was on the ramp and ready to go before I brought out the heavy cases of canned goods and loaded them. I finally got everything loaded between the seats.

The problem with taking off from Ton Son Nhut, however, was that at the end of runway was a cable that hung across it at about 100 feet high. Its purpose was to indicate to pilots taking off that if they couldn't make it over the cable, they needed to abort the flight. Well, the pilot took off, the Otter moving slowly down the runway while I sat on cans of vegetables. Then we were up. I could see a problem, though—weighed down with those cans, we were not going to make it over the cable.

The pilot came back around and we landed. We threw out two cases and tried again. The same thing happened. Back again to the runway. I said to myself, "If we throw out many more, I'm going to have to get a truck to take me and this food back to Go Cong." But that was too damn dangerous, with just me and a driver. So I told the pilot, "Okay, get rid of one more case, but you *have* to make it this time."

We barely made it over the cable. Just barely. After an hour's flight, we were landing at Go Cong with relief.

Near the end of my tour, I was on my way out of the country on December 25. My buddy Carl Robinson said, "Let's head down to the South China Sea." With his Vietnamese girlfriend, we managed to get a local driver and car to take us down to a French resort in Long Hai that had a great beach and was nearly abandoned. The owner was a Communist sympathizer. There was a Special Forces camp near the resort, and I went into it wearing civvies, bought a bottle of Johnnie Walker Red Label scotch whiskey at the Special Forces bar, and brought it back to the hotel. Carl and I and the hotel owner finished the bottle by 4 a.m.. The owner had only one record, Elvis' "Blue Christmas," and we listened to that as the owner rambled on and on about the benefits of Communism. He spoke perfect English. I could not help but give him my definition of Communism from Father Robinson's class at GU: "Communism is a debased society based on the materialistic determination of everything." That just started an argument and ended the evening.

I went up to my room. Our driver was sleeping in my bed. I opened the window, stepped out on the roof with my .45, and emptied my clip into the air—all seven rounds.

When I came back into the room, the driver was gone. I just went to bed and when I woke up later, I had to look for the driver. We finally found him under the bed.

Getting sun on the beach at Long Hai

I got to come home that winter, leaving Vietnam on December 29, 1967. In late November, Westmoreland had addressed the National Press Club, stating that "the Communists were unable to launch a major offensive....I am absolutely certain that whereas in 1965 the enemy was winning, today he is certainly losing...We have reached an important point when the end begins to come into view."

Then on January 30, 1968, North Vietnam, with the Viet Cong, hit South Vietnam with a surprise attack, the beginning of the Tet Offensive. I was lucky to have missed this part of the war; 80,000 North Vietnamese and Viet Cong troops hit more than 100 towns and cities, including some provincial capitals and, of course, Saigon. It was a big deal. The leadership of Hanoi had bet that the offensive would spark a popular uprising, making the South Vietnamese government collapse, but that never happened. There was intense fighting at the Battle of Huê and combat base Khe Sanh. The North Vietnamese executed thousands of innocent Vietnamese in the massacre at Huê, but none of the peace groups in the U.S. protested the massacre. Between 2,800 and 6,000 civilians and POWs (5 to 10 percent of the total population of Huê) were found bound, tortured, buried alive, or clubbed to death by the North Vietnamese.

The offensive shocked the American public, which had been led to believe that the North Vietnamese were being defeated and not capable of launching such an attack. It was a lonely, sad time for me; by the time I came home, I had no idea what we were accomplishing there, but I also soon wished I had been there with my comrades for the Tet Offensive. I maintained contact with some of those remaining on the ground in South Vietnam. Some of the observations they shared with me in our letters during the summer and fall of 1968, as the Tet Offensive proceeded, included these:

> The people failed to support the VC in a general uprising against the Americans, but this doesn't necessarily construe that they therefore love the government of Vietnam (GVN) or that they detest the VC.

> The city dwellers' traditional apathy has been shaken, but apathy continues—a situation which has traditionally helped the VC more than the GVN.

> I believe the people have short memories and now that the VC have been chased out of the cities, the government presence remains. It is up to the latter to produce.

> Pacification has gone to hell. In the Delta, all but three of the 12 RD battalions have been pulled into the cities for security.

> Roads all over the Delta have been pretty well sealed up.

> Province capitals and Saigon are, for all practical purpose, cities under siege, with some produce slipping in, undoubtedly with high taxes imposed by the VC.

> In GC, near where we were billeted, the VC snuck in from the north under a cover of B40 and 82 mortars and attacked the province prison next to the Special Operations Information Center, freeing 120 prisoners, presumably VC. Eventually Major Chou, the deputy province chief, was killed. (*I had been on a couple of operations with the major. He had been very smart and had spoken very good English. He was replaced.*)

Our buddy Stan, the CIA operative who we had gone on operations with, was wounded twice but survived. He resigned from the Army later. A few other Americans were wounded and one was killed.

I also learned that my friend, Army Lieutenant Kelly, was driving a jeep with a load of soldiers to get out of a mortar attack during the 1968 Tet Offensive when the jeep tipped over. Sadly he is now a paraplegic as a result. A few team members visited him some years back.

Some of the lyrics I later wrote into my song "Vietnam Farewell" might say best how I felt about all of this:

> I can hear the voices crying
> Crying lonely in the night
> I can see the people dying
> Will we ever do things right?

The experiences I had there definitely changed me. And when I came back, there was no one interested in hearing about Vietnam, either. Paula and I went to party in Spokane, and after being in Vietnam most of the year I was so tan that people commented on it and asked where I'd been. When they found out it was Vietnam, they changed the subject. Nobody wanted to hear about it.

Carl and I enjoying our last Beer LaRue together

CHAPTER 7: NEW ORDERS, NEW FRIENDS

"I hope my Vietnam buddies
Who have gone ahead
Will welcome me..."

—*John R. Black, "When I Died"*

Back stateside, after my first tour as an infantry officer in Vietnam, I changed branches of the Army to join the Adjutant General Corps. Some of my buddies said I was a chickenshit to move from the infantry, a combat arm, to this support group, but I felt I'd be of greater service to the Army and my country. I got orders to attend the Army's Institute of Personnel Management in Ft. Benjamin Harrison in Indiana. I was there for ten months, through October of 1968, and then we were assigned to Fort Carson in Colorado. I spent a little over two years there in three assignments, first as chief of the personnel management office for the Fourth Infantry Division and for the post, and then I was assistant chief of staff and secretary of the general staff (SGS) for the post, and then assistant deputy post commander. My assignments were challenging and exciting.

As the SGS, I moved to my new office in the command control group, right next to the office of the Fifth Infantry Division SGS. He reported to the division chief of staff and Rogers. I initially reported to the Fort Carson deputy post commander, then the Fort Carson chief of staff. I was endorsed by the deputy post commander and my performance was reviewed by the Fifth Infantry Division commanding general. They all gave me assignments. Right next to my office was that of my counterpart, the division SGS. His office included two former Military Assistance Command—Special

138

Operations Group (MACV—SOG) captains. They did covert missions in Vietnam. We all smoked cigars except when General Rogers came roaring out of his office, madder than hell and throwing his inbox at his chief of staff and SGC. Then we quickly, but temporarily, put our cigars out. It was fun, really. We also provided space to the CG's helicopter crew. Rodgers' chopper was parked out in front of the building. Periodically we might get a ride.

There was a big uproar while I was there. Major General Roland M. Gleszer was the outgoing commanding general, and he called in police dogs and set up barbed wire when he heard Jane Fonda was coming in. At the time, she was a major figure in anti-war protests, sometimes known as "Hanoi Jane." But then Gleezer left in fall of 1969 and was replaced as commanding general by Major General Bernard W. Rogers, a West Point graduate and Rhodes scholar.

Rogers would be in the post from 1969 into 1970. At the time, the Fifth Infantry Division was not well regarded, with a high turnover rate, low morale, and problems with drug abuse and racial conflict. The previous year, William Westmoreland had been reassigned as chief of staff of the U.S. Army after commanding the forces in Vietnam. While in that role he was responsible for the transition to an all-volunteer force, known as Project Volunteer Army (VOLAR). He issued many directives intended to make service more attractive, including efforts to listen more to enlisted men. The effort generated media interest, including a visit by news anchor Walter Cronkite to Fort Carson, where Rogers was beginning to implement Westmoreland's directives, not only to modernize the force but to address the division's overall morale and reputation.

Cronkite was a much-beloved network anchor who'd begun the politicization of America's news media with an infamous broadcast from Vietnam that described the 1968 Tet Offensive as a major victory for the Communists. The attacks and their media coverage significantly turned the American public against the war. In fact, the Tet Offensive had been a military disaster for the NVA and Viet Cong, as later admitted by North Vietnamese military leaders. Decades later, Cronkite admitted he got that story wrong. But by then, the damage was done. Attitudes toward both the war and the military were changing.

Some of that change was positive. Working for Rogers's chief of staff, Colonel David Hughes, I got the assignment to put together the framework for Enlisted Men's Councils at Fort Carson in early 1970. I worked with two enlisted soldiers—brilliant, fun guys, including Specialist 4 Scott M. Gray, a 20-year-old combat veteran who became the Council chair. The other soldier, who spent a lot of time smoking cigarettes and drinking coffee while planning with us in my office, was Specialist 5 William J. Rosendahl. In 1970, Rosendahl told a reporter for The New York Times he, "had just about given up any hope of working for change within the system when Bobby [Kennedy] was shot. Now General Rogers has given me a new faith in that at least some people in the power structure are willing to listen." We all felt the same way.

General Rogers bought the package we put together with help from Colonel Hughes. The result was Fort Carson Regulation No. 600–16, which Rogers issued on February 17, 1970, established the Enlisted Men's Council as a two-way channel of communication for enlisted men to raise grievances and suggest improvements. The council included 20 members who wasted no time. At their first meeting, they pointed out 18 issues and suggested ways of solving them. Agreeing, Rogers ordered their ideas to be implemented.

In addition to attending the meetings, I maintained the records and minutes for the many soldiers' councils Rogers had started. He had difficulty getting the non-commissioned officers (NCOs) to accept the idea that the enlisted men should have input into how the fort was run. He took care of that. In a meeting, he asked those who didn't support the idea to stand up— and those who did were immediately reassigned to Fort Hood, Texas. Seeing that would influence my own understanding of change management for the remainder of my career.

Rogers met twice a month with the councils, taking suggestions and discussing issues that affected working conditions and morale. Council meetings also sought input from local city officials and businesspeople as well as officers and staff. Four months after the council was started, it had discussed nearly 200 issues. More than 100 suggestions were implemented that first year alone, many of which I was involved in while supporting Rogers and performing follow-up. Later, additional councils were created to enable junior officers and soldiers who were members of racial minorities to express their concerns. We also set up a free-speech coffeehouse, complete with folk singers. The new strategy worked. Morale improved, racial tensions were lowered, and re-enlistments rose. Rogers became known as one of the Army's brightest thinkers after he shared these innovations at the 1970 Army Commanders Conference.

Shortly afterward, Time Magazine published a lengthy cover article on efforts like these on December 21, 1970. The article quoted Rogers and included a number of examples, including a reference to the Enlisted Men's Council: "A 19-man group of enlisted men meets regularly with Rogers and has had 70 percent of its suggestions accepted by him." LIFE magazine also did a 1971 cover story on "The New Army" that featured a Fort Carson soldier and the idea that old-school soldiers, shown as familiar cartoon figures by cartoonist Bill Mauldin, might look askance at the changes.

In another departure from traditional Army attitudes, in April 1970 Rogers invited Fonda and about 100 of her scalawags to come right into the fort and headquarters. My office was 20 feet from Rogers's, so before long, one of her protesters stood on my desk and said we were "fucking pigs."

Rogers met with them for a couple of hours in his office and talked with them about the protests and the war, and that seemed to calm her down.

Jane Fonda in the Vietnam visit that earned her the nickname "Hanoi Jane."
CPA Media Pte Ltd/Alamy Stock Photo

The community didn't forget, though. In 1973, while in Germany, I sent a letter to the editor of the Stars and Stripes newspaper as an open letter to Fonda that recounted my memory of her visit. (By then, Jane and the other show business members of her family had been featured on a Time Magazine cover of their own.) In part, it said:

> Your repugnant verbosity through the years about the Vietnam War and our involvement as a nation attests to your disloyalty to our country. I find it now necessary to take my valuable time and tell you what I think of your antics over the past years… I was at Fort Carson when you danced your way through the gates, attempting to play on your presumed disloyalty of our young soldiers who were then deeply involved in the issues of the Modern Volunteer Army under the command of General Rogers. The smelly rabble that was in your attendance turned off the soldiers and your attempted "sick call strike" was a failure. I saw it all, Jane. Your act was bad. The unfortunate thing was that you felt it was progress. Somehow, this nonsense has

gone to your head and you think the people of this world listen when you speak.

I listed the ways I thought she turned soldiers off and plain got the facts wrong, including calling our brave returned POWs "hypocrites and liars." And noted, "Your FTA [Fuck the Army] program has been a flop and so have you. Someday when old and gray, you may understand."

Nearly 40 years later, when Fonda was in the Fort Carson region filming a Netflix movie, her arrival drew plenty of negative comments in local newspapers from community members. Ironically, the troops at Fort Carson didn't appear to mind much, but Hughes, who by then was retired, had a visceral reaction to hearing about Fonda's return to Colorado Springs, as reported in a local newspaper article.

> "I winced and decided I wouldn't go anywhere near it," said Hughes, 88, who served in the Korean and Vietnam wars. "And I'm sure not going to watch any movie she's in. There's a lingering distaste for her for all that time ago. Sitting in an anti-aircraft gun seat was the last straw. I have not and never will forgive her for that."
>
> Hughes remembers Fonda's 1970 visit to Fort Carson during her anti-Vietnam War phase to talk with the commanding general, Gen. Bernard Rogers, and visit the stockade, a military prison that has since closed.
>
> "We invited her to talk to him in his office," said Hughes. "She had been told we were running a political prison called a stockade—disaffected soldiers told her that. We asked if she wanted to see it. We gave her a tour of the prison. She went to the wire and some of her friends were outside the wire on post and she said this is the nicest general I've ever met. That stockade became famous."
>
> Fonda wrote in a Sept. 21 blog post on janefonda.com that she was reunited this fall in the Springs with the woman who snuck her onto the post in the trunk of her car in 1970 to distribute newspapers by the GI Movement. Hughes disputes the story. He doesn't believe she could have either gotten in or stayed on post without anybody noticing her. [A Fort representative] can confirm Fonda visited the base legitimately in 1970 but didn't have any information about her alleged illegal entry.

There was also at least one unhappy person in Florence, another location for "Our Souls at Night." One sign in the back of a pickup said, "Go home, Hanoi Jane," and moved around town to different locations, according to Florence city manager Mike Patterson. He heard a couple of people held signs protesting her visit during the town's Pioneer Days parade.

"The protests were pretty mild," said Melissa Walker, owner of Florence Flower Shop on Main Street. "It was more positive than negative. The extent of protests was writing comments on vehicles. I didn't see any signs or anything."

Rene Pryor, manager of the Iron Gate Antique Mall on Florence's Main Street, also saw a mostly positive response.

"Some people of that (Vietnam) era said they'd rather not worry about it," she said. "Overall what they spent in the town and what they did for the town was phenomenal. I'm sure they spent half a million or a million dollars in Fremont County."

Patterson and the shop owners didn't know of anybody refusing to open their shop in protest, though he said the film crew did ask some owners to close for a day or two during filming and offered them compensation.

In addition to excitement like that, I enjoyed making some music at Fort Carson, too. A group of who liked to sing got together, and after happy hour at the officers' club we would go from door to door in the officers' individual quarters at night and serenade them, including carols at Christmas time.

But one of the best things that happened in Fort Carson was that I got to know Roger H. C. Donlon and his wonderful wife, Norma. We lived on post and the Donlons lived just a few houses down the street from us. When I met him, he was a lieutenant colonel. We hung out together, went to happy hour together on Fridays, and became good friends. Paula and I were even proxy godparents for the baptism of Roger's oldest son, Damian, in Fort Carson on May 31, 1970.

Norma made great martinis, although not as good as A.C.'s. Roger and I were sometimes chewed out by our wives for rolling down the hill from the officer's club to our quarters instead of walking. We've now known each other for 50 years. He'd been a Special Forces officer in Vietnam in 1964 and late that year became the war's first recipient of the Medal of Honor, which was presented to him by President Johnson on December 5, 1964, for his incredible bravery during a five-hour battle in Nam Dong that July.

Roger, Norma, and their sons Jason and Damian

He and I really bonded over a bad incident at Fort Carson. Back then, an Army officer's wife had to meet certain expectations. The fort's Officers Wives Club (OWC) had an annual competition to recognize a new second lieutenant's wife, presenting her with a "Mrs. Lieutenant Award." This prestigious award was presented at the final luncheon of the year. All of the units on the post nominated someone, and the wives' club board members read the résumés and narrowed the search to two finalists.

While we were there, Paula was serving as the club treasurer and Norma Donlon was its secretary. Both had voting rights. At the meeting to select the award recipient, Paula voted for one finalist and Norma voted for the other, who received the most votes. After the meeting, Paula quizzed Norma about why she'd voted as she had. Norma's response was that she was impressed with the candidate's volunteer work with a group called Army Community Service (ACS).

The day before the award was presented, Paula was working as a volunteer at ACS and, while checking some records, found out that the winning candidate had never volunteered there! She had falsified her résumé.

Paula called Norma to tell her what she'd uncovered. Norma took immediate action, calling the OWC president, Jane Short, the wife of a lieutenant colonel. She relayed what Paula had found out and that she would have voted for the other candidate if ACS had not appeared on the second candidate's résumé. The difference would have resulted in a tie vote.

The president responded that she would have broken that tie vote by voting for the candidate who had already won.

Norma said it was not fair to the first candidate to compete against a falsified résumé; perhaps other voting members would also have voted differently if they'd known. She suggested the women call the other board members, inform them of the discrepancy, and let them vote again.

The president replied, "Absolutely not!"

The luncheon was scheduled for the next day. Both Paula and Norma were told to keep their mouths shut and that the award presentation would proceed.

A Christmas with the kids

Both Paula and Norma were champions for fairness, so they decided not to participate in this charade. At the luncheon, they were seated at the head table with the other board members. When the award was presented, however, they did not stand and did not applaud. Their protest was noted by those in attendance, especially by the commanding general's wife, Mrs. Bernard Rogers. She asked the president why two of the board members hadn't participated in the presentation and was told the reason. That night, she reported the incident to her husband and asked him to speak to the husbands of these two wives.

The next morning Major General Rogers called my commander to his office and told him to immediately fire me and have me reassigned. I got called on the carpet and was told the movers would come to my house and I'd be gone within the week—I was being reassigned to Texas, "because I will not have an officer in my command who can't control his wife and whose wife talks about our general officers' wives."

Paula and Norma were having coffee at our quarters that morning when I walked into the dining room, ashen-faced, and said, "Paula, what did you do at the OWC luncheon yesterday? I'm being relieved and reassigned, with packers coming tomorrow to remove us from the post!"

Norma raced home to find out if her husband had met the same fate. Roger had not heard anything about any reassignments for something that happened at the OWC luncheon. Norma argued that they probably couldn't do that to Roger because they would've had to justify the action. Not only that, but he was a Medal of Honor recipient, so there would have been some inquiry if he was fired.

Norma pleaded with Roger into the night to do something to help us. It just wasn't fair that only one officer's career would be damaged when two wives were involved in the same incident.

The next morning, after Roger left for work and without his knowledge, Norma called Lieutenant General Vernon Mock, the commanding general of Fifth Army Headquarters. He was from her home state of Arkansas and had once told her that if he could ever do anything for her, she should call him. So she did! Mock was one rank above Rogers, his boss so to speak, and said he would look into the incident.

Later that day, Rogers stormed out of this office and yelled into the hallway, "Who the hell called General Mock at Fifth Army Headquarters?" The staff was abuzz after the incident leaked out. Not wanting anyone else to get into trouble, Norma stepped up and admitted to making the call and telling General Mock what was happening at Fort Carson.

Rogers called me in and said I wasn't going to be reassigned after all. "But don't ever do it again." I remained at Fort Carson with Paula. Roger was verbally reprimanded for his wife's action, but we both were promoted to our next ranks on time Captain Black to Major and Major Roger Donlon to Lieutenant Colonel

The only fallout was revealed a few years later, in 1970, when Roger received orders to Command and General Staff College. He was given his Officer Efficiency Report (OER), which was signed by his rater and endorser at Fort Carson with no mention of his wife or the OWC incident. He signed off on that report. But the following year, while on temporary duty in Washington, D.C., in preparation for his second tour to Vietnam, he went to the Military Personal Center to check his file. He came upon the Fort Carson OER and discovered that it had been altered after he'd signed it. One paragraph had been added: "This officer should never be given an assignment of responsibility or to represent the United States of America until his wife learns his place." For those who believe in the Army code of honor, someone in the system going through a wife to get to the officer like this is called "chickenshit"—and it is probably illegal. It's hard to know exactly who was to blame, but it's likely that if either General Rogers or the OER rater, a

Lieutenant Colonel Griggs, hadn't put that negative comment in Roger Donlon's personnel file, he would have been a general.

Ben and Heidi making music with their Grandpa Black

In 1971, I was assigned to go back to Vietnam in May. I was disillusioned with the war and I really did not want to go back. I felt that I'd made it out alive the first time; going a second time was pushing my luck. But second tours were not an option. I had no desire to spend my tour in the administrative bureaucracy in Saigon, either. I wrote John Paul Vann, who by then had been given responsibility for II Corps, also known as Military Region II. (He would later would be the subject of Neil Sheehan's 1988 Pulitzer prize-winning book, *A Bright Shining Lie: John Paul Vann and America in Vietnam*). Vann had not signed up for Westmoreland's way of war. Like many of us in the military, he believed that the Vietnam War had to be viewed as a long effort at a lower level of engagement with the enemy, not a short war with large units and a high level of engagement. Sheehan's book includes one of Vann's famous and oft-quoted maxims. It came from Vann's first lessons: "This is a political war and it calls for discrimination in killing. The best weapon for killing would be a knife, but I'm afraid we can't do it that way. The worst is an airplane. The next worse is artillery. Barring a knife, the best is a rifle—you know who you're killing."

I volunteered for duty on Vann's team in the II Corps Tactical Zone in the Central Highlands. First, though, I took my family back to Spokane by way of Yellowstone National Park, and we moved into a place on Walnut Street. Back home, things in the family were changing. We went to a fair in Valley, and that would be the last time I'd see my Aunt Margaret, Uncle Louis' wife. She had an affair with Denny Burya, who was my age, and all hell broke loose. Ultimately she ran off with Denny. I really felt bad for my uncle Louis, a World War II Navy veteran.

After Margaret left him, Uncle Louis sold the homestead house to my Aunt May and Uncle Bill. Uncle Bill was still in the Air Force at the time, and when he retired, they bought a house in Spokane and settled there. So they rented out the homestead. Then they decided to sell it to Nick Skok, a neighbor who lived on the farm next door to the homestead. When Aunt May called Mom and told her what they were planning to do, Mom blew her stack. She was really upset. The next day, Aunt May called back and said that Mom and Dad could have the house, outbuildings, and thirty acres around it. Skok simply bought the rest of the acreage. So when Dad retired from his last job at the Spokane post office in 1970, my parents moved back to the homestead once more. Mom got it back into tip-top shape and it became a great place to visit.

My kids and I with Mom and Dad at Waitts Lake

Being back around family was sometimes great and sometimes a challenge. For instance, my Aunt Fran was a great aunt but a rather interesting person. She had plenty of money and went through three husbands, but she was also a kleptomaniac. She didn't go into Nordstrom's and steal purses or perfume, though. Her specialty was restaurants.

She would take Paula and I out to dinner, where she would point to the set of salt and pepper shakers and say, "Johnny, would you please hand me the salt and pepper?" Of course I would, and then she would put them into her purse. No one would say anything; I don't know why, but I guess since she was taking us to dinner, we felt it would be rude.

By then the waitress would have taken our orders and Aunt Fran would have taken her silverware and put it, too, into her purse. I was thinking, "We are accomplices to a crime or minor theft of some sort!" But we didn't say anything. Before dinner ended, my aunt had also taken a large handful of napkins, too. I'm sure that if we hadn't been there, she would've taken the napkin holder as well.

Some months later, I got a call from Aunt Fran, who said she was going to marry Charlie Coppula, an Italian lawyer and bookmaker, her second husband. In my younger days, I had worked for Charlie, taking phone calls from his clients who called in with bets on football games and other sports. Aunt Fran said the wedding reception would be at her house and she wanted me to tend bar. She paid pretty well and I needed the money, so I agreed.

She said, "I'm going to the liquor store and need you to come up this afternoon." So I went to her house, just a few blocks from ours. She had me come into the kitchen, where five new bottles of various types of liquor sat on the counter alongside empty mason jars.

"Here's what I want you to do, Johnny," she said. "Open each bottle and pour half of it into the mason jar, then fill the liquor bottle back up with water."

I said, "Fran, won't the reception guests notice the difference if you water the liquor down?"

She said, "Everybody always gets drunk, and they never know the difference."

After I finished that task, she told me to get the silverware, napkins, and salt and pepper shakers together for the table setting. I opened the cupboard where she pointed. There were at least 10 napkin holders and plenty of napkins. The next cupboard held many sets of salt and pepper shakers, and the silverware drawer contained many sets of silverware. Basically Aunt Fran had enough table settings to open her own restaurant.

When the event came, I tended bar, white shirt and all, and her party was a great success. Aunt Fran was right, the guests all got sloshed. Nobody said anything about the weak booze.

Then I left home again for Vietnam. I ended up at John Paul Vann's headquarters in Pleiku, in the central highlands of Two (II) Corps, not far from the border with Cambodia. This was a combat area of operations officially named Advisory Team 21, Military Region 2, Military Assistance Command (MACV). Vann was the senior American advisor there. He'd been assigned the military region as American involvement in the war was winding down and troops in the region were being withdrawn. That put him in charge of all U.S. personnel in the region, where he advised the ARVN commander to the region and became the first American civilian to command U.S. regular troops in combat. Although he was technically a civilian, his position was the equivalent in responsibilities to a major general in the U.S. Army.

At the Advisory Team 21 headquarters

My assignment was to be the adjutant general (AG)—the chief administrative officer—and special staff officer at John Paul Vann's headquarters. I hoped my letter to Vann, who at the time was on leave in the U.S., had something to do with this assignment. My job was to directly support the corps headquarters and subordinate combat field elements, which included numerous advisory teams at many locations.

I found out about my assignment while at MACV headquarters in Saigon. I had placed a call to the officer I was replacing at Team 21, an Army AG Corps captain. In the middle of the call he said, "I've got to run, we are under rocket attack." When we talked later, he sounded worried and stressed, but I wasn't impressed with what he told me. My assignment officer said I'd be reporting to or working with another AG major who was misassigned.

"They'll have to figure out what to do with two of you," he said.

"Great job, Black," I muttered sarcastically to myself. "Great job so far managing your career."

I arrived at Pleiku Army Airfield on February 26, 1971, in a C119, called the flying boxcar, with its side windows blown out. An Air Force pilot sat in the left seat and a South Vietnamese Air Force pilot sat in the right seat. Several C119s were being turned over to the South Vietnamese Air Force.

I'd soon also be going back and forth to Nha Trang and Saigon on business and would sometimes take a Vietnam Airlines C47 civilian flight loaded with everything, including farm animals, then catch a small Scatback Air Force jet or other available aircraft.

A moped ride was sometimes the safest transportation choice in Saigon.

Initially I thought, "Well, this won't be too bad. I'll be here for the dry season and can play a little tennis." The rainy season started in May and lasted through November. But you wouldn't call it a great place to visit even in peacetime. The airfield and advisory compound, known as Camp Holloway, was attacked by the VC in February of 1965, leading to the further escalation of the war. To sum it up, in the middle of the night on February 7, the attackers penetrated the camp, opened fire with AK-47 rifles, and mortared the airfield and compound where I'd be living and working. The attack killed eight U.S. soldiers and wounded another 126, destroyed 10 aircraft, and damaged another 15. When the news reached Saigon later that morning General Westmoreland, McGeorge Bundy, and Ambassador Maxwell Taylor flew to Pleiku to check out the damage. Bundy then called President Johnson to request retaliatory air strikes.

Johnson quickly convened the National Security Council while South Vietnam General Nguyễn Khánh met with Westmoreland and Bundy. That same afternoon, Johnson started Operation Flaming Dart to bomb selected North Vietnamese targets in Đồng Hới. Khánh reportedly celebrated with champagne because it bolstered his military's morale by demonstrating more U.S. commitment. The air strikes only prompted another VC attack a few days later, and the war was still on by the time I arrived in 1971.

When I got there, I realized that the situation wasn't what I'd expected. It was clear we'd lost the war and were simply abandoning the South Vietnamese. I took a jeep from the Pleiku airfield to the MACV compound and signed in. I was met by the headquarters company commander, an Army captain. He had the briefing memorized. We walked the facility and I was shown my room to put my gear away. This time I was issued an M16 which would be under my bunk with a fully loaded clip.

On our way down to the area with the officer billets, I asked the Captain about several areas where the buildings were gone but their concrete slab beneath remained. He said those were from past rocket attacks. There was a larger area that used to be the officer's club. I also asked the captain about all the white empty vials along the walkway. He said they were empty heroine vials, that much of the drug traffic came from Cambodia through II Corps' area of operations. "We have those vials picked up every morning." He also alerted me that an unannounced inspection of enlisted barracks took place at least once a week, usually early in the morning. "You'll be participating in those. We have to go through all lockers, all the nooks and crannies, to keep some control and damper the drug problem."

Longing already for Go Cong, I was glad though to see that my room was still standing. All the room doors opened directly to the walkway, but once opened, they protected the occupant via a brick wall so that the VC could not set up machine guns at either end of the walkway to kill advisors as they exited their rooms, as they had in the 1965 attack. My room connected with a bathroom shared with the guy next door, who happened to be another major and the secretary of the General Staff (SGS)—a good guy to know. His boss, Colonel Johnson, MR II chief of staff, would turn out to be my endorser. For now, though, I was only concerned about how the other AG major and I would work out being double boxed—a military term that means you don't know who you're working for and neither does your boss. Our relationship later would be clarified when I met the other AG major, who said, "As your rater, I will start you with a score of 1 (the top) on the five-point scale used in the DA 67.6 Officer Efficiency point scale and then back down depending on your performance." Getting a five would mean you were "dead meat" and your career was over.

I was positive this would all work out.

First I met my rater, lieutenant colonel Harvey, G1 advisor, and Colonel Johnson. Later I met the head of my AG section, which was currently being led by the captain I was replacing. The senior enlisted man was a young staff sergeant with about 20 enlisted administrative Army soldiers. We were housed in a quonset hut lined with poorly prepared sandbags that I'd later get fixed. Harvey and Johnson wanted to be clear with me on the importance of my assignment, that drugs were a big problem, and that I was expected to fix some administrative matters that had fallen through the cracks. My responsibilities included awards and decorations, personnel actions and management, legal matters, morning reports, casualty reporting, supervision of the Corps translation section and many others. I pulled my team together and we got to work.

Outside my officer's billet in Pleiku

One top priority was to get my team together and emphasize discipline, being on time, wearing clean fatigues, haircuts and shaving, no drugs, and above all keeping in mind that we were the support for all the troops in the field. We were considered the administrative experts. There was one question about facial hair or beards, and I told them what they'll tell you in the Special Forces: "Why would you grow hair on your face when it grows wild on your ass?"

In addition, I said I wanted clean desks, with inboxes, outboxes, and work kept up to date. For any reports due, particularly awards and efficiency reports for all grades and ranks, that my only acceptable standard was nothing late—zero. My advice was also to write home, answer letters from your family, go to church on Sunday if duty allowed it, and the expectation was that they were expected to be on duty Sunday through Sunday, unless duty allowed for a game of tennis, horseshoes, badminton, or the movies we provided.

My first priority, however, was to get clear who I was working for. After about two weeks with the other major, listening to his revival tapes from the deep South coming through our shared wall and observing his love/hate relationship with alcohol, I decided I needed a new boss. I became friends with another major who worked in operations. We usually had dinner in the non-commissioned officers (NCO) club, which allowed officers, too. We'd have a beer, talk, and order a barbecued steak and a bottle of wine apiece. Sometimes there would be a great band from the Philippines putting on a show.

Once I got back to my room, there might be a check-in with the SGS from next door. Finally I brought up the subject of my direct reporting relationship. I gave the SGS my background, including ROTC and distinguished military graduate, and said that, as he knew, being rated by an officer of the same grade was the kiss of death. I also told him I could not deal with the peculiar habits of the other major and that I had already slipped a point on his performance rating of me.

The SGS, Dave, said he'd talk to Colonel Johnson. Later I was called into Harvey's office. He told me would be rating me, with Johnson endorsing and General Wear reviewing my OER.

I had plenty to do. I had a standup meeting with my team at about 7 a.m. each morning, which kept the team focused because when standing, you're all looking into each other's eyeballs. Everybody checks in, with no exceptions. The NCO in charge (NCOIC) and I went over our list and the staff had the opportunity to voice their concerns, gripes, or whatever. Both the NCO and I were also informally checking everyone's appearance.

It was easy to spot who was on drugs. MACV policy was that anyone caught with contraband was shipped out immediately or, depending on the issue, the HQ commander had some authority under U.S. Code of Military Justice. Usually a soldier ended up with a dishonorable discharge after he was sent back to the United States.

One morning after our standup meeting, I headed to my office behind the wall of the working area and the NCO's desk. Sitting in my chair and going through my files was the chief of staff, Colonel Johnson. I was startled—that was very unusual. I asked if I could help him.

He said, and would continue to say while I was in Pleiku, "Major, I'm just checking things out."

"Well, for starters do you want to know what my plan is to fix the late awards and efficiency report problem?" When I arrived, the late submission rate for officer efficiency reports for the Corps was 20 to 50 percent. Obviously, he wanted to know.

I told him that was going to get fixed. "The next time you check my file you'll see a detailed plan."

He kept his word, as he had to pass right by my office to get to his. I'd have the chief visiting me at least once a week at no set time of day. Later at Boeing we would call that management by wandering around (MBWA), a concept traced back to executives at Hewlett Packard, who were practicing it in the 1970s. Later MBWA would be used by Tom Peters and Robert H. Waterman Jr. in their 1982 book, *In Search of Excellence*. It was similar to the Japanese gemba walk developed at Toyota.

I liked seeing Colonel Johnson going through my desk because it showed me and my team that he cared about the important work we performed in the middle of rocket alley. Our team could be wiped out in seconds, and the evidence of past attacks was around us every day. But for me it has always been about taking care of the soldier, as it was in Go Cong in the case of my sergeant, A.C. Cunningham.

By the time I left Pleiku, the late submission rate for officer efficiency reports was down to 2 percent. As my endorser, Colonel Johnson echoed my rater, saying, "Major Black took over an AG section which had an unreasonable backlog of recommendations for awards and overdue efficiency reports. He was hampered by a large percentage of drug users within his section. Through his personal efforts he brought the section under control and now has the lowest backlog in any Corps in the Republic of Vietnam. He works with a minimum of supervision, is good judge of people and is responsive to the command. His performance of duty has been truly outstanding in every respect."

While I was there, II Corps closed down activity on the An Khê pass. In the First Indochina War, this had been the site of the Battle of An Khê, also known as the Battle of Mang Yang Pass. It had been the last official battle of that war and one of the French Union's bloodiest defeats, which Dr. Fall had written about at length in his book, *Street Without Joy*.

I was told by the chief of staff to go with Mr. Vann to read the official citation of the closing of our operations. Vann flew in his chopper and I flew separately in a Bell, which had room only for the pilot and me. I told the pilot, "Give me a quick lesson in case you take a round."

Fortunately, I didn't have to fly it, and we arrived at the pass. A Chinook helicopter with a squad of U.S. troops and an honor guard also flew in for the ceremony. It was an historic event. I read the citation, Vann spoke, and that concluded the ceremony. I looked over to where the U.S. troops were getting ready to board the Chinook and spotted an Army captain I knew from a previous assignment at Ft. Carson: Buzz Altshuler.

I went over and asked Buzz how it was going. "Badly," he said.

I said, "How badly?"

"Very fucking badly." He was concerned, as we all were, about the drawdown taking place.

While at Pleiku, however, I enjoyed the time I was able to spend with Warrant Officer Bob Richards, Vann's chopper pilot. He was a bourbon drinker who I couldn't keep up with. He also was a great storyteller. I knew I didn't have the guts to walk in his shoes. As he took a shot of bourbon, with a cigarette in the other hand, his hands would shake. A crew chief in Pleiku had a guitar, and often we'd get together at night to sing. Sometimes I'd make up songs on the fly with guys from the Tactical Operations Center (TOC). The crew chief either made up or found the following lyrics somewhere: "I don't care if it rains or freezes as long as I got my plastic Jesus sittin' on the dashboard of my car....." There were more verses that I don't remember, but we'd sing them together.

The morning I'll never forget was a clear one. About 10 a.m. I told my NCO that I had to walk up to the S2 (combat intelligence) office to make a photocopy. We'd used their copy machine before, and I had established a working relationship with the NCOIC of S2. The copy machine was located about 10 feet from his desk. An African American sergeant soon to complete 30 years of service, he had nine children waiting for him back in Texas. He'd served in World War II, Korea, and now Vietnam. I was in his office when suddenly I heard the sound—the sound I had been told was an incoming rocket. It sounded like a freight train that had left the tracks, but in the air, as if you're standing right next to the tracks—until it goes absolutely silent. Then BAM, it hits.

MACV headquarters was on the hill right next door to the Vietnamese headquarters for Military Region 2, the Central Highlands region in South Vietnam and the second allied combat tactical region. The white building was a great target for the Viet Cong, who would set up rockets at night with the fuses set to fire when the hot morning sun burned off, evaporating the water.

We took probably 10 rockets that day, 122 millimeter Chinese rockets that were big enough to blow a house apart. They could come in at various intervals and could land anywhere, an unknown, silent killer. We could go to sleep at night and never wake up the next day. When the attack started that morning, all personnel knew to get into the bunkers, and my team and I headed there.

Inside the bunker, a Vietnamese woman who was frightened to death asked me to hold her. She was shaking and praying. Harvey and the chaplain ran into the bunker and then, as the attack continued, said they needed to run back out and check on the S2 NCOIC. After about thirty minutes, the all-clear signal sounded and we left the bunkers to back to our office.

The S2 NCOIC, who'd been at his desk a dozen feet to my left as I used the photocopier, had been killed outright and his body taken away. How I escaped, I don't know, but the confusion and panic was terrifying. I went to my own desk and saw that the rocket that had killed him had passed over my desk and landed in the S2 building just across from my office. My desktop was covered with wood splinters and debris, so I was lucky.

The NVA and Viet Cong frequently used bamboo launchers for 122 mm rockets. Our headquarters staff found launchers like that after our rocket attack. Of course, the VC were long gone.

Bamboo rocket launchers like those we found after our attack (AP photo ©1969)

I was told to do a recommendation for a Bronze Star Medal for valor both for my boss and for the chaplain. Later my job was to schedule the awards ceremony and read the citations. In addition, it was my job to write the condolence letter to be signed and sent to the sergeant's family. I found it difficult to write. His family would be notified in person, but the letter from the S2 was standard procedure. My admin team was shaken up, so I told them we were all going to re-sandbag our building. All that physical labor together helped take everyone's mind off the attack.

By then, I had decided that since Paula and I hadn't been able to find our first baby, we should adopt a Vietnamese child instead. It was a way to compensate for what had happened with our first child. I asked to be reassigned to Saigon so that I could take care of that from there. I made several trips to Saigon on Air Vietnam, a C47 prop plane with tickets that cost $15. These trips sometimes included sitting by chickens, pigs, and goats as well as older Vietnamese women chewing betel nut. I became the MACV special services officer there, and Paula came to Saigon as part of the effort. But adopting was just too complicated, and we couldn't make it work.

We helped some local kids, though. On my first tour, while in Go Cong I had worked with the local orphanage and had Paula work with the Catholic parish in Spokane to have parishioners collect and donate children's clothing. Paula then arranged shipment to the orphanage in Go Cong. On October 18, 1967, about 50 boxes arrived from Spokane and were accepted by the orphanage's Mother Superior. It was quite an undertaking that Paula gets the credit for. About 40 orphans whose parents had been killed by the Viet Cong received those new clothes and were overjoyed.

Go Cong orphans with the shipment of clothing Paula and I arranged

Things were not great between us at that time, but with a West Point graduate named Rick Wilbur, who was my deputy, I rented a car and the two of us stayed at a hotel with our wives. Two days after we left, that hotel took a rocket and was destroyed. That's what can happen in a combat zone.

Roger Donlon and I ended up in Vietnam together during my second tour there. By then he'd been promoted to major and was assigned as special advisor to a district chief in the South China Sea. He came by to visit me on his way to his district. I was the recreation officer for our team in Saigon, and over a couple of beers, he mentioned that he'd sure like some sports equipment for his team. I told him I'd deliver some, not sure how to do it without making it a mini combat operation—and I'd have preferred to die John Wayne-style, rather than with a baseball mitt in one hand and a horseshoe in the other! But one day I got a bunch of stuff together, like baseball bats and mitts. I absconded with a riverine boat and for a small fee, its Vietnamese pilot. I had to convince him that we'd be safe and that this mission had priority. We showed up at a dock in Roger's district with all this stuff. He couldn't believe I'd done that. Grateful, he saw us off again with a cold beer. It sounds like a small thing, but helping to improve the morale of the troops was a high priority for me, regardless of the difficulty or danger involved. I carried that priority with me throughout my whole career, both in the military and afterward.

With Roger on Pattaya Beach during a visit to Thailand with our wives

Roger had an 18-month tour and his wife, Norma, was in Bangkok. Since we were close friends, I arranged my next rest and recuperation (R&R) leave for Bangkok and had Paula come, too. He and I flew in there together, met our wives, and stayed at Roger's place. After that R&R, I went back to Saigon, and Paula followed me. I received approval to host her in Saigon, and we spent some time at Vung Tau beach, an in-country R&R center for the Army. Afterward, I said goodbye to her and had her routed for a stop in Hong Kong to do some shopping.

For better or worse, my second Vietnam tour ended in May 1972 when I contracted hepatitis in Saigon. I was medevacked with a bunch of other military passengers to Guam and then on to Hawaii. En route to Hawaii, we hit a terrible storm. The airplane turned black inside. The nurses buckled us down the best they could, the plane was passing through violent turbulence and lighting strikes.

The pilot came on the speaker to say, "We may be lost; I'm doing the best I can." Finally, after what seemed like an eternity, we began breaking out of the weather system we were in. The pilot came on again and said, "I apologize. We have been lost, but now we are on a more direct route to Hickam Field in Hawaii."

Once we landed at Hickam, we expected that we'd be taken off the plane, but we were told we were all too infected. We had to stay on board for another five hours. After finally getting to Travis Air Force Base, we stayed overnight before being moved to Madigan Army Hospital in Tacoma, Washington.

I was laid up at Madigan for a month, but I'd made it out of Vietnam alive not once but twice. There were plenty of others who didn't.

Among them was John Paul Vann. He was killed in 1972, after I'd been reassigned to Saigon not long before my Vietnam tour ended. Before his death, he won a magnificent 1972 victory over the North Vietnamese Army in the Battle of Kontum. That was one of the great victories of the Vietnam War. Within a matter of months, however, Kontum was given away at the Paris Peace Talks so that Nixon and Kissinger could run for reelection on having "ended" the Vietnam war.

After the battle, Vann's pilot, Bob Richards, deserved a much-needed R&R break. He was replaced by a 26-year-old pilot, Lieutenant Ronald Doughtie. With Doughtie at the controls, Vann's chopper went down in Kontum on June 9, the evening of the day the town was declared fully secure. It crashed into a grove of trees near a village cemetery. The investigation of the crash concluded that the pilot probably experienced vertigo. He did not have Richards' hardcore experience to deal with what some pilots call the graveyard spiral.

When he was killed, Vann was only 47 years old. President Richard Nixon posthumously awarded him the Presidential Medal of Freedom, the nation's highest civilian citation, for his ten years of service in South Vietnam. Although as a civilian he was ineligible for the Medal of Honor, he was also posthumously awarded the Distinguished Service Cross for his actions over April 23 and 24, 1972. The only civilian so honored in Vietnam, he was buried in Section II of Arlington Cemetery. His funeral was attended by notables such as General Westmoreland, Major General Lansdale, Lieutenant Colonel Lucien Conein, Senator Ted Kennedy, and writer and military analyst Daniel Ellsberg. A footnote I found interesting was that the Vietnamese communists paid Vann a reverse tribute by exulting in his end. They gave far more attention to his death than they had to the occasional deaths earlier in the war of ordinary American generals. Liberation radio noted, "his removal constitutes a stunning blow" for the U.S. and the Saigon side of the war.

Once I recovered, I was assigned again to Germany, Heidelberg this time. We'd be there nearly six years. My kids were getting older and I started singing and making music with them, too. In fact, Shane, Heidi, and Ben sang "A Girl Named Paula" with me in a Heidelberg talent show we entered, and we won first place. The prize was a trip to the U.S., and we couldn't go! But it was still a big award. The kids also stayed busy with activities of their own. Heidi was in Brownies; Shane played baseball and soccer; and Ben also liked sports as well as music. The kids and I built rockets together, and we skied all over Europe.

Talent show winners!

We lived adjacent to a shared stairwell in our Heidelberg military housing. It was a partying stairwell—all of us socialized together. Mom and Dad came to visit us there in Germany, along with my brother, James. We rented an extra car and toured Germany, staying in camping sites and visiting relatives in Yugoslavia.

Paula and I were in Germany five years that time, though, and over two summers, Paula took the kids and went home to my parents' homestead, so I was sometimes alone. Living below our apartment were Hugh and his wife Jerry. I once met Jerry in a hotel. I wrote a song for her, too, called, "Flower Child of Springtime." Many years later I finally recorded that song on the *Original Rockabilly* album I released in 2018. She called me years later, after I was back in the United States, to tell me she had pancreatic cancer and didn't have long to live. She wanted to say goodbye. Long after she passed away, her daughter Debbie called me and told me that her mother had chosen to die pretty much alone, and that her Dad had eventually remarried.

Another summer in Germany, which Paula and the kids were spending at the Tomsha homestead north of Spokane, I was assigned to the Second Signal Group. I got a call at work from a woman I knew who was named Mitzi. She invited me to her house for dinner while her husband was gone on training. We had dinner, danced, and we ended up in bed several times.

In Heidelberg, I started performing in plays, including a play called *George Washington Slept Here*. In the cast was a beautiful blond named Elizabeth (Liz). She was married to an officer who lived in our housing complex. While the play was in rehearsal, she came to me after a stage party and asked for a ride home. We stopped on the way and made out. Finally she asked if we could meet at a local hotel, which we did. She wanted to continue seeing me and I her, but we were both living in Heidelberg government housing, close to each other, and knew it wouldn't work.

Then there was Mary, a young Army second lieutenant who was getting a divorce from her husband, a sergeant. I met her at the Dining In, which was a very formal military dinner only for service members or others who worked for the Army. I danced with her there. Later she came to my office and asked if I would help her map out her career, which I did. We started to see each other in a relationship. It ended, but later she came to my office and we started seeing each other romantically again.

When I had to attend a two-week Army seminar offsite in Augsburg, I asked Mary to take the train and spend the weekend with me. That weekend, Paula wanted me to come home to Spokane. I told her I had assignments and couldn't do it. Instead, Mary and I danced the night away at the local disco. We continued to see each other periodically until I left Germany for reassignment.

My family left Germany before I did. While I was still there, Mary asked a friend to call me and let me know she wanted me to stop by and tell her goodbye before I left. I should have, but I didn't do it. I didn't have the guts to tell her good-bye face to face. I knew it would be painful and sad.

When I rotated back to the States for reassignment, I called her office in Heidelberg and was told she'd been reassigned. The scene in my imagination of her waiting in her room that morning, waiting for me to knock and tell her goodbye, which I never did, has stayed with me. I think often about it, and I eventually wrote a song about her, "Rock and Roll Mary."

Meanwhile, my family knew about Liz, who ran a Service Club for soldiers. I had to visit her club, which was near where I worked. She later said that when I walked in, looking pretty sharp in my uniform, she about fell apart. In her office, we just talked, but we kept connecting elsewhere. By then, I was in a play called "Bus Stop." I played the part of a cowboy, and the director said I had to sing, so I wrote a song for it, "Lonesome Cowboy Dreams." At a performance one night, Liz asked me for a ride home. She lived in an apartment on the Neckar River, near our housing area. When we got there, she asked me to come in and have a drink. We sat and talked, then she motioned for me to come into her bedroom. I did.

That was the start of a relationship which became complicated. My family went ahead to Lewiston, Idaho, to stay with Paula's mother. I would come later, and we would house-hunt to settle near Seattle, since we knew I would be discharged after finishing my assignment at Fort Lewis nearby. Once my family was gone, I went on with Liz to Majorca, an island off the coast of Spain. I was drinking heavily, feeling the guilt of Paula and the kids leaving without me as well as the guilt of leaving Mary without seeing her while I also saw Liz. Plus I felt the stress of my impending separation from the Army and knowing I'd have to start another career.

Liz would later visit my family in the States. She had a great relationship with my kids and Paula. Later, my kids figured out I was having a relationship with Liz and, when they were in high school, they confronted me.

"We know about Liz, Dad," they said, adding that they knew it had started in Germany as well as that she'd eventually stay in our house.

I told them the honest truth: "Yes, I did." As far as I know, they didn't talk to Paula about it—or at least, she never discussed it with me, although I knew that she knew. It never came up with my family again.

Singing with the kids

Throughout this time, I was also preparing for a life after the military. The University of Oklahoma had a representative at U.S. Army Europe, and you could take a course every quarter that involved two-week intensives with a professor from the university. Through that program I received my masters' degree in human relations from the UO in 1975. My advisor was an African American who ran the human resources department, and between him, the courses, and all my various Army training, I was headed toward a career in human resources management.

From 1974 to 1976, summer and winter, I helped create biannual seminars of leaders to present problems they had not been able to solve. It was a unique way to approach problem-solving in the military. I felt the Army could use a lot of changes to make it more people-oriented. We called these seminars "human-oriented command assistance teams." While leading them, I traveled over 6,000 miles by Army sedan and helicopter to visit 160 fixed station communication sites in Germany, England, and the Benelux countries. My team checked 53 functional areas, identified the best ideas at each site, and shared them with all sites.

We then brought the leaders of those sites together in a four-day seminar to continue tackling what worked and what didn't. These were designed as unstructured sessions. One of the highlights was a seminar I held in Germany in these years focused on the feminist movement. I felt this subject should be tackled. We held the first seminar in Europe on this subject using this unique forum.

We brought together a panel of five women to discuss the role of the modern woman, which was pretty much a taboo subject back in the early 1970s, at least in the military. We brought in Rose Judge, the Federal Women's Program coordinator for United States Army Europe. She and other female leaders spoke about myths about women in the USAE. One was that a woman couldn't handle the responsibilities of an executive position. Not true, they said, noting that women traditionally had not been offered high positions. Other myths pictured a woman worker as emotional, indecisive, overzealous, and seductive, despised by the male workers' wives. It was pointed out that women then made up about 43 percent of the Department of Army Civilians workforce, yet accounted for less than eight percent of those holding the top eight pay grades. Men held 99.5 percent of the GS-13 pay grade and above, which was equivalent to a colonel or higher in the Department of the Army. But they said the number one problem facing women soldiers was ridicule. They told us that male soldiers were still looking on the Women's Army Corps (WACs) as either promiscuous or homosexual, with no middle ground. I was proud to have started a constructive conversation about it.

My next assignment in Europe was in the Human Resource Development Division, at Headquarters U.S. Army Europe. The Division was led by a combat arms colonel and had five branches: leadership, race relations/education, drug and alcohol abuse, and statistical. I was assigned as the race relations/education staff officer. All branch officers were from the combat arms: infantry, armor, or artillery, and my boss was an African American artillery lieutenant colonel.

My job was to design and put into place a three-phase race relations education program (RREP) for U.S. Army Europe during fiscal year 1977. The single holdover was a 12-hour orientation seminar for new arrivals. Incoming soldiers, as well as Department of Army Civilians in grade GS-7 and others, would be required to attend a seminar after arrival. My job was to integrate the principles of organizational effectiveness into the RREP Executive Seminar concept by organizing workshops of instructors and commanders throughout Europe. I also had to produce guidance for commanders, lesson outline modules and tasking, and supporting public information releases.

As the United States was getting out of Vietnam, the Army was downsizing. As a reserve major, I would've had to make regular army major to stay in. At one point after my second tour in Vietnam, prior to working with the race relations program, however, I'd been assigned in Europe to report to a Colonel Busby. When I reported for duty, I wore my "greens," which were normal to wear when reporting for. The first thing he said was, "You know, if you're attempting to impress me by wearing all your ribbons, you haven't."

I had no more ribbons than any officer coming from two tours in Vietnam. I said, "Colonel, this is my uniform—how we're supposed to report." But we didn't get off on the right foot. The nail in the coffin was Paula, who was always outspoken. All the women smoked then, and Paula didn't like smoking, so already she didn't fit in with Busby's wife. Then she was at an event with them, and Mrs. Busby said, "I want all you girls to be volunteering." Paula said she wasn't going to. "I'm going to get a job, we need the money," she said. That went over like a lead balloon

Colonel Busby called me in the next day and said she had a bad attitude. I said, "I'm sorry, I'll talk to my wife," and I did. I told her to knock it off. This was a repeat of what happened at Fort Carson. It might be hard today to believe this was how the Army worked, but it was.

Then we were undergoing a big inspection, and I pulled everyone through it. We got high marks. Still, the colonel said to me, "Don't think you're going to get all the credit for this." He just didn't like me. It's no wonder I wasn't promoted afterward.

I left the regular Army in 1978 as a major after I didn't receive a promotion. Once that was decided, my last six months would be spent back in Washington at Fort Lewis, and then I joined the Army Reserves for eight years in order to retire as a lieutenant colonel with a full 20 years of service. During those eight years, I took two weeks away from the Boeing Company each year for reserve duty. My reserve duty station was the Pentagon, where I was assigned to the Office of the Deputy Chief of Staff for Personnel (DCSPER) and made responsible for special projects.

In the meantime, Paula and I returned to the states in 1978, moved from Spokane to Western Washington, and bought our first house at 14809 72nd Avenue East in Puyallup. That home cost $45,000 and had four bedrooms and a big yard for the kids, who were getting to be teenagers and attended Rogers High School. We did quite a bit of remodeling. We were all very happy, or so I thought, because we'd been living in a four-bedroom apartment in Germany.

I served the last six months of my Army career in the Equal Employment

Opportunity (EEO) office at Fort Lewis. The base was then headed up by Major General Richard Cavazos, deputy chief of staff for personnel and commanding general of the Ninth Infantry Division there at Fort Lewis. He would ultimately become a four-star general, and he liked me. I was assigned as the EEO staff officer for the Ninth and Fort Lewis.

I stepped into the assignment with major issues around the chain of command within the office. It was run by a Department of the Army (DAC) civilian GS13, the equivalent of a colonel, and I was a major. There were three non-commissioned officers (NCOs) assigned as race relations instructors and EO Specialists. They all reported to the GS-13, who was African American. Two of the NCOs were African American, too, while the other was Caucasian. I met first with the NCOs and then the GS-13 before meeting with Cavazos.

The NCOs hated their civil servant boss. They told me they were mistreated by him, that he constantly berated them. At five p.m. I'd send someone for a six-pack, and we'd talk about it. They asked me for help. Once I met with the GS-13, I could understand what they meant. In my meeting with General Cavazos I told him what I thought the issues were and that I would come back to him with my recommendations. I did that, quickly reporting back to him with the recommendation that the NCOs should not report to the DAC but to me. We got the civilian out of the EEO office and its staff reported to me instead. They were overjoyed.

I also told Cavazos the Fort and the Ninth Division needed a new focus, with five guiding principles to follow in design of the new EO program:

- To further increase the channels for command involvement with EO problems.
- To establish an orientation and sustainment type of training in human relations.
- To provide maximum flexibility in design for the commanders who supervised the program.
- To minimize record keeping.
- To also satisfy the requirement of specialized programs for senior supervisory personnel.

I told the general that these recommendations were the results of a study group I had put together composed of soldiers from various units that I had met with for ten days. The soldiers had gone back to their units, briefed their commanders, and come back with feedback. Then we'd put together a final plan, coordinated with the unit commanders and briefed the general with those commanders present.

The plan was approved. It included building-block training conducted around the unit level, and we called it "People with People Day." The plan called for feeding EO issues up through the chain of command, with the Commanders Panel for Affirmative Actions as the channel for communicating back down the chain. We also put into place a Fort Lewis Rainbow Week, which we used to establish harmony between racial and ethnic groups by showing and celebrating similarities in music, art, food, and dress and to create an appreciation for the heritage and culture of others.

Cavazos took care of his soldiers, saw what I was doing, and was really impressed. He wanted to keep me in the Army and, since I was due to be discharged, he went to the Pentagon's Department of the Army about it. He asked that I be retained on active duty. They said I'd have to become a warrant officer, and I didn't want to do that. I was looking forward to joining the Boeing Company instead. So I got out of the regular Army and joined the reserves.

By the time I formally retired from the Army on my birthday in 2000, I'd received a number of awards. These began with two Bronze Star Medals for Meritorious Achievement in Ground Combat Operations against hostile forces in the Republic of Vietnam for the years 1967 and 1972. I then was awarded three Meritorious Service Medals, one in 1977 from the Fifth Signal Command, the first oak leaf cluster in March 1978 from the Ninth Infantry Division and Fort Lewis, Washington, and the third presented in 1992 from the Adjutant General and Secretary of the Army for the previous ten years of service in the Pentagon as a citizen soldier. The Fifth Signal Command also honored me with a Certificate of Achievement in August 1975.

I also received an Army Commendation Medal for Meritorious Service at Fort Carson, Colorado, in 1971; the first oak leaf cluster for Meritorious Service at the Fifth Signal Command in 1976; and the second oak leaf cluster for Meritorious Service at Headquarters U.S. Army Europe and Seventh Army in 1977; as well as the Combat Infantryman badge and Airborne badge.

Finally, I received an award called the Republic of Vietnam Staff Service Medal, First Class. It was awarded by the Republic of South Vietnam's Military Region 2 for the period from February 26, 1971, to October 12, 1971. During that time I was serving as the adjutant general for Advisory Team 21 in Military Region 2 of Vietnam's Military Assistance Command. It notes, "Major Black demonstrated outstanding initiative and devotion to his assigned staff duty during the stated period of service."

We all appreciate rewards and recognition as part of doing our jobs, whether in the military or civilian world. I'll not toot my horn about the awards I received in combat, where we were expected to perform, including risking our lives if necessary. Being a civilian would be a different matter, especially when corporate politics raised its ugly head, but in either case not for General Patton. Patton led his soldiers by example, and he was always willing to personally get into the fight, whether political or on the battlefield. For example, he was shot in the leg during World War I after exposing himself repeatedly to enemy fire.

Patton didn't mince words and some of you reading my story may have wished I'd minced a few. Shortly after the Japanese bombed Pearl Harbor on Dec. 7, 1941, Patton began giving his now-famous "blood and guts" speeches at Fort Benning. They were often profane, but direct. "This individual heroic stuff is pure horse shit," he told troops on June 5, 1944, before D-Day. "The bilious bastards who write that kind of stuff for the *Saturday Evening Post* don't know any more about real fighting under fire than they know about fucking!" I certainly was no Patton, and I can't think of any time in combat where I deliberately exposed myself to enemy fire. I'm proud of all my military awards, but I'm most proud of the military and, later, civilian awards I would receive for improving workplace conditions and bringing people together to solve problems.

My Vietnam experiences would continue to haunt me, sometimes in nightmares and other ways I wasn't consciously aware of. But it would be another decade before I finally turned to music to help me exorcise those ghosts and reconnect with both the good memories and bad that I had from those years.

CHAPTER 8: NEW BEGINNINGS & A LONG-SIMMERING ENDING

How does it feel?
How does it feel
To be without a home
With no direction home
Like a complete unknown?
Like a rolling stone?

—*Bob Dylan, "Like a Rolling Stone"*

When I left the Army, I took a job in racial relations education and training with Boeing's commercial airplane division. My first title there was Equal Employment Opportunity (EEO) officer. It was a really tough job, having to deal with a lot of sensitive issues without getting management upset at you and getting fired. For instance, a woman named Eleanor, one of the few women superintendents at Boeing in 1979, came to me about a friend of hers who was a secretary. She said this woman's boss, a vice president, was chasing her around the desk all the time. Eleanor asked if I could help this woman out.

I wrote up a letter addressed to the guy, saying, "We are aware of the fact you're discriminating by harassing your secretary. It's a violation of company policy and you'd better stop immediately." I didn't sign it, so he didn't know who it was from. But the next day, he called her in and apologized, and he didn't bother her again. That's the kind of stuff I did—figuring out how to help people but not making any boss so mad that the wrong person got fired. I always tried to protect those with a legitimate issue.

While in that job, I designed an equal opportunity program that included comprehensive training to support line managers. I accomplished it by working at all levels in the chain of command, down to the factory floor crews. I also brought in a consulting company specializing in EEO management to help me put together a detailed presentation showing overall progress on upward mobility for women and minorities in the company for the past five years by division and department.

We kicked off the program in the large cafeteria of Boeing's Renton Division facility. All supervisors, general foremen, and superintendents, plus managers at the first level and above, were required to attend. That included the directors of operations, manufacturing, and human resources. The 737 jet assembled at Renton had already been in production for a decade and was on its way to becoming the most-ordered plane in commercial history, a milestone it would reach by 1987. More than 10,000 are in service today. In 1978, many thousands of employees and managers were involved onsite in its production.

Introduced by the director of operations, I presented a detailed plan, with copies for all those present, that outlined clearly defined goals and objectives for recruitment and upward mobility of women and minorities. The presentation included the overall status at that time and the plan to increase the number of minorities and women among the employees and improve their upward mobility. Communication and examples set by the senior leaders would help make changes in behavior. I presented slide after slide that demonstrated minimal progress to that point; the lines on the charts were pretty much flat.

Right in the middle of my presentation, Eleanor stood up on the desk where she was sitting and in a booming voice said something like, "This is absolutely horseshit. I've had to claw my way to the top to become a superintendent. There is no way, Mr. Black, that the management in this room is going to embrace and support the tough goals and objectives in this plan." When she sat down, I said, "Well, Eleanor, I disagree because every manager in this room will be measured by their support of this program, and those who do not support it will have their own upward mobility impacted."

I got high marks for the plan, and there were clear marching orders for all leaders present to move forward. Finally we were beginning to make progress. The Renton Division EEO program became the model for Boeing. The effort was estimated to have saved Boeing millions of dollars in potential lawsuits by addressing complaints and issues immediately, before they could become formal complaints and move to arbitration.

I was learning that Boeing leaders above me didn't subscribe to the common belief that the higher you go up the chain of command, the more you talk and the less you listen. Many Boeing leaders listened to me, at least, all the way to the corporate office.

For instance, in walking through the factory as I did every day, I observed a general foreman named George who had a bad habit of walking along with a cigarette in one hand, kicking over the cans that contained scrap and letting go a long streak of profanities. I asked to see him in his office. I suggested that rather than kick the cans over and yell at workers he might try stopping and talking to them, asking them how they are doing. He stopped the behavior after our talk.

I also was successful in developing good relationships with the corporate EEO office, which resulted in the spread of my efforts throughout Boeing. It was tough working with factory managers who had tough production goals to achieve, but my experience as an Army officer in combat roles had given me communication skills that worked.

In December 1978, I got a Special Incentive Award and commendation letter from CEO and Chairman of the Board Thornton "T.A." Wilson and President E.H. "Tex" Boullioun. The company's first incentive award given for EEO assignments, it came with a $1,000 award. Those were hard awards to get! The letter cited my outstanding contribution toward the implementation of an equal opportunity awareness and development program so widely accepted that other divisions of the company had or were in the process of adopting similar programs.

I also received a Certificate of Outstanding Performance from the superintendent of the largest factory organization, known as R-3300. It said in part, "Your dedication and creativity have resulted in an EEO program that is not only beneficial to the R-3300 organization, but to the Boeing Company in general. The time and effort you have put into this endeavor has been exceptional and the results most gratifying." Also, received the same from my boss which said, "Special attention is given to your achievement in developing an awareness of EEO with all levels of management and employees in the Division which exceeds all previous efforts."

I was soon promoted, first to personnel manager in the 737 factory and then to productivity manager for the 757 division. I was the first to introduce the ideas of quality gurus Dr. W. Edwards Deming and Dr. Joseph Juran to the company, and I eventually got Boeing management to commit to using the Toyota Production System (Lean). A lot of that story is in my business books, especially my first book, *A World Class Production System* (Crisp Management Library, 1998), as well as *Lean Production: Implementing a World Class System* (Industrial Press, 2008), and both editions of *The Toyota Way to Healthcare Excellence* (Health Administration Press, 2008 and 2016). I was in the trenches of the "quality revolution" of the 1980s, first in 1980 for the Boeing Commercial Airplane Company (BCAC) 757 airplane program, moving to Boeing Aerospace (the company's military division) in 1983, where I was named productivity manager. I worked for BCAC again in 1985. The Lean transformation at Boeing was an incredible challenge, and I loved it.

A Christmas with Grandma Harootunian in the 1970s

I got employees much more involved in Boeing's quality improvement and productivity efforts, and I was responsible for training thousands of employees in the quality principles and processes championed by Toyota. In 1982, Ernie Fenn, vice president and general manager of Boeing's 757 program, asked me, "What can we do to make the 757 program into a more participative culture?"

I told him that we couldn't change how employees behaved without changing how managers behaved and that, to succeed, this change had to start with him. He asked me how long it would take to answer his question in more detail. After some research and discussion with leaders and employees at many levels, I appeared in his office a month later with a four-foot-by-six-foot cardboard model I'd put together.

"This is it," I told Fenn. "This is our process for increasing employee involvement, and we should get to work on implementing it."

He agreed. I reported to a great human resources director and brilliant guy, John Bassett. He supported my efforts completely and went with me to every session with Ernie. The model became a plan, the plan became a handbook, and the handbook in turn became a process that permeated Boeing's 757 production program.

Some of my productivity work with the 757 program involved a special assignment at Eastern Airlines in 1982. The 757 employee involvement program had become so successful that Phil Condit, chief engineer and later vice president, briefed a customer about it—former astronaut Frank Borman, who'd circled the moon in Apollo 8 and later became chairman and CEO of

Eastern Airlines. Afterward, Borman asked that I be assigned to Eastern to help them implement a similar program. I was sent to Eastern headquarters in Miami to try to work with the company and the unions for the pilots, the flight attendants, and the machinists. I reported to Borman, who was a former astronaut, and Marv Amos, the senior vice president of personnel. They'd been struggling, and Borman had shut off the fountain in their outer lobby and told people that it wasn't going to be turned back on again until they got things turned around.

Two senior Boeing executives—the directors of manufacturing and of program management—went with me to get started at Eastern. I'm sure they were a bit nervous as I was still only a supervisor and had not made it into management yet. But Conduit had sold me as a game-changer and I did not intend to disappoint my bosses or Boeing. We met Borman and his team, and I was officially handed over to Eastern as the 757 employee involvement guru. I was to report on a dotted-line relationship to Marv Amos, with an office next to his, and on a direct reporting line to Borman. When I walked my Boeing bosses out to the limo that would take them back to the airport and Seattle, I asked, "How long do you want me to stay here?"

Seven weeks, they told me, and then we'd see how things were going. Midway through the assignment, since I was away from home every month, I requested approval for Eastern to bring my three children to Miami so they could visit Disney World. My kids were excited to come with me, and I appreciated Eastern's generosity.

Over eight months later, I had made many trips to Miami, working with Borman and his management team, including Charlie Bryan, the head of Eastern's Machinists Union, as well as the union leaders representing the airline pilots, transportation workers, and flight attendants. I told them that the first thing we needed to do was form a planning team, with representation from all the unions, to identify what needed to be improved, including the relationship with those unions and how Eastern could be more profitable. Amos gave me a list of who he wanted on the planning committee. I took the list and showed it to a bunch of union people, who said, "That's Amos' list, that's not who we'd want."

So I put the people the unions wanted, including some of their leaders, on the team instead. Amos raised hell with me. He had a Folger's coffee can on his desk that was full of quarters, because his secretary insisted he drop a quarter into this swear jar every time he cursed. It was half full already and he should've filled it, because he swore and chewed me out a lot when he heard what I'd done.

I said, "This is who we're going to have on the committee, and I'll go to Frank Borman if I need to." I also described the training and team-building we were going to do. He swore some more.

"You don't have a budget," he said. "You can't do this."

I asked him what he knew about the American Productivity Center and told him I'd talk to them about it.

"No, you're not," he said, but I talked to people at the center, and they told me they'd send Dick Siegle, a famous arbitrator, to help. I signed a $17,000 contract for Siegle's support. He flew to Miami, and when he got off the plane he was carrying this big briefcase that was obviously very heavy.

I told him we had to go talk to Amos, and that he was going to yell but how we'd handle it. Siegle, who was shorter than Amos, was very nervous.

When we went into Amos' office, he was on the phone, so we were waiting, standing behind this huge glass coffee table. Dick's briefcase was shaking, but I told him to calm down.

Finally Amos slams the phone down and said to me, "What do you want now?"

"I'd like to introduce Dick Siegle," I said.

Amos stood up. "You son of a bitch!"

Dick dropped his briefcase in the center of the coffee table. *Crash!* It broke in half, with both pieces passing each other through the air, glass and chaos everywhere. The secretary ran in. Things went downhill from there.

But I just kept going in that assignment, despite Amos, and we got a lot done. The first thing I required of Borman was that he and his team, along with other senior leaders and the union leaders, go through an exercise called Desert Survival that we had used extensively at Boeing. He and Amos objected. They asked me the wrong question: "Why?"

I told them, "Because my initial assessment of your culture, after personally interviewing workers, managers, and executives, is that all of your direct reports think everything is going great but the rest of the chain of command doesn't. They seem to like your authoritarian style of management, but the rest of the team down to the hourly employees believe you are trying to rule your people, and it isn't working. If Eastern is going to survive in the tough business you're in, then you and your direct reports and board members need to adopt a democratic style of leadership. This means listening, not directing, and including everyone in the decision-making process."

I then took a deep breath and explained Desert Survival, which would take place in two teams at the local Marriott hotel. Dick Siegal, an American Productivity Center consultant and recognized labor/management expert, would help me facilitate. "The $17,000 consulting fee you paid covers Dick Siegal's time." As I explained, they continued to look more and more irritated.

I briefly covered the situation that the exercise would place them and the rest of their team in—a crash landing in a desert. I added, "Mr. Borman, I'm making you the team leader. Your job will be to get your people out alive after the crash by taking input from your team members in a participative way, putting the team and their survival first. That is the mission. The question you will need to ask yourself is, 'Does the EAL team have what it takes to survive?'

After the exercise was completed, I was disheartened to announce that the Borman team scored the lowest of any management teams that had done the exercise at Boeing Aerospace or Boeing Commercial.

I went back and forth between Seattle and Miami about eight times, and ultimately got really high marks for the job I did there. The people on my team were great, including Edwina "Winnie" Gilbert, who eventually became the company's vice president of in-flight service. They were big into quality circles, and their success rubbed Amos the wrong way, but the project got a good writeup in a *Harvard Business Review* case study. The *Review* noted:

> "Boeing as a company had the credibility with Eastern that they needed, and Black—as the designer of the 757 participation program which had so impressed Eastern managers to begin with—had his own influence. The consultants leaned for a while on Black's credibility until they were able to develop sufficient credibility of their own."

With support from Boeing, I received my MBA from City University. Prior to 1983 I started putting together the commercial airplane group's first team of quality circles. Ten million employees in Japan participated in such groups, and like many companies in the United States, the Fabrication Division was engaging in a similar program. Circles became a hit at Boeing, a home run with the union and with the hourly employees who participated. The circles were collecting data, and despite only meeting weekly as a team, they were making significant improvements.

Boeing's corporate media team had produced a great video about quality circles and it was shown throughout the company. The industrial engineers were not fond of the concept, however; they felt getting rid of waste was their job. They perceived the work I was doing—training all employees to identify and eliminate waste using basic Japanese total quality problem-solving tools—as a threat to how they wanted to manage work. I thought the opposite and stuck to my guns. As a result, I was told that the directors of operations and human resources wanted me reassigned.

I had great bosses, who prepared an outstanding letter about my work and circulated it throughout the company. If my bosses had just bowed to pressure and sacked me, Boeing might never have sent managers to Japan or reaped the benefits of a massive infusion of the Toyota Production System, the moving production line, or the Japanese consultants who saved Boeing thousands of labor hours with their Total Quality approach—on and on.

Instead, in 1983 I found myself reporting to Bill Selby, director of operations for the Defense and Space Division of Boeing Aerospace. Bill said to me, "Okay, John Black, what should we do? I've got the Air Force breathing down my neck about poor quality. Can you help me?"

I told Bill, "Absolutely." I told him I'd brought with me five file cabinets full of research and training materials from my work on the Boeing 757 program, as well as the insight I'd gained from Eastern Airlines. We soon embarked on a holistic, people-focused change process. Selby led a continuous quality improvement (CQI) steering committee that I organized, and we became the first at Boeing to start "quality of work life" programs based on concepts being introduced at that time by General Motors and Ford. We sent three bright industrial engineers (one woman and two men) to training at the Quality of Work Life Institute in Dearborn, Michigan, and we were the only aerospace company to participate in GM's culture-change efforts.

Under Selby's direction, we benchmarked several leading companies that he and I visited together. First, though, Bill wanted to present our plan and proposed trip to his boss, Dan Penick, for approval.

What a meeting that was! I sat there as Bill did the pitch and then proceeded to be torn apart by his boss. Bill received a General Patton ass-chewing while I sat there, terrified. Bill Selby did not back down or give in, however. He stuck to his guns. As a result, then, of Selby's leadership, vision, blood and guts attitude, and plain common sense, we went on the trip. When we came back, Bill led the draft of the first Boeing quality plan, and he established the company's first quality center.

Selby and I also conducted the first Boeing supplier symposium focused on quality improvement. The guest speaker was none other than John Wooden, world class basketball superhero and coach. Our program was touted by Boeing Chairman Malcom Stamper as the model that all Boeing sites should be following. Stamper had launched Operation Eagle, a cost-cutting program with big-ass cost-cutting targets—which are much different than targets to eliminate waste, improve flow, and achieve total quality, which *then* gives you big cost reductions. Bill got us a meeting with Stamper, who was a legend. Sitting on his desk were three HP laptop prototypes that weighed about 15 pounds each. He had them all linked together and running some type of experiment. He had just returned from a Boeing film shoot of Stamper in a boat, fishing in Canada with eagles flying everywhere, hence the name Operation Eagle.

Bill briefed Stamper on what Boeing Aerospace was doing and Stamper said, "Well, that's what we are going to do, because that looks like Operation Eagle to me." The cost-cutting guys were not happy, but it was very successful. Before we left Stamper's office I mentioned that I was heading to the Pentagon to do my two weeks of reserve duty in the Office of the Deputy

Chief of Staff for Personnel. Could I borrow one of his portable HPs to try it while impressing the Pentagon that Boeing was always on the cutting edge of technology?

Stamper said, "Absolutely, and please come back and tell me how it went." That's what I did.

In early 1985, BCAC executives came to Selby and said that, based on the success of quality and productivity efforts in Boeing Aerospace, which John Black was key to making happen, "We would like him back." Commercial airplane customers were writing angry letters to the CEO about poor quality becoming commonplace on planes that were in process and delivered. "And our competition is breathing down our necks, taking advantage of the situation." They emphasized that the situation was urgent.

Bill was gracious. The BCAC that had sent me on my way now wanted me back badly. They made me an offer I could not refuse, and I took my six file cabinets back to Boeing Commercial (after I had Selby's team copy it all). Shortly thereafter, I was assigned to report to Jim Blue, vice president of a newly established, central quality assurance organization. I came back to Blue just like I came back to Fenn—with a plan that required we form a quality improvement center (QIC). The vision and wherewithal to tackle this challenge stemmed from my previous military assignments in human resource development and from my initial assignment creating Boeing's EEO program. Those experiences prepared me well to form dynamic teams that could bring about difficult cultural transformation.

As director of the center, my first assignment was to build a team of the best and the brightest, who would quickly figure out how Boeing could improve quality and productivity. The challenge was huge, and we needed an array of firepower. BCAC had 86,000 employees, most of whom had to be taught to do things differently. In addition, many of our managers believed that having the largest market share automatically made Boeing world-class, even though metrics showed that we were not. To kick-start the improvement engine and get us started on the road to true world-class performance, I created a highly skilled "special operations" core team that provided technical support and horsepower. I recruited Joanne Poggetti, an organizational development consultant and president of her own firm. She would lead the development of team leader training, working with Boeing statisticians, two systems administrators, and other key managers, who would document progress and communicate results. Next, I selected 13 upwardly mobile, executive-potential ("expo") candidates representing all of the company's major functional organizations for an intensive, two-year learn/do experience. Everyone was sent to offsite seminars conducted personally by Deming and Juran, who were legendary, and with Bill Conway of Conway Quality.

When the team members came back, they designed and launched 18 quality improvement courses and seminars that would be attended by more than 34,000 employees. We also sent hundreds more managers to seminars by Deming and Juran. In addition, we created innovative partnerships with both of Boeing's major unions, which represented over 30,000 employees. The union business managers eventually had offices next to mine and participated in all training. I personally contacted CEOs and invited them to speak at our two-day "Managing Quality" seminars. They came willingly, with no fee. Due to high demand, these seminars were held at local hotels. Each session was attended by 250 managers, and between 1986 and 1989, a total of 7,297 were educated. Attendees heard from CEOs who were leading quality revolutions at IBM, Ford, Alcoa, Caterpillar, Federal Express, General Dynamics, Harley Davidson, Hewlett-Packard, Honeywell, and Xerox. We had dinners with the visiting CEOs and key Boeing executives to continue the learning.

I also contracted with Bill Conway to conduct one-day seminars at the University of Washington, and we bussed Boeing managers to the university 400 at a time. Conway covered the details of the Toyota Production System and the teachings of Deming, who had been a consultant to Conway's former company. A total of 6,894 managers attended the Conway seminars between 1986 and 1989. At the QIC during the same period, we trained a total of 15,497 people in courses on facilitation, team leadership, team membership, introduction to process control, and quality improvement.

CEO Colin Fox and his firm, Deltapoint Consulting, helped us launch world-class competitiveness training for what eventually became more than 100,000 employees, not only those in our own organization but also in Boeing Aerospace, which was renamed the Defense and Space Group. Over the next ten years, we implemented what by then was becoming known as Lean, adapting Japanese methods to the Boeing culture and sending hundreds of managers to Shingijutsu Kaizen Seminars in Japan.

Soon, people from around the world were coming to see what the Boeing QIC was doing. My first model of implementation for Lean consisted of four steps, and it has been used successfully by others over and over again:

1. Form a team of leaders.
2. Educate them.
3. Establish a sense of urgency.
4. Once they learn, have them do.

On December 1, 1986, I received a Special Incentive Award presented by Dean D. Thornton, then president of Boeing Commercial Airplane Company (BCAC), along with of $3,000. This award recognized my outstanding contribution toward the successful implementation of BCAC's quality process and productivity program. It wouldn't have been a success, however, without the hard work and leadership of Joanne Poggetti and the rest of my team. After three years with Boeing, Joanne returned to her successful consulting practice. She began traveling with Dr. Deming. Japan credits him as one of the inspirations for what became known as Japan's post-war economic miracle of 1950-1960, when the country rose from the ashes of war to become the second largest economy in the world through processes partially influenced by the ideas Deming taught. Joanne was instrumental in getting Boeing management to listen to Deming's wise words about improving quality and productivity. Bruce Gissing, who retired from Boeing in 1994 as executive vice president of operations, was another instrumental leader of Boeing's total quality revolution whom I'll talk more about below.

Ten years later, these efforts would be recognized by a Nov. 11, 1994, *Boeing News* article by Scott Kaseburg, an employee on the A-3200 team.

Time to Celebrate Successes

Let's celebrate our successes. Continous Quality Improvement was started 10 years ago, and it continues to become an integral part of The Boeing Company. Although other CQI-type efforts began earlier, 1984 was the year that Bill Selby, with the assistance of John Black, convinced the top management of the Boeing Aerospace Company that we needed something more to drive improvement than recognition and banners. Early in 1986, both Selby and Black moved to Boeing Commercial Airplane Group and CQI has steadly grown across the entire company ever since.

When CQI was first presented to the 90 Series managers at Aerospace, a bull-of-the-woods manager stood up and said that he had managed in the company for more than 30 years, we were successful with our management methods, and that we wouldn't and couldn't change. Mark Miller, then Executive VP of Aerospace, responded—"You're wrong; we must and we can change."

Volumes should be written about the pain, risk and joy of Bill Selby and John Black who teamed together to make a difference. Although there have been many people who have picked up the CQI vision over the years and made it what it is today, hats off to two individuals who have literally changed the course of an entire company!

One highlight of my career in the 1980s was being appointed to President Reagan's White House Council on Productivity, which advised U.S. defense contractors on improving their productivity. In that capacity, I was present in a closed-door meeting of aerospace executives at the Pentagon; we'd just presented our findings about how the industry could improve productivity to the secretary of state. President Reagan entered the room and personally thanked all of us and our companies for an outstanding piece of work that he'd already reviewed. That work also earned a letter from the White House included in my file at Boeing.

For one special assignment, I went to Van Nuys, California, the location of Nordskog, a Boeing supplier who was building the galleys for the 747. We were having lots of problems with them, so Boeing sent 85 hourly employees to the supplier's factory to help get them on track, and I went down as the team's personnel supervisor. They had an production supervisor, too, but my job was to get everybody paid; as the HR representative, I paid all the employees in cash every two weeks with a draw from the Boeing account at Bank of America. I was also there to help keep up morale, because it was a tough assignment. A lot of drinking went on, and drugs were a problem. Every morning the Boeing supervisor and I would have to go to individual hotel rooms to make sure some of the employees got out of bed.

At the L.A. airport, I met all flights that brought Boeing hourly employees. On one flight with a large number of hourly people, a company executive I didn't know recognized my badge and stood me at attention as he left the plane. He dressed me down for what he thought was inappropriate behavior by our employees on the flight. Later, Boeing's operations executive, Bruce Gissing, had me come to Seattle for a meeting of his direct reports to provide details about the performance issues we were facing, including behavior on the flights and the supplier site.

One day four hourly employees came to me and told me they wanted to take me to Tijuana and show me a good time as a thank-you for being a good supervisor. Two of the guys were Hispanic so they'd pick out the club. We all drove down in my red Pontiac Firebird and went into this club, where we drank all afternoon. I made my record of 20 small martinis for this special event. We probably paid the mariachi band playing the music enough to retire that day, or to buy the club. Nobody had eaten anything, so when we headed back to Van Nuys, the guys asked me to buy them dinner. Their specific request was, "Mr. Black, we know you senior guys go out and have big dinners and drinks, so would you please do the same for us before we go back to the hotel?"

I agreed. As we cruised up toward Van Nuys, I quickly pulled into San Clemente, and I asked around for a good restaurant. We ended up at this fancy restaurant, the maître d' meeting us at the door, despite the fact that we were all casually dressed, with some of the guys wearing overalls. When the waiter came over, I asked him to bring each of us a bottle of wine.

"Are you sure?" he asked. "A bottle each?"

"Yes," I said. Then I ordered a dozen oysters on the half shell for each of us, steak dinners, dessert, and after-dinner drinks. When we got back in the car, the employees were really happy for this great dinner on Boeing.

"You are a great supervisor and we are proud to be working for Boeing," they told me.

The bill was about $800, but I just submitted it on my expense report. The personnel director called me and said, "What the hell are you doing?"

I told him productivity was important, and it had been going down, but that after I took those guys to dinner, it went up.

"Bullshit," he said. "Show me a chart that shows productivity going up after you gave three people dinner."

I told him it had affected the whole team, and I sent him a chart showing productivity low and then rising. He approved my expense report, but he told me that if I ever did it again, I was going to be fired.

In 1983, the *Seattle Times* published a lengthy write-up about the history of the 757 and its design, manufacture, and sale, which in many ways were outside the norm for the company and the industry. Productivity was a key topic, along with the company's culture and employee involvement and motivation, so I was among the managers quoted in the story: "'Pride in the company and its airplanes must be maintained,' said Black, who is enthusiastically proud of both. He even wrote a country-Western song, '757 Fly,' which he calls 'a statement of Boeing culture.' The company had the song recorded in Los Angeles."

The article reprinted some of the lyrics that I'd written in 1981 as a member of the 757 rollout team. I had my music producer in Hollywood record it, as I couldn't make it to the session in Los Angeles. The song was never released as a single, but many copies were provided to employees. After the song's debut, I received many manager and employee requests for a cassette for them to play at the many rollout and singalong parties employees attended.

The 1982 rollout of the 757
(Photo © Boeing; used with permission)

757 Fly
Copyright 1981, words and music by John R. Black, vocals by John Frawley

I was workin' down in L.A., workin' for the railway
When I got a call on the telephone
The man said son you're the lucky one
I happen to be the Boeing recruitin' man
We want you to come up North
By Lake Washington
We're buildin' the world
A new generation plane
(and then he said)

Seven five seven fly, we do more than try
We're the Boeing Airplane Company
And we're callin' you
Seven five seven fly
Buildin' freedom birds for a sky
Full of old Bill's dreams a comin' true.

I packed my bags on the run
Traveled for two days

To report down on the production line
The boss shook my hand
Said, "I'm the factory man"
We'll pay you good and treat you mighty fine.
I'm workin' hard for my pay
But that's what they all say
I know we're buildin' the very best damn planes
(and then he said)

Seven five seven fly
Where angels fear to go
Boeing people build 'em best
Best is all we know
Seven five seven fly
From east to western shore
Planes keep rollin' off the line
The world keeps wantin' more

Now my son is workin,' workin' on the line
Gettin' top dollar for a job he likes to do
I've been workin' here many years
Been through toil and tears
Seen many of my dreams comin' true.
This airplane company
Seems to have a hold on me
We'll be buildin' airplanes 'til the end of time
(and then they'll say)

Keep those airplanes flyin'
Keep those airplanes flyin'
Keep those airplanes flyin'
Seven five seven fly.

Another highlight was the work I did helping to create the aerospace industry's first moving assembly line for the 737, which was based on the Lean principles of the Toyota Production System. The executive leading that effort, Carolyn Corvi, worked tirelessly to make it happen and later became general manager of all airplane production.

In 1990 I was reporting to Bruce Gissing, executive vice president of operations for the Boeing Commercial Airplane Group (BCAG). Early that year, I helped Bruce lead a team of Boeing executives who were involved in leading the company's total quality effort as we embarked on the company's first study mission to Japan. The trips itself took 17 days, and the preparation included 45 hours of classroom training, which in turn required reading five books about the Japanese quality revolution. During the trip, we visited eight companies that were all well into their quality journeys, including the Union of Japanese Scientists and Engineers and, of course, Toyota. As one Boeing executive said, "Thank God Toyota is not in the aerospace industry." On our return Bruce put us on a rigid schedule to implement our action plans from Japan. The formation of the BCAG Strategy Council in February 1991 set the stage for a major full court press focused on world-class competitiveness principles learned in Japan. The rest is history. Six more teams would follow through the end of 1991, a total of 99 executives, including chairman and CEO Frank Shrontz and all of Boeing's presidents, general managers, and other executives down to the director level.

These visits taught us that the basis of competitive success was shifting away from technology as a competitive advantage toward greater efficiency in manufacturing and process development by applying total quality control as the management system.

Many executives and managers didn't want to read the books before these trips, saying, "We don't have time." So CEO Frank Shrontz told me, "Black, go into the Boeing studio and do an audio tape for each book so my executives and I can listen in the car." That way they'd be able to pass the quizzes on each book.

Boeing's studio set me up, and I read *Kaizen* by Masaaki Imai, *Companywide Total Quality Control* by Shigeru Mizuno, and *Attaining Manufacturing Excellence* by Robert Hall. Thanks to my music background, I've got a good speaking voice, and in addition to reading the books, I highlighted key areas and winged it. Everybody listened to the audio, passed the quizzes, and felt they learned something valuable, so I was a hero.

In the years since I'd worked directly for him, Bill Selby had been reassigned to the Commercial Division as director of operations at the Everett plant, and later he'd be asked to run the Auburn division. He went with Bruce Gissing's team and me to Japan in 1990 on the Boeing's first Japan study mission. Bruce was impressed with Bill's performance in Japan. After we came back, Selby was the only—yes, the only—executive participant who asked to take a team of his own to Japan. Gissing approved that trip, too. Selby and his team came back and began aggressively implementing at Auburn what he had learned on both trips. He was a true quality leader who helped spread the ideas through the organization.

The leadership development process I'd created through the quality improvement center in the 1980s evolved in the 1990s into the Boeing Production Systems Specialists Program, which in 2002 evolved further into a program called Kaizen Fellows, technicians focused on Total Quality.

By 1996, I'd become director of Lean manufacturing education and training support, responsible for best practices, managing all external consultants, expanding our Lean knowledge base, and handling employee training and certification. Boeing soon began to focus on kaizen events. In 1997, we called them Accelerated Improvement Workshops, and we conducted more than 100 in the first two months of that year. More than 6,000 employees participated in 756 kaizen events over two years, demonstrating the degree to which improvement was becoming part of their jobs. Between 1997 and March 1999, these workshops saved $900 million in costs; reduced inventory by 313,689 units for a savings of $156 million; and cut distances traveled by workers by nearly 7 million feet (almost 1,300 miles!), saving $342 million in labor hours. They also reduced cycle times by 43,173 hours for a savings of $4.3 million; eliminated 48,680 hours of lead time, saving $4.8 million; reduced setup times by 5,303 hours, saving $1 million; and freed 146,443 square feet of floor space, saving $286 million. That adds up to a lot of savings!

By the time I retired in 1999, I'd earned a certificate of achievement for the 757 airplane program, which was presented by Erne Fenn, vice president and general manager, in February 1982; two special incentive awards, one in 1978 and one in 1986; and numerous other awards and letters of recommendation.

My music was going well, too. Before heading to Germany, I'd bought a four-track Sony recorder, and while still in Heidelberg, a couple of friends and I had used it in Liz's apartment to record three songs I've already mentioned: "Lonely Cowboy Dreams," "Flower Child of Springtime," and "Rock and Roll Mary." Back in the States, our house had a garage that became a great place to record more songs with that Sony.

My sister Julie and I had both been writing songs, and that four-track recording setup gave my brother James, Julie, and me the opportunity to do some recording together. By then, I'd written but not recorded more than a dozen songs since 1962:

> The Day You Left Town
> A Dead Man's Tale
> Hope That I Don't Die
> I'm Tired
> Jennie Ann
> Ma-Ling-Na
> The Undertaker
> The End
> The Western Blues
> Donkey Go My Way

Once living there in Puyallup, I recorded many of those and a few more in our garage. The new ones included:

Jennie Ann
People Talk
New Life
Out Along this Way

When Mt. St. Helens erupted in 1980, I also wrote a song called "Harry Truman's Mountain." Harry lived on the mountain, and he refused to move when the area was evacuated. He died in his cabin. Right after Mt. St. Helens blew, Air Force pilot Bill McLure and I wrote and recorded the song together. It got play on Seattle radio stations. In addition, my sons Shane and Ben had fun working up and recording four more songs, "I'm All Shook Up," "Be Poppa," "Trip Around the World," and "Life of Bog Wog" on the Sony four-track.

In the mid-1980s, I also began working with a producer in California, and took a couple of trips to record with him in a studio there. When we could afford it, Paula also continued to spend occasional summers at the family homestead. After one summertime trip she'd taken home from Germany with the kids, my Mom told me Paula was thinking of not coming back.

Nonetheless, we stayed together. I think all my affairs came right out of my abuse by Father Knecht. I never really trusted male friends, and I really don't have many male friends even now. Though there were plenty of military colleagues I drank and partied with, I felt like I could only trust women, and I think that's why I was so inclined to affairs. Those women all had some issue with their husbands, too, whether it was wanting to leave them, or being beaten or abused.

And Paula had her own demons, which didn't help. One of those was an inability to control her spending. As a result, our family finances were often in a terrible state, and she was constantly bouncing checks, sometimes writing hot checks to get from one payday to the next. That affected not only our marriage but also my career. I went to Consumer Credit to set up a good plan for paying off debts and getting our finances back on track, and I cashed in favors to get her an hourly job at Boeing that paid well to help bring in more money. She quit that job the first day. I asked her why, because the Boeing HR rep was upset with me; he'd pulled strings to get Paula hired. All she said was, "All the women smoked."

The abuse I'd suffered in childhood kept haunting our family, too, sometimes in ways we didn't realize right away. After we moved to Puyallup, we reconnected with Father Reinard Beaver. I knew Father Beaver from Gonzaga University, where I'd seen him several times riding around campus in the back seat of a convertible, along with several college guys and a jug of beer. He'd been the priest for Spokane's St. Aloysius parish. I also knew that Beaver had been involved in taking the Chad Mitchell Trio, which started there at the college, to New York to help launch their careers.

Father Beaver had been assigned to Fort Carson while we were there, too. The kids remembered him from their childhood there as well as his visits to Spokane during the Vietnam years.

What I didn't know then was that Father Beaver was also an abusive priest. Eventually he retired as a lieutenant colonel after working as a chaplain for Madigan Army Hospital, and he continued to occasionally serve Mass at Fort Lewis, where we attended as a family. He became like our family priest, coming over to our house and officiating at family events, and several times our whole family stayed overnight at Beaver's house in Steilacoom.

He betrayed us completely. Beaver would abuse my son Ben. I later would learn that Ben was first victimized at age twelve or thirteen by Father David Jaeger while at a Catholic Youth Organization (CYO) camp, Camp Don Bosco, in the early 1980s. Jaeger was from the Seattle Archdiocese. Ben didn't mention what had happened, of course, no more than I'd told my parents about similar abuse. He didn't even have words for what had happened to him, thinking only that it was shameful and not to be discussed.

Unfortunately, Ben's trauma didn't end there. Beaver began grooming him when he was about thirteen or fourteen and then sexually abused him for roughly three years. Meanwhile, Beaver—our family's representative of God—visited with our family at holidays, gave Paula advice, counseled the kids, promised to help Ben with his music, and took him along on short trips such as to Canada, Oregon, and Eastern Washington. We agreed to those trips, thinking they were a great opportunity for Ben. In fact, the abuse happened in hotel rooms and in Beaver's house.

"We trusted and loved him, but he was grooming me," Ben recalled later. Beaver took advantage of him when we all spent the night at Beaver's house by sometimes putting the boys up in a bed right next to his own. Alcohol was apparently often involved in the abuse.

As parents, you think, "This is a priest, he wouldn't abuse anyone," and maybe part of the problem was that I hadn't really come to grips with the abuse that had happened to me, but even I thought Beaver was different from Knecht. It later came out that he wasn't.

Not until after our family disintegrated, though. Paula and I both had a lot of anger that unfortunately we took out on each other and the kids. Before we married, she'd told me she was abused by an uncle of hers in Lewiston starting when she was twelve. I also found out, though she never told me, that she'd had a baby by a fellow student while in high school in Lewiston. Her sister, Susie, also may have had children out of wedlock. Both girls might have been searching for love they didn't get at home, because Paula told me her mother had beaten them with a shoehorn on many occasions. She recalled one incident when she was about four or five years old when her mother caught her doing something she didn't like: "I was beaten within an inch of my life, which happened often." When she tried to talk about the sexual abuse she was suffering, she was called a sinner and was told she was no good and cursed by the devil. Even in later life her mother, Magda, refused to believe that Paula had been abused.

Apparently her mother didn't mellow with time, either. The first time I was in Vietnam, Paula visited me on our Hawaii R&R that year. To do so, she left the kids with her mother. Later, Shane said, "Don't ever leave us with Grandma Magda again. She treated us terribly."

I often felt that Paula's intense anger, which came out towards me, was partially a result of this abuse, while the anger that came out from me was a result of alcohol and my own abuse by Father Knecht. We had terrible fights.

That kind of anger affected the kids, too. Paula and Heidi had a fight while Heidi was in high school, and Heidi ran out of the house. As soon as she graduated, she moved away to Seattle, and we didn't see her at all for a year. That made me sad. Toward the end of her life, Paula wrote a three-page letter to me and the kids, explaining some of her anger and the abuse that had caused it and begging us to forgive her.

Meanwhile, I had another affair. Paula and I, with another member of our parish, were working on raising money for the Tacoma opera. In doing so, we went to the house of a woman named Janet, who was from a wealthy family. She was married to a retired military officer who she said abused her. In my opinion, she also was bipolar, so very unpredictable. For instance, one night we were riding around in her red Pontiac and she pulled into a Ford dealer in Tacoma. A new Ford sedan had just come out, and she decided to buy one right there on the spot. We drove away in the new Ford. I introduced her to my kids, wrote her a song called "Forever Please Love Me," and took her with me to one of my recording sessions in California, where I recorded it.

My job at Boeing was going very well. I worked closely with Joanne Poggetti, who I'd hired, and I got to know her well and respect her. After she left Boeing, we stayed in touch.

My marriage to Paula was just about over. I was seeing Janet and I continued to drink, coming home to have a martini and then a couple glasses of wine. As our kids grew older, Paula got involved in more volunteer activities in the community. Plus, in 1986, she started a catering business she called Parties by Paula. Heidi and Shane had already left home for Seattle, with Shane attending the University of Washington there. He graduated in 1986, which made me proud. Heidi was entering the automotive business and, with hard work, would become a general manager. Ben, who turned 20 the year Shane graduated from the UW, followed shortly behind them. After attending Edmonds Community College and touring the West Coast with a vocal jazz group, he enrolled at Seattle's Cornish College of the Arts, where

I covered some of his tuition. He completed two years there but did not get a degree because he was struggling with PTSD related to abuse and addiction, though I didn't realize all that at the time. His departure from school disappointed me, as he is a gifted musician, but he did continue to pursue music, releasing CDs and performing.

So our nest had been emptied, but my life was about to take an even bigger turn. By late 1987 or early 1988, I started meeting Joanne for coffee, now that we no longer worked together. Realizing that I needed a therapist who could help me with my drinking problem, I found one. I told the therapist I had a problem. She said, "Let's see if you really do. Come back next week and tell me you haven't had a drink." I came back in a week and told her I'd had a drink every night, so she advised treatment.

I took her advice. Boeing had a 30-day alcoholism treatment program that I entered in February 1988. The treatment program was like a military setting, with bunk beds. My journal entry for February 17, 1988, reveals my thoughts then:

> I am in the Care Unit in Kirkland. I did not exactly come voluntarily. I am vacillating between whether I have or do not have a problem with alcohol. I don't drink a fifth a day, but I drink every day. I am dependent on drinking something every day. Plus, I have been drinking and driving. If I get a DWI I will be in big trouble, court costs, etc. So, what I am doing is prevention. I drink too much. I always have. I have to have the final drink. I'm the last one to have the last drink. I am going to miss not drinking because I really enjoy it. Having a cold beer after work is great—but I don't need it, it is not necessary. Not having a clear head was great in Vietnam because everyone either had a hangover or was stoned. I have just talked to the people in my office and they all support what I'm doing. So does everyone else. What Pablo Casals says is true: "The main thing in life is not to be afraid to be human."

My time in the care unit was a Godsend. I felt the love, hope, and trust of the other patients. Many put handwritten notes in my diary, and one in particular brought tears to my eyes:

> "John, the Care Unit has done so much for me that I will never forget it, and you, John, are one of those that really make it work. I was impressed with you from the first time I saw you—straightforward, no nonsense, all

business—but then you sang your song for the first time and I knew that was just a shell—inside was a sentimental old softy."

It was a relief to stop drinking. I'd known for a long time that it was a problem. Paula had probably been right when she'd said it would hurt my career if I'd gone into treatment sooner; in many ways the military was powered by alcohol. But now that I was retired from the military, that was no longer an issue.

The therapists in the program were great. We dealt with all these issues, from my parents' drinking to my abuse by Father Knecht. This is when I told my parents and the rest of my family about that abuse; it all came out. That was like a dam bursting—not only my abuse, but Ben's, too. He and I were mostly estranged at that point, but when I revealed the sexual abuse I had suffered, Ben told me what had happened with Father Beaver. He had decided previously that when it came to Beaver "messing with him," he "wouldn't tell Mom and Dad."

"You just don't talk about this," Ben says now. "But then we had this one-on-one while Dad was in alcohol treatment and I just blurted it out. I told him Father Beaver had messed with me. I didn't have the words yet to call it sexual abuse."

Of course I was horrified. I had plenty of reason to believe him, however, whereas my mother and dad had a hard time believing my abuse by Father Knecht. I told Mom I thought she and Dad had problems with alcohol, too. They did not want to have anything to do with that. They couldn't believe what I was doing and did not want to admit they had any issue, but they did. I remember taking the family to visit them after they'd moved from Spokane back to the family homestead. One time we all went together to the store and Mom picked up a big jug of wine. Shane told her, "You shouldn't do that." She replied, "We're social drinkers, we can do what we want."

I wanted to put issues like that behind me, and when I got out of treatment, it felt as though I was starting a whole new life. I attended Alcoholics Anonymous (AA) meetings, and Paula and I separated in May 1988. I moved out of our family house in Puyallup, got an apartment in Des Moines, closer to Boeing, and filed for divorce. Once the divorce was final, my Aunt Fran helped me to pay some alimony. I later paid her back for some of it, but couldn't pay it all, as I gave Paula about $2,500 a month. At the hearing, my attorney said to the judge presiding over our case, "Your honor, we are requesting that the payment of alimony be concluded per the date you set previously." The female judge extended the payment period past the settlement date, saying, "Mr. Black is an executive at Boeing; they pay well and he can afford it."

I had moved into an apartment near Seattle and was still seeing Janet. She told me she was going to Hawaii for two weeks and that maybe we should end our relationship. I didn't think I'd be seeing her again, and was both relieved and yet hoping we'd see each other again.

One night very late came a knock at my door. It was Janet. She said, "I need to spend the night here with you." I was glad to see her. Early the next morning, I heard someone at the front door and realized I hadn't locked it after letting her in. I looked through the curtain and saw it was her husband, who by then was slowly opening the door. I became very anxious because Janet had told me he kept a gun in his car. I also knew also he had beaten her.

What then took place was very bizarre. Her husband came in and sat down on the couch with no gun that I could see.

"Would you like a cup of coffee?" I asked him. I could see Janet getting dressed in the bedroom as I started to make the coffee. When it was ready, I brought Janet's husband a cup and we started to talk.

Janet walked in, all dressed. Her husband said, "Thanks for the coffee, John. We have to go." I breathed a sigh of relief as they walked out the door, quickly locking it after them.

I was starting a new life, all right. But not everything about that was exciting. Fortunately, the music that had been a part of my entire life was one of the things I'd carry forward into my new life.

CHAPTER 9: MUSIC, NEW LOVE, & HEALING

Will I ever know your name?
Will you come and sleep with me
Forever in the morning dew?
Will you come and hold me close
and take my heart so true?

—*John R. Black, "Flower Child of Springtime"*

After leaving Paula, I spent the 1988 holidays at my parents' homestead. It was an introspective winter homecoming for me. I was single for the first time in more than 20 years. My kids were grown and there was significant distance between us. Vietnam continued to haunt me in many ways, often without me being aware of it, but there at the homestead, something just clicked. I realized that, among other things, the time had come to face my Vietnam past and how it was still affecting me.

I wrote three songs to try to exorcise the demons. I'd also written "Vietnam, I'm Dreamin', Dreamin' On" while still in treatment. When I got out of treatment, I hosted a dinner and invited my boss at Boeing, Executive Vice President Bruce Gissing. I thanked him and the company for their support and handing out autographed and framed copies of the song. All these songs helped me confront my nightmares, my guilt, my despair, and the idea materialized for my first album, *Vietnam Farewell*. I didn't pretend to know the answers, and I still don't, but music gave me a way to try to figure out my Vietnam experience.

Then I relapsed. One mistake I made was going to Boeing's vice president of quality and suggesting to him that Boeing give Janet a Pride in Excellence

Award, a company award that wasn't normally given to community members. I explained that I'd been working with someone in Tacoma who'd done great work in getting opera better established in the community, and that the award might help Boeing community relations. He agreed and she got the award, which included a lunch in Boeing's executive dining room.

Then the VP found out I was having an affair with her. He was really pissed about it, and I got a written reprimand and 90 days to get my act together, which included reporting back to him. It's probably a wonder I wasn't fired, but my direct boss spoke to the VP and convinced him not to fire me. "That's what recovering alcoholics do," he explained. I apologized and met the requirements for fixing my behavior. It was a good reminder about how the road to recovery sometimes includes backsliding.

I spent more time with Joanne and ended the relationship with Janet. Janet had come to visit me during my treatment, but I knew Joanne had to be part of my new future. I moved into Joanne's Seattle home in November 1989, and we married on November 25. I was happy to be marrying her and starting a new life, but I would never forget Paula, either. We'd spent so many years together.

But military service is hard not only on soldiers but their families. It's not a regular 9-to-5 job. The hours vary, so family time often suffers. At best, spouses and kids face frequent moves away from other family members, friends, and schools and lengthy absences by the soldier for training or deployments. During times like the Vietnam War, these hardships are complicated by battlefield deployments and constant fear of loss. Before the Internet, communication was limited to letters and the occasional audio tape or phone call, and those were few and far apart. Even once the soldier returns home, reintegration is no easy task. Family routines are completely disrupted, and kids have to get to know the serving parent all over again—and that's not even taking into consideration the effect of injuries, substance abuse habits picked up on deployment, or post-traumatic stress disorder (PTSD).

Today, the annual divorce rate for military families is very close to that for the general population, but a 2003 Brigham Young University study found that Vietnam combat veterans faced divorce 28 percent more often than civilians. (Korean war vets had it even worse.) My marriage to Paula certainly suffered from my career, as well as from the emotional baggage we both carried.

My children didn't attend my wedding with Joanne, and that made me sad, but I understood. Not only had I divorced their mother, but they knew about at least some of my affairs.

Joanne married me in 1989.

Joanne and I didn't have much money to go on a honeymoon, but we did manage to scrape together enough for coach plane tickets to New Zealand. We hitch-hiked and camped our way across that beautiful country in a month-long backpacking trip that started on the North Island. Luckily I took my Boeing business cards with me, which helped our hitchhiking. We'd get picked up by IBM salesmen, and when I handed them a Boeing business card, they were more than happy to drop us where we needed to go.

We made it to the South Island to hike the Milford Trek. I signed us up for the corporate version for $800 a person, as I didn't want to relive Vietnam operations in the forest, which we nearly did anyway because Joanne cancelled my plans and went with the $100 backpacker's version of the trek. She reminded me again, "You are broke, John Black." So we stayed in huts and slept on makeshift bunks. The three-day hike is billed as one of the most beautiful in the world. For us, it rained three days straight, bringing floods that washed out the trail and many of the huts. Our last day, we had to rope up and follow guides for 14 miles to safety. There were 20 hikers in our group, and half of those were statisticians whom Joanne bonded with. At one point, we were waist deep in water and I told Joanne, "This is not a honeymoon; this is like Vietnam."

We finally arrived at Milford Sound. The statisticians invited us to come to the hostel with them. I put my foot down and said, "Not only no, Joanne, but hell no. We are going to stay at the five-star tourist hotel."

With Joanne's dad after our wedding

The hotel was a high-class place that catered to Japanese tourists. We had not bathed for a week, and now we had dirty hiking clothes and bandannas around our heads. Obviously we were no match for the spiffily dressed tourists. I went up to the desk clerk, who was also formally dressed. Behind me, Joanne leaned against the wall, exhausted, with our backpacks propped against her.

In the best English accent, the clerk said, "Sir? May I help you, sir?"

I said, "Yes. You see that woman over there leaning against the wall? That's my wife and we are on our honeymoon, having just escaped with our lives from a flood. We need a room."

He said, "But sir, we have no rooms. No rooms, sir."

"We have not bathed in four days, we're exhausted, we're on our honeymoon from America, and I'm a Vietnam veteran."

He repeated, "But sir, we have no rooms."

"Please go talk to your manager," I said. "Plainly tell him our circumstances and that if you don't give us a room, as a Vietnam veteran, I will burn your hotel down."

"Yes sir. Right away, sir."

About ten minutes later he came back and said, "Sir, we have found a room for you."

I signed us in with a credit card and told Joanne we had a room. In fact, it was a very nice room. Once we got inside, she asked me how I got the room. I told her that once I'd mentioned that I was a Vietnam veteran, that did the trick.

That night we ate rack of lamb in the five-star dining room and had our fellow backpacker statisticians come over from the hostel next door. We treated them to dinner. Joanne and I walked through the dining room in our dirty hiking garb, both of us in ours socks, as if nothing were out of the ordinary.

Paula died ten years later at only 59 years old after complications from an eight-hour heart surgery. She died in Tacoma General Hospital's intensive care unit at about 1:00 a.m. Our three children were with her. The surgeon came into the waiting room after the surgery and said he'd done everything he could.

My kids called me at home, all terribly shaken and sobbing over the phone. As we'd been divorcing, Paula had sent a letter to Shane, Heidi, and Ben, which said in part:

> "I have come to realize how very wrongly I have acted and reacted toward all the terrible things that have happened in the past months. I don't want a divorce, never even thought of that happening to your Dad and I, but here I am in the midst of one. I still love very much the loving father, the loving husband, the loving John that I married 25 years ago. I again ask your forgiveness for all my failings. I want to leave the past in the past and get on with the business of living, not existing."

She never had a chance because I didn't give her a chance. She was a wonderful mother, a wonderful loving wife. Her deteriorating health and death were tragedies, particularly hard on our kids, and my behavior and drinking and the toll of two Vietnam tours certainly contributed to her early death. The bottom line was that I failed Paula. She didn't fail me.

After my marriage to Joanne, I tried to channel the emotions and difficulties of my past into my music projects. Joanne was very supportive of my Vietnam album. Once I got started, I was determined to finish it, for myself and for my fellow Vietnam veterans. About 1991 I went to a book signing by Lewis B. Puller, Junior. He was the son of Marine "Chesty" Puller, a World War II top gun who had been the subject of two books, and he wrote more about his father as part of his own story in *Fortunate Son: An Autobiography* by Lewis B. Puller, Jr. He'd had both legs and most of both hands blown off in a Vietnam mine field, which had prompted his famous father to break down in tears when he first saw his son in the hospital room. Nonetheless, Lewis had later run for Congress, though he lost, and that day, he autographed my copy. Sadly, although his book won the 1992 Pulitzer Prize, he became dependent on drugs and committed suicide a few years later.

Even before then, meeting him helped me to realize how lucky I'd been in Vietnam and that I had no reason to complain about anything. I focused on making music that might help other vets who hadn't been so lucky.

My first recorded album

Once I had the songs written, my good friend Charlie Childers, a Vietnam vet, formed Silver Star Productions to get the project started, and several other generous supporters contributed. Producer John Frawley and sound engineer Richard Rosing deserved special mention for helping me weave my musical story and give name and shape to my grief. The songs on this album included:

> Vietnam Farewell
> Saigon Girl
> Vietnam, I'm Dreamin', Dreamin' On
> Ricky, I'm Right Behind
> I Want to Be Free
> Who Did I Leave Behind?
> Ho Ho Ho Chi Minh
> Oh, Mr. War Memorial
> The Women on the Wall
> I'm Home
> We Don't Have to Worry Anymore
> Vietnam Farewell (Reprise)

I released the album in 1991, and my colleagues at Boeing—many of them veterans, too—were also highly supportive. The Boeing newsletter had an article about me and the album on July 2, 1992, for the Fourth of July, and another in August. The company also paid all the shipping to have free copies of the album sent to nearly 200 Veterans' Centers throughout North America. The album was dedicated to all those vets, and my hope was that the work might help them in some small way just as it was helping me.

I sold copies of the album at the Chewelah Chatauqua Festival in 1992; the festival started around the nation's bicentennial in 1976 and is the valley's longest-running and largest event. The album also was written up in the *Seattle Post-Intelligencer* at the end of that July.

Joanne at my Vietnam Farewell booth in Chewelah

Another article in the *Post-Intelligencer* dated November 11, 1992, and written by Patrick Pilcher said, "Black has been asked to appear at the Sylvan Theater in Washington D.C., for National Reconciliation Day this month to perform songs from the album. He will be a guest at an awards dinner sponsored by a national veteran's organization as a benefit for the founders of the Vietnam Memorial. Boeing has strongly supported his efforts and will pay for his travel expenses."

An article in the *Boeing News* about a week later also referred to the visit in D.C.: "Black reflected on the names of the eight Army and Air Force nurses killed in Vietnam, women he had paid tribute to in his song, 'Women on the Wall.' After the concert he visited the memorial wall and touched their names." I felt really close to those women, and the article quoted me as saying so. It went on, "It is common for visitors to the memorial to place a piece of paper on a name and rub it with a marker.

Transferred to the paper, they become keepsakes." I'd never made any rubbings before but while in D.C. I made rubbings of the names of two veterans I knew, Leonard G. Marcum and Hardy W. Peeples.

My *Vietnam Farewell* album, and several to follow, prompted hundreds of Vietnam vets to contact me, and it was really healing for all of us to connect. I performed some of my songs live at many veterans' centers around the country as well as at the tenth anniversary commemoration of the Vietnam Veterans' Memorial in Washington, D.C., in 1992. I've since performed at the memorial many more times.

Those were highlights of my music career, but more were to come. One veteran, a staff sergeant who served with the First Squadron, First Calvary (1-1 CAV) in Vietnam, sent me a card I thought said it all: "Life's journey is not to arrive at the grave safely in a well preserved body, but rather to skid in sideways, totally worn out, shouting 'Holy shit, what a ride!'"

Cover art by Maria

My youngest daughter, Maria, was born February 9, 1993. We named her in honor of Joanne's mother Marie, and we started her in music early. In fact, my second album, *Maria and Me*, contains songs that Joanne, Maria, and I wrote in a collaborative effort and sometimes sang together. Maria also did the cover art, and she was featured on six of the ten songs:

Maria & Me
Who Ya Gonna Play with Today?
How Old Is Maria?
Abba Dabba Do
What Do You Want to Be When You Grow Up?

Fly Me to Heaven
Shanti Dog
Alligator Man
Where Is Nonnie?
My Sleepy Gal

In some cases, such as "Fly Me To Heaven," Maria wrote and sang the song solo. That one is my favorite:

Fly Me to Heaven
Copyright 1999, music and words by John R. Black and Maria P. Black

Before I go to sleep at night
I kneel down and pray
To my guardian angel
I pray I'll be safe tonight
And my dreams will be
All about my angel
Oh angel way up in the sky
Fly, fly, fly and fly
Fly me to Heaven
Angels up, angels down
Angels flying all around
Fly me to Heaven
Fly me to Heaven
Fly me to Heaven.

After that, I returned to the Vietnam theme. In 1992, I'd met Lieutenant General Harold G. "Hal" Moore and Joe Galloway, the authors of *We Were Soldiers Once and Young.* The soldier pictured on the cover of their book is Lieutenant Rick Rescorla, a highly decorated soldier of the battle. He retired from the military and became a security guard at the World Trade Center in New York. On 9/11 he raced into the building, saving many lives but dying in the tower. There's now a statue to his memory at the 9/11 memorial.

Joe Galloway, Hal Moore, and me in D.C., where I played "Ia Drang"

At the Seventh Cavalry Reunion in Washington, D.C., Moore and Galloway autographed my copy of their book, writing, "For John Black—who put part of this story into a song." It still sits proudly on my shelf, part of my memory of that event, where I performed another of my songs, "Ia Drang." The music video for this song, which is on my website, contains actual footage of the battle synchronized to the lyrics. It was produced by my friend and new American citizen, Joseph Assi.

On November 11, 1993, I participated in the dedication of the Vietnam Women's Memorial, and I returned to celebrate its fifth anniversary in 1998. I would be remiss in this book if I didn't include my long-term brother-and-sister relationship with Diane Carlson Evans, founder and chair of the memorial project. It was Diane who inspired me to write "The Women on the Wall," a song on my *Vietnam Farewell* album that is dedicated to the eight U.S. military women who were lost in the war and whose names are inscribed on the memorial.

At the Vietnam Women's Memorial dedication with Diane Evans

Diane went through her own personal hell during the war. She was a captain in the Army Nurse Corps, but nothing in her training prepared her for the burns, wounds, and suffering she saw during 1968 and 1969, when she was at Vung Tau and Pleiku.

Back home in the 1970s, she married and had children, becoming a full-time mom and traveling to Germany with her husband, who was assigned as Chief of Surgery at the 130th Station Hospital in Heidelberg. She was haunted by memories and nightmares—whirring helicopters, blaring sirens, screams and groans, gaping bloody wounds, limbless torsos, eyeless sockets, napalm and white phosphorous burns, punji stick infections, pit viper snakebites, torture marks—all the sounds and stench of death.

She had a vision, however, and the energy to reach it. She tells her whole remarkable, gut-wrenching story in her book with Bob Welch, *Healing Wounds: A Vietnam War Combat Nurse's 10-Year Fight to Win Women a Place of Honor in Washington, D.C.* (Permuted Press, 2020). I ordered an advance copy and had to read it twice. Pages 47 through 139 made me cry. Right after I finished it, I sent her an email that said, "Diane, you entered the fray with grit that came with the roots of being raised on a farm. You mustered unyielding courage in the face of hardship and danger. You were tested in Vietnam, you volunteered for Vietnam, you volunteered to join the heat of battle as a nurse, then you came home and didn't stop. You kept going with a vision that became the Vietnam Women's Memorial."

She launched the design of the memorial at an event in Washington D.C., that was attended by General Westmoreland. I met him there because I served on the memorial's board for ten years, helping with fundraising and promotion, including through the sale of T-shirts. At that event, I introduced myself to Westmoreland. He asked me, "Do you think your service in Vietnam was valuable?"

I was holding Maria at the time, and I didn't have the guts to say, "No," because he looked so depressed that I felt sorry for him.

Westmoreland, me, and Maria at the Vietnam Women's Memorial design launch

The Vietnam Women's Memorial went forward. It was dedicated on the grounds of the Vietnam Veterans Memorial. I was there as a board member, While still working at Boeing, I'd arranged for the company to host a trip for Diane to Seattle and to make a contribution.

In writing this book I am reminded over and over again of the words of an old French war song: "To each his turn. Today yours, tomorrow mine." War is hell, as they say. You may wonder what that means, and then you read about it but still don't understand.

In their monumental book, Hal Moore and Joe Galloway wrote:

> We were children of the 1950s and John F. Kennedy's
> young stalwarts of the early 1960s. He told the world that
> Americans would "pay any price, bear any burden, meet
> any hardship" in the defense of freedom. We were the
> down payment on that costly contract, but the man who
> signed it was not there when we fulfilled his promise.
> John F. Kennedy waited for us on a hill in Arlington
> National Cemetery, and in time we came by the
> thousands to fill those slopes with our white marble
> markers and to ask on the murmur of the wind if that
> was truly the future he had envisioned for us.

You read that and think of men, soldiers marching off to war, heading for
some distant land to fight an enemy we didn't or don't really understand. And
then you think again about the women and what they did—the women who
went to war. How many times do we not think of them, particularly the
nurses? How many times?

This country had a Civil War where tens of thousands of women were
forced to fend for themselves when the men went off to war. Katharine
Prescott Wormeley knew. She was a U.S. Sanitary Commission volunteer
serving in a Union transport ship in June 1862, moving wounded from
the peninsula battles to hospitals. She said:

> We went on board, and such a scene as we entered and
> lived for two days I trust never to see again. Men in every
> condition of horror, shattered and shrieking, were being
> brought in on stretchers borne by contrabands who
> dumped them anywhere. Men shattered in the thigh and
> even cases of amputation were shoveled into top berths
> without thought or mercy.

Katharine Wormeley knew, and so did Laura Frost in World War I. Near
the battered medieval town of Ypres, she wrote:

> Our casualties were 20 and 30 percent gassed. It caused
> huge blisters on the men and they suffered painfully. We
> became very fond of our patients, a young fellow with a
> bullet hole right in the middle of his forehead. We kept
> trying to get him to talk. All he could say was "glass" but
> he wasn't paralyzed. When he wanted something we

would keep asking him until we hit the right thing and he would nod his head.

But it didn't end with Katharine and Laura, did it? In World War II women served in every branch of the military as clerks, mechanics, administrators, radio operators, photo interpreters, cooks, meteorologists, supply sergeants, test and transport pilots, nurses, and more. They did everything but engage in combat, and General Eisenhower said he couldn't have won the war without them. But they knew about war and they had their personal hell, with their male colleagues telling cruel jokes about them if not actually harassing them. The same was probably not often true of the wounded and their treatment of nurses.

And then Korea and then Vietnam and some still don't understand it all— the women and the war, stories told and then forgotten. Before we came to Vietnam, the "Angel of Dien Bien Phu" knew that war was hell. Geneviève de Galard-Terraube, a French flight nurse, brought a piece of heaven to that hell, much like her female counterparts from the United States would do later. At Dien Bien Phu, surrounded and doomed, she helped horribly wounded men—men with amputations, often double, even triple; men with gaping abdominal wounds; blinded men; men with their brains showing through rents in their skulls; men crying out for their mothers; men with holes where their privates had been. This was Geneviève in Vietnam.

And so the stories go. Some said it was a nice little war, a war in a land of tigers and elephants. We stumbled into a war some wanted forgotten before it started. And there he was, Lewis B. Puller Jr., who wrote *Fortunate Son* and who killed himself in 1994, a casualty of Vietnam. He wrote about his angels of mercy, the women of Vietnam, after he was seriously wounded while a Marine on a tour of duty in Vietnam in 1968:

> I had lost massive portions of both buttocks, my scrotum had been split, my right hand was missing a thumb and little finger, my left hand had only a thumb and half a forefinger. I had lost my right leg at the torso and only a six-inch stump remained of my left thigh. But the dedicated professionals in Da Nang and Yokosuka saved me. They worked tirelessly every day in a world of blood and gore that would have broken men and women of lesser stature. There were also Red Cross volunteers who spent hours at my side as I began, throughout a narcotic underworld, to assimilate the magnitude of my personal loss.

Then I remember Edie McCoy Meeks, a nurse in Vietnam who was quoted in a story celebrating the dedication of the Vietnam Women's Memorial in 1993: "I don't have to recover from killing somebody. I have to recover because I couldn't save anyone."

Lieutenant Colonel Edith Knox, a 42-year-old native of Kilgore, Texas, was the chief nurse at the 67th Evacuation Hospital in Qui Nhon, South Vietnam. In John Combs' book, *Mercy Warriors*, she reported wanting to run the first time she saw battlefield casualties brought in:

> I walked into the receiving and emergency room just after they had brought in four young men, all with amputated legs. I just took one look at it and I thought, I'm not sure I can handle this. And I left the room immediately and went outside and then I thought to myself, No, I'm the chief nurse, and those nurses that are working in there have to handle this every day, and I have to learn to handle it. So then I walked back in. But it's just, I think, that I had never seen anything quite like that. And the first time it really hit me, and I'm sure it did every nurse that was over there.

So I write about these stories because it should be part of our job to remember the stories. We cannot forget the 265,000 women who served in the military during the war, 11,000 in Vietnam. Of those, 90 percent were nurses. Others served as doctors, air traffic controllers, intelligence officers, and clerks. Nearly all volunteered for Vietnam service. We need to honor women who served in the Army, Navy, Air Force, and Marines as well as volunteers for the Red Cross and other international relief agencies—them and the professions they represented.

I wrote already about my medevac ride home after my second Vietnam tour was almost over. I think about the nurses who cared for me as I went to Saigon, to Manila, to Guam, to Hawaii, to Travis, and finally to Madigan Army Hospital. I think of their tenderness, compassion, and unselfish love as our flying hospital ship took off from Ton Son Nhut loaded with stretchers, full of the sick and wounded, bound for glory land. It was our freedom bird, our passage home.

Later, when I visited our family homestead and walked the hills of my childhood, I would listen as the wind blew and the summer sun set, ending another day. It was quiet. My heart swelled and tears came to my eyes. I listened closely. I heard the voices calling to me from my past, the voices of my fellow soldiers in Vietnam, gunned down in their youth. But then I paused and thought again. I thought about the Women on the Wall who weren't coming home and the women after them, some of whom entered a personal hell. Then I heard the lyrics of my song echoing, repeating, almost silently in my mind over and over again.

The Women on the Wall
Copyright 1991, words and music by John R. Black

On this earth at another time
You gave your life to save mine
In that war so far away
You cared for me in a special way
I heard your voice as you spoke to me
You gave up what you could be
You nursed me through the lonely nights
As the rockets came 'til dawn's early light

Oh oh farewell – *(Carol Drazba 1966)*
Oh oh farewell – *(Elizabeth Jones 1966)*
Women on the wall
Your spirit is strong
Women on the wall
The boys say so long
Women on the wall
God bless you all
We'll always remember
The women on the wall

At Saigon, Chu Lai and Pleiku
Your tenderness was all we knew
You gave us strength, kept hope alive
You gave your love so we'd survive

Oh oh farewell *(Eleanor Alexander 1967)*
Oh oh farewell *(Hedwig Orlowski 1967)*
Women on the wall
Your spirit is strong
Women on the wall
The boys say so long
Women on the wall
God bless you all
We'll always remember
The women on the wall

Carol and Elizabeth, you're living on
Eleanor and Hedwig, not really gone

Pamela and Sharon, history will tell
Annie and Mary, we'll remember you well

Oh oh farewell (*Pamela Donovan 1968, Sharon Lane 1969*)
Oh oh farewell (*Annie Graham 1968, Mary Klinker 1975*)
Women on the wall
Your spirit is strong
Women on the wall
The boys say so long
Women on the wall
God bless you all
We'll always remember
The women on the wall

Women on the wall
Your spirit is strong
Women on the wall
The boys say so long
Women on the wall
God bless you all
We'll always remember
The women on the wall

Live on in our hearts
The women on the wall
Always remember
The women on the wall

In 1995, my dad died at 92 years old after having been diagnosed with Alzheimer's. He'd recently gone into the Alzheimer's unit in the Colville, Washington, hospital. He was buried in the same cemetery at St. Joseph's Mission Church with my grandparents and great-grandparents.

Over the next few years, my sisters Julie and Judy began conniving behind the scenes. Our brother James lived next to the homestead for many years (and still does), and since he had a business, he would periodically visit Mom and help her with her taxes. We had been told that the four of us kids—me, James, Julie, and Judy—were all in our parents' wills, though of course in our community-property state, Mom had simply inherited everything of Dad's. At one point while James was there helping her with paperwork, he found a document that indicated that her will had been changed to take James and me out, leaving everything to Julie and Judy alone. James confronted Mom about it and learned that "Julie made her do it." Mom said that Julie's reasoning had been that they did not marry into wealth, while Julie believed that James and I did, though our wives were only rich in Julie's opinion. On the other hand, both of my sisters eventually divorced their husbands. Judy's second marriage also ended in divorce. So they somehow felt that it was not right that James or I should benefit from any share of the inheritance.

James called Julie to question her about this and was told that, contrary to what Mom had said, this had all been Mom's idea. I talked to both Mom and Julie and could tell they were lying. I can only assume that our sisters put Mom up to it. Like James, Judy lived near the homestead, while our sister Julie was in California.

One of the last visits that my brother James and I had with Uncle Louis

By then, we all could tell that Mom, too, was fading. As her health and mental condition deteriorated, Judy got a durable power of attorney. At one point I called Mom to ask how she was doing, and she didn't seem to really understand where she was. Then Judy came on the phone, screaming about how she was putting a restraining order against me and not to call again. We exchanged some harsh words between us. Judy did go to the local sheriff to take out a restraining order against my brother and I, cutting off all communication between us and Mom.

Judy then proceeded to sell everything from the homestead it was possible to sell, setting up a private auction so that the rest of us could not even bid on family possessions. She even logged the timber on the homestead and then sold the house, taking all the proceeds. That was the end of the Tomsha homestead. It was all legal, since she'd persuaded Mom to give her power of attorney while Mom was still capable of it.

Before too long, Mom entered the same Alzheimer's unit where Dad had died—in fact, she was in the same bed. We could visit her there, but by then her mind was gone. We knew she wasn't long for the world.

Joanne, Maria, and I moved to a new home in Seattle in 1997, and I left Boeing in 1999 to open my own consulting firm with Joanne, John Black and Associates. Between then and 2017, I would spend 18 years sharing Lean quality improvement techniques with global leaders in a variety of industries, notably health care. Without Joanne's groundbreaking work, we wouldn't have been as successful. But those accomplishments are recorded in my other books. On a personal level, I was focused on my family and music.

The same year I retired from Boeing, I released a third album, *Vietnam Farewell II (I Don't Know Where the Time Has Gone)*. This album was a long time coming, but it again was distributed to all 220 Veterans' Centers in North America, the Virgin Islands, Puerto Rico and Guam, as well as to all members of Congress.

I don't know where the time has gone
John R. black

My second album, Vietnam Farewell II

The songs on this album include one I wrote for Joanne, another for my dad, and many more:

I Don't Know Where the Time Has Gone
Rock and Roll Mary
Dear Dad
Take Me Home Freedom Bird
I'm Asking These Questions Joanne
Out Along This Way
Maimoona
God Help Us Lyndon
I Think I'll Go to China
You Took My Picture
Dr. Fall
The Stars Are Callin' Me Home (*music by John R. Black,*
      lyrics by Julie Black Brockhaus)
From Deep Inside My Heart to You

While working on this album, I wrote and included a song in honor of Dr. Bernard Fall:

Dr. Fall
Copyright 1998, words and music by John R. Black

Dr. Fall, you told it all, Hell in a very small place called
      Dien Ben Phu
Two Vietnams, Street Without Joy
Why wouldn't those Pentagon boys listen to you?
Dr. Fall, you stood tall
On that sunny day when they took your soul in Quang
      Tri
Those Viet Cong were dangerous guys
Seems to me we were where we weren't supposed to be
Dr. Fall, I dream of you
And all of the things you told us we shouldn't do
Ho Chi Minh, General Giap
They won the war without the high tech stuff we knew
Dr. Fall, we're okay, it's taken quite a while to really
      shake it all
But we did it, Dr. Fall.

As part of this work, I reread my old, torn copy of Fall's 1968 book, *Last Reflections on a War*. I saw that his wife Dorothy Fall had written the preface for it. I picked up the phone and called her in Washington D.C. On a 2001 visit to that city, I had the fortune of meeting her. I met her for the first time at an art show she was attending in Georgetown, and she came with me to a reading I did of Dr. Fall's work at the Vietnam Women's Memorial. We had dinner together and she invited me to her home.

The house was as if Dr. Fall had never left it. She made coffee and went to the basement, where she told me she was working on her husband's memoir. She showed me the many boxes of FBI reports that'd been generated about her husband. She told me FBI agents had even come and searched through their trash cans. President Hoover was paranoid and so intent on suspecting or trying Dr. Fall, a true patriot, for his opposition to the war. That, to me, was disgraceful. Our government seems to slip to a warped level of honesty when confronted with the truth—and more than the basic truth, the absolute statistics and conclusions of a brilliant scholar of guerilla warfare. It is enough to make you wonder where it all leads, and of course, it has now led us into Iraq. I suspect Rumsfeld, like McNamara, never read Fall.

Dorothy was very gracious in her home with me, particularly since she'd never before met me.

I was able to present her with the song I'd written about her husband, "Dr. Fall," and we stayed in contact by email. I sent copies of my Vietnam Farewell II album, which included his song, to her daughters. Dorothy sent a copy to Bernard's sister, Lizette, in Paris, as well as putting a copy into the Bernard Fall archives at the John F. Kennedy Library.

In the meantime, Dorothy's words, "I'm working on his memoir," kept turning in my mind. In phone calls or emails, I would ask her how it was coming. After meeting her, I knew I needed to memorialize her in song as well. So when I started working on my next album—a much bigger project—I wrote a song about her. I told Dorothy about it and I'm sure she probably wondered what I was really up to, but I sent her the lyrics and she seemed to like them. I decided to hire the string section of the Seattle Symphony to help record the string arrangement. (I also used the symphony on my recording of, "The Walls Came Down.") I invited Dorothy to come to the recording session, but she couldn't make it. The song turned out great. In addition, when Dr. Fall's book *Last Reflections on a War* was reissued in 2000 with Dorothy's permission and help from war historian Don Oberdorfer, she presented me with a copy. She inscribed it, "For John, thank you for remembering Bernard's wise words. May 25, 2001."

These were some of the inspirations for my fourth album, *Meet Me in Vietnam*, which I released in 2003. A two-CD compilation containing 31 songs, it is accompanied by a website, www.meetmeinvietnam.net, that tells about my soul-searching journey with this album and provides resources for other vets like myself. My producer, Scott Anderson, and I worked to digitally re-record, remix, and remaster some previous selections from my first two Vietnam albums and we also added new songs. My favorites are "Ia Drang" and "When I Came Home." The other new songs on the album include:

No One Is Left Behind
Storm
I Woke Up This Morning
I'm Just Hangin' On
Shadows
Shut Out the Lights
The Walls Came Down

I sent this new album to Dorothy and was relieved to hear how pleased she was with the album graphics, too. I hadn't realized what an accomplished graphic artist she was until I met her, and once I knew what a wonderful artists she was, I put a copy of one of her works on my album jacket. Dorothy made sure family members received copies of this one, too.

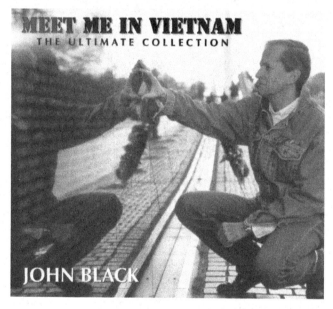

My two-disc collection

Then in 2004, when Maria and I were visiting Paris, I tracked down Lisette, and we had lunch with her on the Champs Elysees, talking about her brother and Dorothy. It was a wonderful meeting, and we learned from her how Falls' parents had been tortured and killed by the Nazis in World War II. Fall himself, at 17, had been part of the French Resistance.

Finally, in 2006, Dorothy published her own book about her husband, *Bernard Fall: Memories of a Soldier-Scholar*, with a forward by David Halberstam. It is a terrific book. As I read it, I noted that it was apparent to me that the great works of war wisdom, including those by Fall and T.E. Lawrence, about previous military and political encounters are not read by most of our present military and political leaders. I noted, "Donald Rumsfeld will be the Robert McNamara of the Iraq war." This is a strategic tragedy, because history repeats itself unless we study lessons learned. This fact to me is stunning. I have read, for example, most of the writings of Ho Chi Minh, Dr. Fall, and Lawrence. They are very clear, first of all with their data (brilliantly coupled with being on the ground) and secondly with the conclusions they reach, which become applicable today. Dorothy's book was wonderful and a great tribute by her to her husband.

Dorothy's book about her husband

I also recorded some music videos for this album and the website. Video producer Brian Lee filmed me singing "Dear Dad" at our family cemetery to create a music video for it. Another video for "I'm Just Hangin' On" was filmed on location at a tavern in Seattle featuring veterans from every U.S. war except World War I. My daughter Maria played a cameo role as a patron with a date. Producer Joseph Assi used my family footage and location scenes near Kingston, Washington, for another music video for "I Don't Know Where the Time Has Gone" as well as videos for "You Took My Picture," "God Help Us Lyndon," and "Ia Drang." Joseph also produced me singing "When I Came Home" for a live video called "John R. Black Live at the Union Gospel Mission," as well as another for "Vietnam, I'm Dreamin', Dreamin' On." The latter was shot at Kingston as well as at the mission with live footage of the homeless men and veterans. Finally, I have a live video of my performance of "The Women on the Wall," which I performed in Washington, D.C. It's on my website.

Researching this album also allowed me to find my old Vietnam friend Carl D. Robinson and his wife Kim Dung, who I found living in Australia. I was reading *Lost Over Laos* by Richard Pyle and Horst Faas, whose book included a reference to Carl. Dorothy Fall and Joe Galloway helped me track him down.

Maria, all grown up

Not everything in these years was rosy, of course. When I started consulting in 1999, I often found myself on long plane rides, which were always a challenge. I'd be sure I had the cross from my grandmother's casket and the rosary I always carried in my briefcase. I also made sure to turn my watch around on my wrist, which is weird, I know, but became a kind of compulsive superstition. But, after ten years of sobriety, I also started to have a drink on the plane.

I told Joanne about this and she convinced me I shouldn't. "When we got married you promised me you wouldn't drink again," she reminded me. But I continued to drink now and then on a plane, which led to more drinks. Plus, when working with my consulting team in far-flung locations, I'd sometimes join them for a beer. This became a pattern I didn't tell Joanne about and that I lied about.

In 2002 I received a phone call from the Colville funeral home. Mom had died at the age of 84, and my sister Judy had the body delivered to them with instructions to call me, since she was leaving the state. She'd told them I should take care of burying Mom. I agreed, of course—what else could I do?—and picked out a casket over the phone based on its color, one Mom had liked. It cost $6,700. I called James and Julie and let them know that we needed to split the cost three ways. Their comments were, "Well, that's expensive," but they agreed to chip in after I said I'd pay the whole tab.

"It's our only mother, and we're hung up on expensive?" I asked. I would have buried my mother in a solid gold casket if necessary.

It was a mistake to have an open casket. Mom probably weighed 80 pounds; her appearance was shocking. She, too, is buried at St. Joseph's Mission Church with my father, and I plan to be buried there as well. Later my brother, James, showed me his plot next to Mom's, as well as one for his wife.

I miss both Dad and Mom every day. My Uncle Louis, my mother's last living sibling, died nearly a decade later at the age of 92. The homestead is no longer in the family, of course; Judy had made certain of that. But it was a huge part of my childhood and later life, and it will always be a happy place in my memories.

CHAPTER 10: COMING FULL CIRCLE

"Learn and obey the rules very well, so you will know how to break them properly."

On a happier note, a good thing happened in these years thanks to the efforts of my oldest son, Shane. After Paula and I divorced in 1989, she started looking again for our first, mysterious baby. She also told Shane, Ben, and Heidi about this sibling who'd been given up for adoption before we were married. Following the state's formal processes, she worked with a confidential intermediary to try to track down this child who'd grown up to adulthood.

By then, of course, the memories of the birth were more than two decades old, and Shane suspects that his mother also might've been confusing some of the details from our child's birth and that of another baby, fathered by another young boyfriend, that she'd given up for adoption before meeting me. She now told the family about that baby, too. Between what were probably traumatic teenage memories and the upheaval of our divorce, it was hard to piece together certain dates or other details, and without those, Paula didn't make much more headway in this effort than we had the first time we'd tried.

After her death in 1999, Shane decided to pick up the effort to find the sibling he thought was a brother. He told the rest of the family what he was doing, but nobody else seemed interested. "It was my thing, but I felt it was appropriate to let them know what I was doing," he said. He went through Paula's paperwork and did some detective work of his own, such as trying to pin down where she'd been working at the time of the birth, to find details that might help the intermediary. Finally the information added up enough for the intermediary to find the birth certificate and identify our daughter.

Lauri Clark, by then married and known as Lauri Cragun, was living with her family in Utah. She'd been born in Spokane, of course, and then lived all over the country, since her adoptive father had been in the janitorial business and had worked jobs from Spokane and Richland, Washington, to Florida and Georgia before settling in Utah in 1975. The intermediary contacted her on March 20, 2000, to verify some information and let her know that she had a full sibling who was interested in contacting her.

Lauri (fourth adult from right) with her husband, children, and grandchildren

Lauri had grown up in the Clark family with three other adopted children. The adoptions had been no mystery to any of them, but she said the contact from the intermediary was still a shock, coming out of left field, and gave her plenty to think about and consider. By then she'd gotten married and already had four wonderful kids of her own. Her adoptive mother had died some twenty years previously. The reminder that she'd had a different birth family and a biological mother who'd abandoned her had to be difficult. "There were lots of emotions and feelings," she said. But she talked it over with her husband, gave the required written consent, and soon received Shane's phone number.

With all my kids (left to right): Ben, Maria, Heidi, Lauri, me, and Shane

She called him. She and Shane talked by phone and then he and Heidi both went to visit Lauri. "We had a sort of family reunion in Utah," Shane noted. Not too long afterward, Lauri visited Seattle so Ben and I could meet her, too. It's too bad we hadn't been able to find her while Paula was still alive to be there, but I'm happy we finally did—and that Lauri existed. If Paula had been able to have an abortion all those years back, would she have done so? Obviously Laurie would not have been born, and neither would her children or their children. How terrible would that have been? I'm glad that today, Lauri and Heidi, in particular, seem to be close.

"We have all your typical family relations," Lauri noted. "Some of us are closer than others, but it's been wonderful to meet my father and his current wife and family, and it's wonderful to have another sister." Not every adoption story has a happy ending, but this one did.

Once my parents were both gone, I decided that another way I could find some healing for past traumas was to file a lawsuit in 2004 against the Spokane Diocese of the Catholic Church. Though at that point we didn't have much of a relationship, I'd already supported Ben in an early 1990s lawsuit against Beaver, the Seattle Archdiocese, and the military ordinariate under which he worked. Ben ultimately won a barely equitable settlement—

not much, but something to help with his healing. He'd been diagnosed with PTSD after his abuse came to light, and he got therapy, in part through a program called Therapy and Renewal Associates (TARA) run on behalf of the Seattle Archdiocese. He did that for more than two years, along with family therapy with Shane and Paula, and those experiences prompted him to get inpatient drug and alcohol treatment, too, which probably saved his life.

More than 80 complaints were ultimately made against Beaver. As the 1990s went on, scores of victims of priests under the authority of the Seattle and Spokane dioceses began coming forward, and the issue of priest pedophilia and abuse started making headlines across the country. In addition to Ben's case, at least three other suits naming Beaver were filed against the Spokane Diocese and Archdiocese for the Military Services by 2005. Beaver had been removed from public ministry in 1988 after complaints, and he was listed by the Spokane Diocese as an abuser in 2002. He'd been abusing boys and teens for at least 25 years by the time he hurt Ben.

He was by no means the only one. By mid-2004, there had been at least 18 multi-million-dollar lawsuits filed against the Spokane Diocese, including mine. Dozens of people, whether they were party to one of those lawsuits or not, accused a couple dozen priests, Jesuits, and other clergy—including Knecht, Jaeger, and Beaver—of abuse. As of 2018, lawsuits by abuse victims have so far forced Catholic dioceses across the United States to pay more than $3 billion in settlements. At least 19 have filed for bankruptcy protection. But money can't repair the harm.

By the time of Ben's lawsuit in the 1990s, Jaeger's abuse had also come to light, with the Archdiocese quietly settling a 1988 complaint against him before more claims and lawsuits were filed. As a young adult in recovery, Ben was able to confront and reconcile with Jaeger about the abuse at summer camp. Jaeger had gone through a treatment program himself and would eventually die in 2014.

Ben's struggle with ongoing PTSD continued, however, and in 2004 he went into a six-week inpatient sexual recovery program in California that was ultimately reimbursed by the Archdiocese of Seattle. Then, in 2005 he received a small settlement from the Archdiocese related to that abuse, which helped pay for therapy.

He and I were estranged at that time, but afterward we reconnected. He says my alcohol treatment gave him a path to follow. "My dad set a good example by going into treatment for alcoholism, because soon after I disclosed the abuse to him, I got into therapy and then inpatient treatment for alcohol and drugs." Ben has now been clean and sober for more than thirty years.

"I am so grateful my dad has been honest about his struggles with alcohol," he adds. "Our experiences together show the different layers of healing from the personal, intergenerational, and collective aspects of abuse and alcoholism in families and communities."

Ben says he's gained a deeper sense of reconciliation, both with the priests and with me, and he's since done a lot of local and international service work to support other survivors in recovery.

My friend Mike Shea is another of Beaver's victims. I can relate to something Mike said in a newspaper report of his 2003 lawsuit—that the abuse has followed him throughout his life, fueling problems with alcohol and relationships.

In my case against Knecht, apologies were issued (for all the good that did), including a January 11, 2008, letter to each of us who were abused at St. Mary's from William Skylstad, the bishop of the Spokane Diocese. My letter, addressed to "Dear John," said in part, "I am writing to apologize for the harm that has been inflicted upon you through sexual abuse by Father Knecht. I realize that your life has been disrupted and impacted each and every day by this painful experience. I wish that I could take the hurt away.... I am also willing and open to meet with you personally."

I didn't take him up on the offer. The Diocese filed for bankruptcy that year, selling off most of its property to pay settlements. By the end of 2008, it had settled with nearly 200 people, including me, paying out nearly $50 million in total. Allegations were still being made against the Diocese as late as 2009, and you only have to read or listen to the daily news to know that the Catholic Church still has a long way to go to really address the problem.

A line in one of the lawsuits really gets to the point. Kent Hoffman, a Spokane psychotherapist, has said, "Unless somebody has been a victim of sexual abuse, there's no way to understand the kind of pain and chaos involved. You just don't get over sexual abuse. You work with it."

My relationship with some of my kids has been difficult over the years. As I've mentioned, for instance, for a time Ben wasn't speaking to me. Then in 2016, he wanted me to go into a session with his counselor, so I went. Unbeknownst to me, he had prepared a multi-page letter about everything he felt I had done to wrong him or the family, including the affairs I'd had, and he read it to me. He and Shane wanted me to know that they knew all about it. I sat there for an hour and took it, but when he was done, I said, "This isn't a therapy session, it's a trial." I suppose it made him feel better, but at the time it didn't seem very productive to me. I think we both have more empathy for each other now.

Music continued to be the place that I turned for healing. I kept writing, recording, rerecording, and releasing my music. In 2008, three of my songs, including "The Women on the Wall," were included in a Vietnam compilation, ...Next Stop Vietnam, produced by Bear Family Records. This huge 13-CD set includes a 304-page hardcover book and 334 musical tracks covering all facets of the war and its aftermath. It features the full gamut of artists, from Connie Francis, Johnny Cash, and Merle Haggard to Bob Dylan, Joan Baez, and Bruce Springsteen to Staff Sergeant Barry Sadler and many other veterans like me with little name recognition but a passion for writing and singing songs that tell a story of the war. I was honored that three of my songs were selected with the greats. The compilation contains all the Vietnam songs of the time that everyone remembers, such as "Where Have All The Flowers Gone?" and "Ballad of the Green Berets," as well as newer tunes about the war like mine. It is the most comprehensive anthology of music inspired by the Vietnam War ever released.

Roger Donlon and I enjoying my boat

I also found a lot of pleasure on the water in a new boat. I'd always wanted one, and in 2004 I went to the Seattle Boat Show. I'm sure Joanne would say, "If you don't want your husband to get a boat, don't let him go to the boat show." I saw a 34-foot Sea Ray there that was really neat. We took it for a trial spin on Lake Union with the salesman, and Joanne said, "We don't need a boat," but I convinced her. Maria was in grade school at the time, and the boat, which had a swim deck and room for several people to sleep, seemed like a good family activity. We took it up into Canadian waters, which was great, and Maria and all her friends, who are now young adults, say those were some of the best times we spent together.

Then in 2008, I went to the boat show again and spotted a 52-foot yacht that slept six, with a master suite, a guest suite, four televisions, a 13-foot Boston Whaler dinghy, you name it. So I took that one for a ride. I really wanted it but Joanne was just not going to go for it. It got to the point where

I had to use some reverse psychology on her. I said, "Maria's getting bigger, we're getting too old, and we need the damn bigger boat, but just forget it. Don't mention it again, but for the record, you said no." A few weeks later, she woke up at 6 a.m. and said, "Okay, get the damn boat."

It was a hard sell the first time and a harder sell the second, but now she just loves the Boston Whaler dinghy, and we really enjoy it.

In fact, Joanne joined Northwest Women in Boating and became such an avid boater that in 2018 she and a friend, Katie Geraghty, took Joanne's 13-foot Boston Whaler to Lewiston, Idaho, launching into the Snake River and following Lewis & Clark's 469-mile route down the Columbia to Astoria, where the river meets the Pacific. They went through the locks of seven dams along the way. Joanne told a newspaper reporter, "I just wondered if it could be done. It's a waterway that could be explored. It's been quite an adventure."

In October 2013, Heidi married a great guy, Kurt Edinger, whose father was a former U.S. Marine. They had a beautiful ceremony at the Delille Winery in Woodinville, Washington, and most of our relatives attended, including Lauri and her family. In those years our family also grew when Shane had a son.

Some tension rose between Joanne and I about then, however. On July 9, 2017, we were flying back from a trip to Phoenix, where I'd gone for imaging of my prostate. We were sitting in first class, and Joanne had stepped away for a moment. The flight attendant came around and asked, "Would you like a gin and tonic?"

Of course I said, "Yes."

When Joanne returned, she said, "Is that a gin and tonic?"

Of course, I lied and said, "No." My dad had done the same thing. My track record of admitting if I had a drink or not was never good. It did no good to argue about drinking or having a drink.

That turned into a real come-to-Jesus moment. I started going back to AA meetings, and I haven't had a drink since that July flight in 2017. That includes during two major trips to Russia, probably the last country you want to visit if, like me, you're a bona fide alcoholic.

In 2016 I released *Back in Time*, which contained both a number of my old tunes and three new ones: "Night Flight," "Baby, Baby, Baby," and "Love's Lonely Road." Then I pulled together a lot of my earliest songs from the 1950s and 1960s to release my *Original Rockabilly* album in 2017. The same year, I compiled the broadcast recordings of my 1964 performances for the Armed Forces Network and released them as Armed Forces Network.

 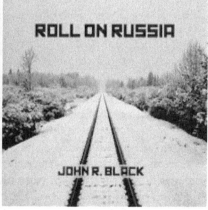

Also in 2017 I decided to do something that had long been on my bucket list: I crossed Russia on the Trans-Siberian Railway. I went with Joanne's cousin, Tom Comerford, a retired doctor who was fun to travel with. We had a great time together. We left on May 8 and ultimately circumnavigated the globe between then and June 23 (47 days). I traveled 21,999 miles by air, chose to cross the ocean on the Queen Mary 2, and both of us rode 6, 700 miles on the railway from Moscow to Vladivostok. We visited 10 Russian cities along the way, including a number of military memorials. Tom and I felt we got a sense of the Russian soul. We ended the trip after a week in Japan, spending time in Kyoto, which has 800 temples.

While crossing Russia, I was inspired to write five rock-and-roll songs about the experience. I wrote the lyrics on the train and then wrote the music at the bar of the Westin Hotel in Kyoto, early in the morning when the bar was closed. The songs "Roll On Russia," "Russian Beauty," "Elena," "Hotel St. Regis," and "Afghanistan" are on my album *Roll on Russia*, which I released in 2018.

Russian Beauty
Copyright 2017, words and music by John R. Black

She was a Russian beauty that stepped off the train
I knew it when I saw her, I said, "What's your name?"
She came close to me, took me by the hand
I said, "Let's meet for dinner." She said, "Yes I can."
We sat down for dinner on a cold winter night
She was sad and lonely. I said, "Are you alright?"
She poured out her story, a sad tale she told
Her lover died in battle, her heartache's grown old.
Oh Russian beauty, where have you been?
I've searched far and wide but to no end
Oh Russian beauty, will you be mine?
I'll love you forever until the end of time.

The following year, I was invited back to Russia as a participant in the Sixth International Patriotic "Machine Gun and Guitar" Festival in Perm, a large city near the Ural Mountains. The festival is a place for veterans of Russian military actions, including those in Afghanistan and Chechnya, to connect, enjoy music by and about other veterans, and heal.

Performing onstage in Russia

I went for the August festival and performed four of my songs from *Roll on Russia*. It was a chance for military veterans to acknowledge the values we shared, regardless of our country, and plea for peace. Between my railway trip and this music festival, I witnessed music's power to bring people together. From the beginning of the festival, a natural common bond of brotherhood and respect was evident.

Fellowship with veterans of Russian wars

My participation was noted by the governor of the Perm region, and I was also interviewed by a reporter for the October 16 issue of Russian daily newspaper *Moskovskij Komsomolets* (*MKRU*). The article that resulted called me, "a man talking about war in absolutely the same words as our veterans." It added, "Without any translators, veterans of different wars understand each other's pain." As the festival organizers had noted, "It turns out that the soldier of our 'most likely opponent' also wants to end the wars on the planet." I hope to still make a third trip to Russia, since I think a lot can be done through cultural exchanges, friendship, and fraternity like that can conquer politics.

I was featured with Russian vets in festival media coverage.

I was asked to write a letter to the governor of Permsky Krai to give him my comments and observations as a guest and participant in the 2018 festival. In part of my October 1, 2018, letter, I said:

> We have a common bond of brotherhood to share through music and I felt as a Vietnam veteran I could join with the Afghan veterans in sharing my music. It was lucky for me your leader Irik Vakilievich Shigabutdinov believed the same. Who knows how many wars on all sides could be avoided if we addressed political issues not with bullets but with songs. The lyrics to the songs written by veterans tell a story that includes hope for the future and ways to approach future conflicts—how sensible to approach political disagreements with a bit more reason and with the spirit of brotherhood than with guns and bullets. And this is exactly what I witnessed at the festival as organized and produced by Irik Shigabutdinov, chief

festival organizer and organization chair. The Perm festival model should be expanded to include not only the John Blacks from America but the veterans from other countries as well, such as Europe and all of Russia.

Before 2018 was over, I'd released another compilation of newer songs, *Stairway of My Mind.*

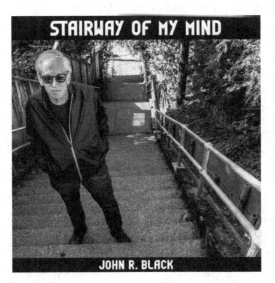

This album includes:

> Roll On River
> I'm Feelin' So Bad
> Away on Time
> Count Me In
> Stairway of My Mind
> Betrayal
> Temptation

I wrote "Roll On River" and "Count Me In" on a 2017 camping trip on the Lochsa River in Idaho. The site is on the Lewis and Clark National Historic Trail, and Joanne and I try to go there every year. I write song lyrics in the early morning, with a cup of coffee and the heat turned on in the car. Later in the year, I wrote "Betrayal" and "Temptation," while "Away on Time" is a 1970s song I had remastered. I wrote "Stairway of My Mind" in 2018 when all the shootings and politics were heading America into a shitstorm. The lyrics says it all for me:

Stairway of My Mind

Copyright 2017, words and music by John R. Black

Empty dumpsters full of sound
Screeches in the night
Vacant streets call out loud
For those we left behind.
Abandoned homes rise at dawn
No-one to awaken
Foundations we relied upon
Now have all been shaken
Oh yeah, oh yeah, oh yeah.

Oh, the stairway of my mind
How many steps do I have to take?
Oh, the stairway of my mind
Got these troubles I can't shake.
Is there a secret stairway you know?
I want out of this hell hole
I want out of this hell hole

Empty rooms in houses
Empty desks and drawers
Memories scattered in the wind
As if they're off to war
Sour love soaked in brine
Like words without a song
No children left to shine a light
On what has gone wrong
Oh yeah, oh yeah, oh yeah

Call a number, get some help
Analyze this plight
For God's sakes can't you see
Nothing is all right
Call the police, state your fear
Your neighbor packs a gun
Who's got the answer here?
I hope there's some
Oh yeah, oh yeah
I hope there's some

Politicians don't give a damn
They say nothing's wrong
They say buck up do your job
Before your job is gone
No use callin' Dr. King
They say he's dead
No use callin' JFK
They shot him in the head
Oh yeah, oh yeah, oh yeah

Oh, the stairway of my mind
How many steps do I have to take?
Oh, the stairway of my mind
Got these troubles I can't shake
Is there a secret stairway you know?
I want out of this hell hole
I want out of this hell hole
You got to show me the secret stairway you know
You got to show me the secret stairway you know
You got to show me the secret stairway you know.

I also released my song about Roger Donlon, "Captain Roger H.C. Donlon," as a single. A year before I had wondered why there was no song written about Roger. I realized there needed to be one, and with Roger and Norma's approval, I wrote it.

On May 12, 2018, I sang "Captain Roger H.C. Donlon" onstage with Roger at NASCAR event at the Kansas City speedway in front of 50,000 people. Norma Donlon knew Pat Warren, the president of the racetrack, which regularly honored U.S. veterans, in part on the prompting of the Donlons. (Perhaps the remarkable thing about true heroes is that they never stop giving of themselves in the behalf of others.) Roger had been honored there before, along with others, and his story had been published in a book he wrote with Warren Rogers called *Outpost of Freedom* and another written with General William C. Westmoreland called *Beyond Nam Dong*, as well as in many other publications. In short, in May 1964 his team of Special Forces established an outpost at Nam Dong, near the border of Laos. Early in the morning of July 6, 1964, the base was attacked by a large force of Vietcong. Under Roger's leadership the two-battalion attack was repelled, for which he received the war's first Medal of Honor.

For this event, which Norma helped to arrange, he and many other veterans were brought out on stage after the drivers were introduced to the crowd. They were, like me, graduates of the Command and General Staff College, who have held what we call a Wild Goose Reunion every year. Then Roger stepped forward. After he was introduced to the crowd, I stood with him and sang the tune I'd written for him. The national anthem followed, and then the start of the race.

Onstage with Roger at the Kansas City Speedway

The event was videotaped and widely viewed, and subsequently I was asked to perform the song at a special Medal of Honor tribute to him in Bangor, Maine, hosted by Wreaths Across America, as well as for a July 19 ceremony for the Vietnam Traveling Memorial Wall. The Wreaths Across America organization also had their Education Trailer present at the Kansas City racetrack for the crowds to explore.

Captain Roger H. C. Donlon
Copyright 2017, words and music by John R. Black

(words spoken:)
There's a story told, a legend known afar
About Captain Donlon, in the Vietnam War
Born in Saugerties, New York, in 1934
Eighth child of ten, let me tell you more
Mother's name was Marian, father known as Paul
Captain Donlon joined the Special Forces
Answered JFK's call.

In the early morning, July of '64
The enemy came on, knockin' at the door
Donlon led his forces for five hours long
While mortar rounds were raining, slowed the Viet Cong
The assault came on, a VC battalion
Over 800 strong attacked Nam Dong

Oh Captain Donlon, God's grace flows your way
You fought for our freedom in that war far away
You wear the Medal of Honor, the first in the war
Thank you for your service, America asks for no more.

Under heavy fire through the dark of night
Long waited daylight ended the fight
The enemy retreated, the assault overcome
The battle was over, Special Forces had won
Master Sergeant Alamo, Sergeant Houston, too
W.O. Conway died for me and you

That same year, my brother, James, invited me to go to Nashville with him to buy a guitar. We spent a week touring, seeing the Grand Old Opry, and buying tickets to the backstage area, where we met the performers. It was a blast and I was very appreciative of my brother for bringing me along. He bought a great guitar, too.

With James in Nashville

Coming off the stage in Perm, Russia, in August 2018, I started noticing pain in my left foot. It continued in my hotel room for days despite big doses of ibuprofen. My 13-hour flight home to Seattle became the flight from hell, the pain soon reaching screaming levels. The ibuprofen didn't last long, and drinking wasn't an option. I had to tough it out.

As I tossed and turned in my seat, my thoughts flashed back to 1996, when I'd been diagnosed with prostate cancer. I had three surgeries and multiple sets of radiation, and my cancer had metastasized. Earlier in 2018, I'd undergone sixty hour-long treatments in the hyperbaric chamber at Virginia Mason with only limited results. More treatments were coming. What was next?

When I got home, I found out. I was diagnosed with Complex Regional Pain Syndrome (CRPS). It had attacked my body, particularly my left foot, and there wasn't a cure.

"You're going to need to be managed by our pain clinic, and you may end up being disabled," said the doctor. He also warned me of mental health issues caused by the constant pain. He added, "CRPS patients have contemplated suicide."

I was soon put on a nine-month course of hormone therapy for my cancer. The debilitating treatment causes severe depression, on top of a painful injection in my stomach monthly and, later, a course of radiation. The mental health cards were really stacked against me.

At my first CRPS rehab session, the trainer handed me two walking sticks, saying, "You'll be using these for quite a while." I was prescribed opiates, too, though they soon changed that to a different drug, gabapentin, six tablets a night. My doctors also approved multiple doses of CBD so I could try to sleep. Without Joanne holding my foot at night, I couldn't sleep, or I would scream myself to sleep. Without her care I would not have made it, but I charged ahead.

I'd agreed to trailer the dingy from our boat from my daughter Heidi's location Potholes, Idaho, to Lewiston, Idaho, for Joanne's Columbia River trip, which I mentioned earlier. I wasn't going to renege on that promise. My daughter Maria would come along to drive me back to Seattle.

The pain during this trip was intense. In Lewiston, Joanne had to get me to the hospital to make sure I wasn't suffering a blood clot. The exam was negative, but I still faced the eight-hour drive home to Seattle with Maria at the wheel.

To distract myself, I talked with Maria about my life. She asked many questions. The first edition of this memoir had just been published, and we also recalled a special gift my oldest daughter, Lauri, had given me on my birthday in 2003. It was a journal called "A Father's Legacy," with questions and blank space to answer, telling your life story in your own words. One question was, "Share some principles from scripture on which you have chosen to build your life." My answer was: "The main message is to do unto others as you would have them do unto you. For me this has been very difficult. I have been too judgmental of others including my friends, family, and children. I have been too long in forgiveness and too righteous in my thinking. This is without a doubt my main character flaw."

I filled out all the answers and Kinkos put the document into booklets with spine binding – gave a copy to all my children and grandchildren, hoping they would read it, which they said they did.

So I was thinking about the importance of history on this long ride back to Seattle and wondering about our family's history. I'd filled out all the answers in Lauri's journal and made copies for all my children and grandchildren. I'd also digitized family videos and old 8 mm films to share them. But who was going to archive our shared history? It was a "come to Jesus" moment.

My cancer was not going away, having spread to my lymph nodes, and now with CRPS, would my left foot need to be amputated? Would I survive two major illnesses? I'd be 80 soon.

What about all the family scrapbooks and photo albums, the letters from relatives written during the World War ll? Shouldn't they be safeguarded for the family's new babies and grandchildren, with possibly more to come? I decided to take on a family archive project that I thought would take several years to complete. The Black Family Legacy has now been distributed, but I won't say it's complete, as I hope others will continue to add to it over time.

My 60-year reunion at Gonzaga Prep

Meanwhile, in 2019 I attended my Gonzaga Prep 60-year reunion, connecting with several old friends there. I'm dealing with my health issues and my rehab is working. I've recently dropped first one and then the other walking sticks, no longer needed. I have a stubborn limp, but I'm working on it in physical therapy.

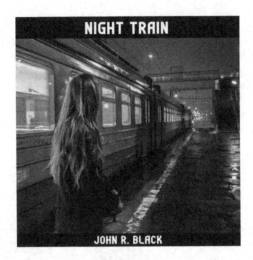

That March, I learned my old friend and Boeing boss Bill Selby passed away on March 21, 2019, after living with Parkinson's disease for 25 years. Bill, whose full name was William Edwin Selby, had been hired by Boeing in 1958 and worked in both the Aerospace and the Commercial divisions before retiring as vice president and general manager of the Renton site in 1994, five years before I left the company, too. But I'm still here, and I'm still writing music. Some of my most recent work includes the songs "Julia," "Night Train," and "When I Died." But my songs about Vietnam bring me the most mail.

CHAPTER 11: CARRYING ON

"But we must carry on. Blessings."

I continue to receive great letters from veterans about my music. One I received was from a veteran's widow whose husband had died from complications of Agent Orange exposure in 2009. She had ordered a copy of my album *Meet Me in Vietnam*, as well as an early edition of this book.

She wrote, "Dear John, you are a good man, John Black, don't ever forget that. I read your book and I see you have lived it well. I tend to watch others live. I'm sorry to say I haven't heard your music yet. My CD player is not working correctly. I will listen to it much once I start. About the priests, I am not a Catholic, but there is incest in my family's past. People tell me it is quite common in America. I don't want to think it is. But we don't expect our religious leaders to do these things. But we must carry on. Blessings."

I also received a call from a U.S. Navy veteran living in a nursing home in Oklahoma. He'd been declared 100 percent disabled in 1964, and his wife and daughter had passed away. We had a long conversation about his life, then he called me again to tell me he had received the old Vietnam maps I had sent him. He was a mapmaker in Vietnam in 1961 through 1964 and had been captured and tortured by the North Vietnamese. Cam Ranh Bay hadn't been built yet, and he made the maps for it. He called me several times to talk about his experiences and my book, about which he said, "I'm passing your book around the nursing home for others to read." Connections like that are gratifying.

Vietnam is still frequently on my mind. I spoke with many of my friends in 2018, when the 18-hour Ken Burns documentary, *The Vietnam War*, came out for television. It was billed as "the epic story of one of the most consequential, divisive, and controversial events in American history as it has never before been told on film." Some of my friends told me they could only watch part of it; other watched it all and were glad they had so they could finally understand what happened.

When the program aired, I went to a University of Washington discussion group sponsored by the Vietnam Veterans for Peace in partnership with the university's International Relations department. The panel was chaired by the head of the department, and it was attended mostly by college students. It was basically a meeting to criticize the Ken Burns documentary and particularly the war. I was the only veteran at the event who had carried a rifle, and those of us in the audience could get in line to make comments.

I did so and talked about Dr. Fall, who wasn't even mentioned in the film despite being an authority on the Vietnam War. I talked about the Revolutionary Development Program I was part of, but no one in the room, including the international relations professor hosting the event, wanted to listen. Later I called Dorothy Fall, the wife of Dr. Fall. Dorothy and her daughters had contacted Burns and asked him why Dr. Fall was not included in the documentary. He gave a weak answer, saying that Dr. Fall had been a historian, not a real journalist. This despite the fact that Fall had died in northern South Vietnam on February 21, 1967, when he stepped on a mine while patrolling with U.S. Marines. By then, he had already authored seven books on Vietnam, most notably *Street Without Joy*, an indictment of French intrusion into Indochina and a warning to American forces just beginning to get involved.

So how was the war lost? H. R. McMaster's 1997 book, *Dereliction of Duty*, tells it all. When it was published, he was a major in the United States Army. (He became National Security Advisor in 2017 after rising in rank to lieutenant general). The book presents an open-and-shut case that indicts Johnson, McNamara, General Maxwell Taylor, McGeorge Bundy, and other top aides who deliberately deceived the Joint Chiefs of Staff, the U.S. Congress, and the American public.

The Gulf of Tonkin incident, in particular, was a pretext for war. It certainly wasn't the first; various commentators have suggested that presidents from Polk to FDR to George H.W. Bush may have similarly misled officials and the public, too eager to embark on a war. "It was fortunate for Johnson that Americans of his own time did not learn that soon after Congress passed the Tonkin Resolution, he was secretly informed that thanks to further investigation by the Pentagon and U.S. intelligence, there was probably never any Aug. 4 attack by the North Vietnamese," notes Michael Beschloss, the author of Presidents of War: The Epic Story from 1807 to Modern Times. But President Johnson wouldn't risk sharing that insight with Congress or the public, and while he remained skeptical of subsequent evidence, real or imagined, of hostility, he didn't put the brakes on, either. He proceeded with the charade, and we went to war under a made-up story.

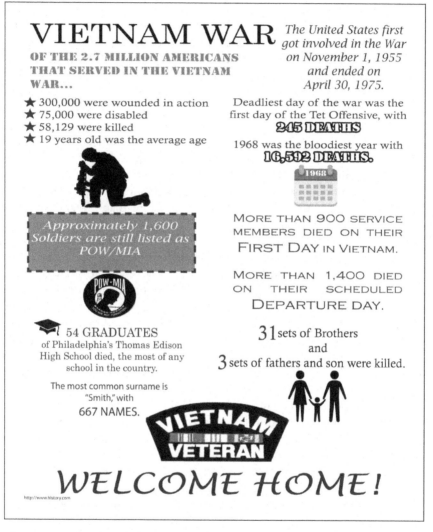

VIETNAM WAR

The United States first got involved in the War on November 1, 1955 and ended on April 30, 1975.

OF THE 2.7 MILLION AMERICANS THAT SERVED IN THE VIETNAM WAR...

★ 300,000 were wounded in action
★ 75,000 were disabled
★ 58,129 were killed
★ 19 years old was the average age

Deadliest day of the war was the first day of the Tet Offensive, with **245 DEATHS**

1968 was the bloodiest year with **16,592 DEATHS.**

Approximately 1,600 Soldiers are still listed as POW/MIA

MORE THAN 900 SERVICE MEMBERS DIED ON THEIR FIRST DAY IN VIETNAM.

MORE THAN 1,400 DIED ON THEIR SCHEDULED DEPARTURE DAY.

54 GRADUATES of Philadelphia's Thomas Edison High School died, the most of any school in the country.

The most common surname is "Smith," with **667 NAMES.**

31 sets of Brothers
and
3 sets of fathers and son were killed.

VIETNAM VETERAN

WELCOME HOME!

http://www.history.com

A summary of sad statistics courtesy of Wreaths Across America, whose mission is coordinating wreath-laying ceremonies each December on National Wreaths Across America Day. They "Remember, Honor, and Teach" throughout the year, too. Go to WreathsAcrossAmerica.org to donate or volunteer.

As early as January 1968, other U.S. leaders were suspicious or actually investigating this story, but their work was withheld from the public, most of it for many decades. As Beschloss makes clear, the alternative might have been a Johnson impeachment. Those politics ultimately led to our losing the war.

Another leadership failure that's since been revealed was outlined by Army intelligence officer Hamilton Gregory in *McNamara's Folly: The Use of Low-IQ Troops in the Vietnam War*. Secretary of Defense Robert McNamara instituted a policy that amounted to dumbing-down the Army. In 1966, as the war effort began requiring more and more troops, McNamara lowered the admissions standards late in the year. It was an attempt to cast a wider net, since there were plenty of young American men in the right age group, but a significant number of those candidates were in college, serving in the National Guard, the sons of people with influence, or otherwise able to avoid draft eligibility. Accepting young men who would have failed the previous physical or mental tests became known as Project 100,000, which was expected to enlist an addition 100,000 soldiers a year.

Westmoreland and other military leaders and support staff disapproved of the program, but by the end of the war, more than 350,000 of these people—known informally as McNamara's Morons or by other derogatory names—had been inducted. Most went to Vietnam, and those who did were killed at a rate three times that of other troops. Although some of these men merely had performed poorly on the tests and were able to draw on other talents to succeed, those were probably the exception. Many others were slow learners, functionally illiterate, or simply incompetent in combat. Some would probably by identified today as developmentally delayed or disabled. They endangered troops around them as well as themselves, including through friendly fire incidents—but they allowed the war to continue with less demand on the sons of middle- and upper-class voters. In essence, they became cannon fodder.

This shocking elimination of standards extended to officers, too, according to Westmoreland. It contributed to such disasters as the 1968 My Lai massacre as well as to overall casualty rates. My experience with the 100,000 was limited, though we all heard plenty of stories where that wasn't the case. My radio operators on my first tour were smart as hell. They were grunts and so was I, as a green horn infantry Captain. Near the end of Chapter 5 I tell the story of how my radio operator, Jim Rode, and I walked into a VC ambush. We were lucky that we kept our wits about us and didn't panic so that once we were under fire, we could figure out what to do. We were separated by the length of our radio comm cord and both stayed in place until we could move forward without getting mowed down.

In another case also described in that chapter, Jim and I were floating across a canal and came under friendly fire. In combat, soldiers look to their leader to give them direction, but sometimes it's every man for himself based on the circumstances.

In hindsight, McNamara's policy ranks with other historical wrongs committed by U.S. military leaders: The foot-dragging that prevented the rescue of more Jewish refugees in World War II, for instance, not to mention the abusive treatment of African American troops prior to, and even after, the Civil Rights era. Project 100,000 was one more terribly shameful example of how we deliberately mistreated our fellow human beings, and I think most Vietnam vets, including me, were completely unaware of the policy at the time. Many still may be, but that needs to change so we can stop repeating the same awful mistakes.

With that in mind, I've also read and studied the writings and testimonies of Dr. Bernard Fall as well as those of Ho Chi Minh and Vietnamese generals Hoang Van Thai, Vo Nguyen Giap, and Bay Cao. Between that reading and my own experiences, I'd give people the following message again and again, as brilliantly summarized by North Vietnamese General Bay Cao when he was interviewed by David Haskell Hackworth. (Hackworth, who was also known as Hack, was a military journalist and former U.S. Army colonel who was decorated in both the Korean and Vietnam wars. He amassed a collection of combat decorations that few veterans of the war equaled, much less exceeded: two Distinguished Service Crosses, ten Silver Star medals, and eight Purple Hearts, in addition to his Korean War valor awards. He died of cancer in Tijuana, Mexico, on May 4, 2005, at age 74.) Hackworth included Cao's comments in his book *Hazardous Duty*, which came out in 1996:

> First we needed to get enough experience fighting you. Second, develop tactics to counter your mobility and machines. Third, wear you down. We were patient. We were prepared to fight a long and protracted war. You were not. We studied your tactics, monitored your radios. You Americans talked too much on the radio. You gave us much intelligence. We even knew when your B-52 bombing attacks would come. Spies told us. We had spies everywhere. Spies are the most important soldiers in the war. We always knew your plans. First come your helicopters, circling like hawks. Then your air strikes and then your troops. Our aim was not to stand and fight, but to run away, unless we could win tactically, or, as in Tet of 1968, we could win a great psychological victory. After the Tet Offensive, we knew beyond any doubt the Viet Cong were going to win, and that is how South Vietnam was liberated.

Visiting the Johnny Cash museum in Nashville with Maria and Joanne

"Inspiration doesn't stay with a lot of artists long, then you're in the game and you've got to sustain it. You notice it—like one-trick wonders or two good albums, then they peter out. To sustain a gift for a long time is rare."
— Joni Mitchell

I'll end my story, for now, with the lyrics to a song I released in 2019. It's called "When I Died." I started writing this song years ago. I would be in a deep sleep and dreaming that I was in my coffin, having died but trying to get out. I could never get out no matter how I tried. It was terrifying. I finally finished the song while in Russia after having contacted a rare nerve disease called complex regional pain syndrome. The pain was unbearable, but I could only load up with Russian ibuprofen at the local drugstore. As a result, my 14-hour plane ride home from Moscow was hell. I had finished reading Bob Dylan's book *Chronicles* and was having flashbacks to coming home from my first Vietnam tour.

On pages 292 and 293 of his book, Dylan said it for me and all the vets about our flights coming home:

In a few years' time a shitstorm would be unleashed. Things would begin to burn. Bras, draft cards, American flags, bridges, too—everybody would be dreaming of getting it on. The national psyche would change and in a lot of ways it would resemble *The Night of the Living Dead*. The road out would be treacherous, and I didn't know where it would lead, but I followed it anyway. It was a strange world ahead that would unfold, a thunderhead of a world with jagged lightning edges. Many got it wrong and never did get it right. I went straight into it. I was wide open. One thing for sure, not only was it not run by God, but it wasn't run by the devil either.

That's exactly what I did in those years, too: I went right into it head first, all 135 pounds of me. That was what I weighed when the Boeing 707 bringing me home out of 'Nam in December 1967 landed at Travis Air Force Base in California.

When I Died
Copyright 2018, words and music by John R. Black

I woke up in this dream where I like to hide
There was the morning news that said I had died
I rolled over in a daze and no matter how I tried
Could I understand the morning when I died

I've got to leave this dream where I like to hide
Go read the morning news the morning when I died
Oh Momma don't you cry, oh Daddy I'm comin' home
Now I'm going to see you, we'll never be alone

I really wasn't ready to leave so soon
Had a great vacation planned, now those plans are ruined
My payments will be late, my woman will be sad
My dog will be in mourning, things are lookin' bad

I hope my Vietnam buddies who have gone ahead
Will welcome me and tell me that I'm really dead
They will say the war is over, we all did what we could
You made it into Heaven like we knew you would.

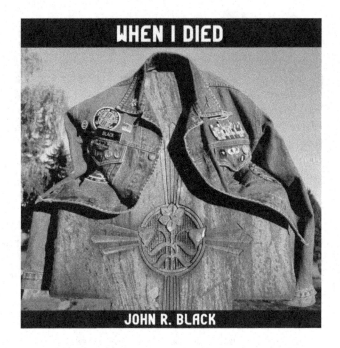

WHEN I DIED

JOHN R. BLACK

IN MEMORY

Barnard G. Marcum
Born Sept. 20, 1939
Died August 2, 1967

Jerry Marcum and I served together in the First Battalion, 19th Infantry, Augsburg Germany (24th Infantry Division). His wife's name was Kathy. Jerry was killed while I was in Vietnam. He was badly wounded in the Mekong Delta and was medevacked to Camp Zama, Japan. His wife Kathy came from Oregon. He died in Japan.

Hardy W. Peeples
Born October 18, 1940
Died January 21, 1967

Harry Peeples is in my song "Vietnam Farewell." I met him when I was first assigned to the Delta. He was an infantry captain, the Ranger advisor to the South Vietnamese Ranger Battalion operating out of My Tho (Seventh Infanty Division Headquarters.) I stayed at the seminary about four days on my way to Go Cong. I bought a can of Merit cigars and we smoked one together. Two weeks later his jeep was blown up by a mine.

BIBLIOGRAPHY

Anderson, Scott. *Lawrence in Arabia: War, Deceit, Imperial Folly and the Making of the Modern Middle East*. New York: Doubleday, 2013

Beschloss, Michael. *Presidents of War: The Epic Story from 1807 to Modern Times*. New York: Crown, 2018.

Colby, William and James McCargar. *Lost Victory*. Chicago: Contemporary Books, 1989

Combs, John. *Mercy Warriors: Saving Lives Under Fire*. 2003. Bloomington: Trafford, 2012

Donlon, Roger H.C. Beyond Nam Dong. R & R Publishers, 1998

Duiker, William J. *Ho Chi Minh: A Life*. New York: Hachette, 2000

Dylan, Bob. *Chronicles, Volume One*. New York: Simon & Schuster, 2004

Evans, Diane and Bob Welch. *Healing Wounds: A Vietnam War Combat Nurse's 10-Year Fight to Win Women a Place of Honor in Washington, D.C.* Permuted Press, 2020

Fall, Bernard. *Hell in a Very Small Place: The Siege of Dien Bien Phu*. New York: Vingate, 1966

--- *Last Reflections on a War*. Mechanicsburg, PA: Stackpole Books, 2000

--- *Street Without Joy: The French Debacle in Indonesia*. 1961. Mechanicsburg, PA: Stackpole Books, 1994

--- *The Two Viet-Nams: A Political and Military Analysis*. 1963. Revised edition, 1967

Fall, Dorothy. *Bernard Fall: Memories of a Soldier Scholar*. Potomac Books, 2006

de Galard, Geneviève. *Angel of Dien Bien Phu: The Lone French Woman at the Decisive Battle for Vietnam*. Annapolis, Naval Institute Press, 2010.

Garrison, Webb. *Amazing Women of the Civil War*. Nashville: Rutledge Hill, 1999

Gavin, Lettie. *American Women in World War I: They Also Served*. Niwot, CO: University Press of Colorado, 1997

Gregory, Hamilton. *McNamara's Folly: The Use of Low-IQ Troops in the Vietnam War*. West Conshohocken, PA: Infinity Publishing, 2015.

Gunther, John. *D-Day: What Preceded It, What Followed*. New York: Harper, 1944

Hackworth, David H. and Tom Mathews. *Hazardous Duty*. 1996. New York: Morrow, 1997

Ho, Chi Minh. *President Ho Chi Minh's Testament*. Vietnam: The Central Committee of The Communist Party of Vietnam, 1989

--- *Selected Writings*, 1920 – 1969. 1973. Hanoi, 1977

--- *Prison Diary*. Aileen Palmer, trans. New York: Bantam, 1971

Hoang, Van Thai. *How South Vietnam Was Liberated*. Hanoi, 1992

Lawrence, T. E. *Revolt in the Desert*. 1927. Revised edition, 2005

Lawrence, T. E. *Seven Pillars of Wisdom: A Triumph*. London: The Folio Society, 1926

Maraniss, David. *They Marched into Sunlight: War and Peace, Vietnam and America, October 1967*. 2003. New York: Simon & Schuster, 2004

McMaster, H. R. *Dereliction of Duty: Johnson, McNamara, the Joint Chiefs of Staff, and the Lies that Led to Vietnam*. New York: Harper, 2017

McNamara, Robert S. and Brian VanDeMark. *In Retrospect: The Tragedy and Lessons of Vietnam*. New York: Crown, 1995

Moore, Harold G. and Joseph L. Galloway. *We Were Soldiers Once... and Young: Ia Drang—The Battle That Changed the War in Vietnam*. New York: Random House, 1992

O'Brien, Tim. *The Things They Carried*. 1990. Paperback. New York, Houghton Mifflin/Mariner Books, 2009

Powell, Colin, and Joseph E. Persico. *My American Journey*. New York: Random House, 1995

Puller, Louis B., Jr. *Fortunate Son: The Healing of a Vietnam Vet*. New York: Grove Press, 1991

Pyle, Richard and Horst Faas. *Lost Over Laos: A True Story of Tragedy, Mystery, and Friendship*. Boston: De Capo Press, 2003

Sheehan, Neil. *A Bright Shining Lie: John Paul Vann and America in Vietnam*. 1988. Vintage Books edition. New York: Vintage Books, 2009

Tomsha, Louis A. *For Whom the Bell Has Tolled*. Colville, WA: Statesman-Examiner, 1990

Vo, Nguyen Giap. *Unforgettable Days*. 1975. Second edition. Soviet Union: Foreign Language Publishing House, 1978

Westmoreland, William C. *A Soldier Reports*. New York: Doubleday, 1976

Wilson, Jeremy. *Lawrence of Arabia: The Authorized Biography of T.E. Lawrence*. New York: Atheneum, 1990

ABOUT THE AUTHOR

John R. Black's career of service to country and corporate America spans five decades. As the president and founder of JBA Associates, he became known as a pioneer and expert on the application of the Toyota Production System to the healthcare industry. He is the author of four books on Lean operations: *A World Class Production System* (1998), *Lean Production: Implementing a World-Class System* (2008), and two editions of *The Toyota Way to Healthcare Excellence: Increase Efficiency and Improve Quality with Lean* (2008 and 2016).

Prior to his corporate career, Black served two military tours during the Vietnam War and another two in the Cold War. His awards included three Meritorious Service Medals, two Bronze Star Medals for Meritorious Achievement in Ground Combat Operations in Vietnam, two Army Commendation Medals, as well as the Combat Infantryman Badge and Airborne, plus the Republic of Vietnam Staff Service Medal, First Class.

Black holds degrees in sociology, business, and human relations, and he is also a graduate of the U.S. Army's Command and General Staff College. In 2012, he was included in the *Universal Who's Who Among Business and Professional Achievers*.

His war experiences have significantly informed his music career. Between 1991 and 2017 he released multiple albums, the most recent of which is *Roll on Russia*. His work is available on iTunes and at www.meetmeinvietnam.net.